AN
ALTERNATIVE
HISTORY OF
CLEVELAND

Jon Wlasiuk

Illustrations by
Libby Geboy

Belt Publishing

Excerpt from "Carpal Tunnel" by John O'Connor,
reprinted by permission of the author.

Printed in the United States of America
First Edition, 2024
ISBN: 978-1-953368-799

Belt Publishing
6101 Penn Avenue, Suite 201, Pittsburgh PA 15206
www.beltpublishing.com

Cover design by David Wilson

To Miles Gamez, Barbara Martin,
and all the Clevelanders who
didn't get to tell their own story.

Table of Contents

Author's Note

Where possible, I use endonyms, or the names a group of people use to identify themselves rather than exonyms, the names applied to them by others. For example, the names "Lakota" and "Haudenosaunee" are used, except in cases where their historical exonyms, "Sioux" and "Iroquois," respectively, are cited.

The following narrative is neither exhaustive nor entirely representative of the over ten thousand years of human history on the eastern shore of Lake Erie. Although I focus on the relationship between humans and the environment, it is but one factor in a much larger story.

Prologue

Hambden Orchard Wildlife Area is a good place to look for a beginning to the story of northeast Ohio. Located about thirty miles east of downtown Cleveland, the wildlife area lacks just about every amenity you might expect at a national, state, or local park. There are no interpretive signs, benches, or even marked trails here. Aside from a rough circle of gravel and a single wooden sign with the name of the location, you are on your own to push your way through 842 acres of second-growth hardwood forest sprinkled with stands of pine and invasive honeysuckle. The Ohio Department of Natural Resources' (ODNR) Division of Wildlife has managed this site since the 1950s, when the state purchased the land with the aim of surrendering a few acres of apple trees to habitat for wildlife. Aside from a scattering of spindly crab apples, the nonhuman world has fully reclaimed this area, a reminder that the land beneath our feet is a living force guided by a natural order that we did not create and have often failed to understand.

When I visited the wildlife area in late November 2022, a storm was kicking up over Lake Erie. Steel-colored clouds crowded out the sun, and locals were making a last-minute rush for groceries and gasoline. This is the heart of the snow belt in Ohio, and residents take the weather seriously. Northern Geauga County regularly records snowfall in excess of one hundred inches per year. The lake effect snow, combined with sandstone ridges reaching 1,300 feet above sea level, are enough to offer even modest skiing. It will never compete with Aspen, but it's enough to keep a few ski lifts churning during the winter.

The interplay between the lake and the Allegheny Plateau east of Cleveland is also responsible for something else I was looking for. As I made my way from the gravel parking lot and into a thicket of chokeberry brush, my feet carefully navigated icy mud. Each step I took created a crunch-squish that was strangely delightful, as though I was walking on a field of crème brûlée. Around a bend, I met a teenage girl in hunter orange—her bright, acrylic nails gripping her shotgun—who greeted me with a nod. I asked her if my passing to the east would spoil her chances at a deer, but she waved me by and laughed, telling me her fellow hunters were posted up in the other direction and I was fine to go on my way.

This landscape is mostly forest, but make no mistake, this is also a wetland environment. Although the official site is just a few miles to the east in a ditch off Clay Street, this marshy forest is the headwaters of the Cuyahoga River, author of the greater Cleveland landscape. I've trekked out to this half-frozen field in search of the source of the crooked river. Like blood vessels that deliver oxygen to a web of capillaries throughout our bodies, rivers don't issue from a single, definitive source. The fractal geometry of nature always finds a way to divide and subdivide until the line between a riverbank and dry land blurs into a wetland.

Although nature often evades our attempts to fit it into hard and fast boundaries, this landscape has remained the source of the region's primary river for more than ten thousand years and will continue to fulfill that role well into the future. For all the books that have been written about Cleveland's history, most ignore this ground truth: the river, the lake, and the climate have structured the lives of people here far more profoundly than the ephemeral relationships involved in economic and political systems. It is a lesson we've struggled to learn, despite having the information widely available for more than a century.

Standing out on this half-frozen field, it's difficult to connect the weight of the river's place in history to this landscape. If you have ever visited a historic battlefield, building, or roadside historical marker, you are familiar with the underwhelming feeling of being a little late to the party. Yet, we should rethink unheralded spots like this one because this river, and the land it drains, have an important story to tell us. For the past thirteen thousand years, humans have made a life in the Cuyahoga watershed. In that time, a spectacular array of diverse cultures have provided different models for how to live on this land. The purpose of this book is to recover some of those experiments and consider them in the light of our present challenges.

Currently, one of our largest obstacles is one of the imagination. Modern Americans are enthralled by a linear view of history, where the present is the culmination and fulfillment of a long arc of progress out of barbarism. In this view, the further we go back in time, the worse things get. What use is history when the past is but the awkward list of misadventures of our species' adolescence? Better to throw all that out like last year's shoes.

Regardless of our preference for the present, though, we have more in common with the first humans who made a life in this landscape than we are willing to admit. Although the hunters I met at the headwaters of the Cuyahoga are equipped with modern firearms, and though their clothes (and acrylic nails) are composed of petroleum polymers, they are participating in the first economy humans brought to this landscape: earning a meal from the forest. If you are a reclusive city-dweller, you aren't much different. When any resident of Cleveland turns on a tap, they are at the end of a long technological system that connects them to Lake Erie, the crooked Cuyahoga's ultimate destination.

Of course, our recent history suggests that humanity has made a plaything of northeast Ohio's natural systems. Since the founding of Cleveland in 1796, we have dammed its rivers, poured so much fertilizer onto our lawns and crops that the lake turns green in the summer, and remade our shorelines and riverbeds to accommodate industry. We have even disrupted the day-night cycle, as the entire region burns as bright as a second sun each night with the help of nuclear power. We have created machines so loud that birds have altered their mating habits. We have chopped (or burned) down 95 percent of the state's forest and drained a swamp the size of Rhode Island. We have also built fantastical complexes to entertain, educate, and feed our growing population. We have even set rivers on fire.

Despite all this, our seeming mastery over the environment is an illusion. Just because we can wrap ourselves in a technological cocoon does not negate the power of climate and geology to structure our lives. The river, lake, and the land itself abide by their own laws, and we ignore them at our peril.

Consider the events of August 14, 2003. The sun rose on fair skies, calm winds, and a comfortable sixty-five degrees. It was a typical, late-summer day in Cleveland. Although the temperature rose to eighty-seven by 2:00 p.m., nearly five degrees higher than the historical average, the gradual increase was well within the means of the power grid's ability to accommodate it.

Accounting for what a power grid can handle is no easy task. It is difficult to accurately measure the present state of even a regional power system, which is why power grid operators employ complicated telemetry software. One such program, known as the "state estimator," assembles all the instrument measurements within the system and projects estimated values for all the gaps between measurements at five-minute intervals. Imagine if your house had a thermostat in every room and a computer capable of calculating the temperature of your couch based on that data, and you will begin to have an idea of the complexity of the state estimator.

Just after noon, an engineer monitoring the power grid covering much of the Midwest noticed an anomalous reading. He discovered the software had erroneously included an out-of-service line as active, corrected the error, and went to lunch. Even in an era of "smart" appliances, our machines still require a human touch, like mentally accounting for an oven that runs hot, a slow clock, or a robotic vacuum that gets stuck under our bed. A system as technologically complex as the power grid also requires human engineers to account for the messiness of the real world. But on this day, the engineer did something even well-trained and well-educated people do all the time: he made a simple mistake.

In manually correcting the error, he forgot to reengage the interval setting, effectively freezing the data in stasis. Without subsequent iterations to relay real-time data into the software, the computers negotiating the complex electric grid for Cleveland were flying blind. The thermostat, so to speak, had been disconnected from the real world, and it entered a positive feedback loop. Over the next fifteen minutes, computer errors accumulated and knocked out critical servers, tripping the FirstEnergy generating plant in Eastlake. When the plant went down, the grid compensated by pulling in energy from other plants, a protocol that puts an additional burden on the power lines that is normally well within standard tolerances. If you've ever experienced a flicker in your lights or a brownout, you've witnessed such a redirection of power.

Although we tend to think of our power grid (if we think of it at all) as a magical machine operated by faraway engineers, complex computer systems, and lineworkers in hard hats, it's also a real, material object. The lines are made of conducting metals like copper and aluminum. On particularly hot days, they can sag, sometimes dramatically, as the metals expand. The amount of current running through a line can also change the nature of the wires. The US Energy Information Administration reports that, on average, 5 percent of the energy transmitted through the grid is lost, some of it as heat. And the more energy coursing through a transmission line, the warmer it gets. On this hot August day, the power lines in Cleveland began to sag as additional current flowed through them. Under normal conditions, this is to be expected. It's why line crews maintain wide clearance around our power lines: they stretch and contract with changing temperatures and conditions. Again, human labor is required to bridge the gap between our technology and nature. Unfortunately, when human labor is subject to economic imperatives, it doesn't always meet its obligations.

What happened next is the subject of some debate. What we know for sure is that after the failure of the Eastlake plant, multiple lines across northeast Ohio made contact with tree limbs, resulting in a short circuit. When a line makes contact with an object, it triggers an automatic safeguard that takes the entire line out of commission. As the lines tripped and power began to flow through the grid in an increasingly chaotic manner, power stations went into safe mode—a type of electronic quarantine—to avoid the damage caused by the surges. Fail-safes and redundancies began to fall like dominoes as one city after another suffered a surge and a blackout. From west to east, the metropolitan areas of Detroit, Toledo, Cleveland, London and Toronto in Ontario, Buffalo, Rochester, Baltimore, and Newark all lost power.

Desperate to contain the cascade, engineers began to sever cities from the grid. Shortly after four in the afternoon, the international connection between Canada and the US failed, and New York separated itself from the New England grid to prevent further damage. Over fourteen million people in New York City were affected by the blackout, and many would remain without power until the following day. The headquarters of the UN went dark, and hundreds of subway cars were trapped between stations. Traffic signals throughout Manhattan blinked out, and people were trapped in elevators. With the terrorist attacks of 9/11 fresh in everyone's memory, many reported feelings of panic and fear as their city was once again paralyzed by forces beyond its control.

The cascade of failures continued until it engulfed hundreds of power plants and substations, creating the largest blackout in the history of North America. Fifty-five million people across eight US states and the province of Ontario were affected. Ohio's lakeshore in and around Cleveland faced some of the blackout's more serious consequences. Cleveland Mayor Jane Campbell was surprised to discover the blackout's far-reaching consequences in its earliest hours. When the city's water commissioner informed Mayor Campbell that the people farthest from the lake would only have running water for about three hours, she asked, "Water? I thought the electric was out."[1] Without electricity to power pumps, though, water service ceased throughout the region, threatening a widespread humanitarian crisis.

Cedar Point amusement park lost power while rides were in motion. Staff were able to use generators to pull some of the frozen roller-coaster cars over their lift hills so gravity could work its magic. Magnum XL-200, one of the tallest roller coasters on the planet, had a car stuck on its 205-foot initial ascent, and the generators didn't have enough energy to overcome that hump. A safety crew escorted frightened guests down the steel coaster, which offers a nauseating view under the best of conditions. Rumors swirled among the thirty thousand guests at the park that Al-Qaeda had pulled off another attack.

As night fell, though, something incredible also took place: Millions of people across North America stepped outside into the warm summer night and encountered a dark sky free of light pollution. Amid the chaos and uncertainty, the curtain of civilization peeled back briefly and gave Clevelanders a momentary view of their home from a different perspective. The full depth of a night sky filled with stars, including the white splash of the Milky Way, wheeled over downtown. It was a sky that once greeted every resident of this land beginning with the first humans who arrived at the close of the Ice Age, before the age of gas and electricity extinguished the cosmic spectacle in the twentieth century.

The soundscape changed too. Without electricity, the night air was uncluttered by thundering air-conditioning units or commercial aircraft. Corner stores held cash-only blackout sales of cold drinks and ice cream, hoping to clear inventory. Neighbors gathered in quiet streets, in doorways, and on porches and shared what little information or terrifying rumors they had heard during the day.

With the exception of automobile traffic and the occasional generator, the sensory world became more intimate, briefly unmoored from our technological interface with nature. Through it all, plants continued to photosynthesize, bacteria continued their work of decomposing, our bodies metabolized food, and the Cuyahoga River flowed from the trickle near Hambden Orchard to its mouth on Lake Erie in downtown Cleveland.

Clevelanders have a strange nostalgia for the 2003 blackout—a mixture of fear, excitement, boredom, and annoyance. Although the blackout imperiled their supplies, Pat and Dan Conway of Great Lakes Brewing Company vividly remember how bright the moon appeared over their brewery that August night. The two celebrated the event by introducing Blackout Stout, complete with a label depicting Clevelanders gathered on a dark porch with candles and, of course, beer.

The loss of power was so complete it caught Clevelanders in every stage of life and death. Danielle Lannings was at lunch in her middle school when the lights turned the cafeteria black and caused the assembled students to scream in terror.[2] Little Italy, which never lets an opportunity to party go to waste, had to call off its festivities for the Feast of the Assumption. And in Garfield Heights, Denise Samide was at the bedside of her dying mother at Marymount Hospital when the power went out and the backup generators kicked in. "It was surreal," she said of the experience.[3]

In the blackout's immediate aftermath, a bilateral, American-Canadian commission produced a 238-page report to better understand how a seemingly small problem snowballed into such a colossal failure.[4] Through interviews and an investigation, they found FirstEnergy had been negligent in clearing tree limbs from the "designated clearance area" around power lines. Multiple power lines in northeast Ohio tripped on the afternoon of August 14 because the company had failed to perform simple tree-trimming maintenance. What began as a software glitch manifested into a real-world crisis, all on account of a few trees in Parma and Walton Hills. The report noted that tree-to-line contacts "are not unusual in the summer across North America" because most tree growth occurs in the spring and summer months. Despite our astonishing achievements in asserting technological control over the natural world, we still have trouble accounting for something as simple as the annual growth of plant life.

Assigning a singular cause to such a large event is as hopeless as finding the exact spot where the Cuyahoga begins. We can get you in the ballpark (or marshy field), but ultimately, it's kinda everywhere. Fussy software, human error, some tree limbs in the wrong place at the wrong time, and decades of deregulation increased the odds of a system collapse. FirstEnergy had spent the previous years focused on buying out competitors rather than maintaining safe clearance around their power lines, and government regulators lacked the power to levy fines against negligent practices because political rhetoric had associated government regulation with tyranny.

The 2003 blackout is a story of a complex, technological system coming into contact with nature. It reveals some of the consequences of constructing a built environment with little regard to how it interfaces with the land beneath our feet. Sadly, this is not a new story in northeast Ohio. Fortunately, our history also holds lessons we could benefit from if we desire to forge a less adversarial relationship with our environment.

In 1961, the historian Lewis Mumford pondered the role of the city in human history with the goal of solving the emerging problems of urban decay in America's great metropolises. Mumford believed humans had reached a fork in the road—we would have to decide if we wanted to continue developing "the now almost automatic forces" we had set in motion to live in comfortable bliss, or choose a life of engagement with our communities and the natural world that would lead to the development of our "deepest humanity." He feared the allure of comfort from an automated landscape would "bring with it the progressive loss of feeling, emotion, creative audacity, and finally consciousness."[5] Mid-century American intellectuals like Mumford didn't spend much time thinking about the middle ground between utopia and apocalypse, which is where most of us live.

Mumford's grim perspective on the future trajectory of the American project would be shared by a generation of urban reformers and cultural critics. Such criticism often came with a sense of fatalism about reform efforts, including the cruel belief that the people who lived within failing cities somehow deserved their fate. If you are from Cleveland and of a certain age, you probably have a chip on your shoulder about how your hometown became a caricature of everything wrong with urban life. Lest we forget, this criticism was also rooted in a real crisis. Prior to the environmental reforms of the latter twentieth century, the city had entirely corrupted the elemental foundations of life: our water, air, and soil.

By raising the stakes to apocalyptic levels, twentieth-century reformers like Mumford set some of the battle lines for the culture wars of the present. Although his rhetoric failed to convince Americans, his observation about the relationship between the city, communities, and the natural world remains true. Today, the city of Cleveland is bound to nature, despite our best efforts to liberate ourselves from its limits.

The present plays a cruel trick on us. As a landscape, the very architecture of the city crystalizes some elements of the past and ignores others. The glow of our streetlights obscures the heavens above our heads, and the turn of a faucet hides our connection to the lake and the river that feeds it. We should interrogate and reexamine our city to reveal a complete picture of the land and our place in it. This book is an exploration of the history of our built environment and how it structures our relationship with the natural world. It's also an attempt to uncover glimpses of the former world—the land and the people who lived on it before Moses Cleaveland arrived in 1796. Two inescapable facts emerge from this deep-time perspective. First, the human relationship with the land goes back further than our memorials and statues suggest, at least as far back as the last ice age that created our Great Lakes. Second, our complex cultural and technological achievements obscure our most critical resource: the land beneath our feet.

Today, Cleveland's relationship to the natural world is stronger than it has been for nearly two centuries. Fish species and raptors are returning to the Cuyahoga River, critical habitat is being protected, and a mixture of scientists, activists, and volunteers are measuring the impact of the built environment on wildlife in order to work with nature, not against it. Unfortunately, the bar for a healthy relationship with the natural world is quite low. The last two centuries haven't given us many high-water marks of environmental resilience. Major challenges remain, such as the maintenance of our critical infrastructure and preparing for the largest shift in climate since the Pleistocene epoch. Hopefully, it won't take another systemic collapse for us to engage with the world around us and decide what kind of city we want to live in.

CHAPTER 1
Here Be Dragons

You can tell a lot about what people value by paying attention to what point in time they choose to begin their histories. Russell Means had been thinking a lot about his own story when he loaded up his wife and two children into the family car and headed to Cleveland in 1968. An Oglala Lakota, Means had spent his early years searching for a place "where I could let my hair grow long and live as an Indian should."[1] By the late 1960s, he had tried his hand in a variety of fields: government work, the rodeo, and dance instruction. Despite his dream of staying true to Lakota traditions, however, life on the Rosebud Indian Reservation was taking a toll on him and his young family. Means and his wife, Betty, decided to take advantage of a new policy from the Bureau of Indian Affairs (BIA) that would provide job training and living stipends to reservation Indians who wanted a fresh start in urban America. So he pointed the couple's car toward Cleveland, Ohio. In the coming years, he would make the city an unlikely center for Indigenous activism that challenged the way Americans imagined their history.

The Indian Relocation Act of 1956, a policy referred to simply as "relocation," designated metropolises with growing economies that would offer opportunities for Natives looking to escape the grinding poverty of reservation life. Using data from the 1950 census, the BIA selected Cleveland as the relocation program's easternmost destination. The city had reached a high-water point by boasting nearly a million residents, making it the seventh-largest city in the country. "I applied for Cleveland, figuring it was about as far away from Indians as we could get," Means wrote in his autobiography. "There was no Indian center in Cleveland, and no Indian bars—and that, we thought, would improve our family life."[2] When the BIA settled Means's young family in a rat-infested hotel on Euclid Avenue that was frequented by sex workers, he successfully pressured the administrators into relocating them to a comfortable hotel in Lakewood. He took a job as an accountant at the Council for Economic Opportunity, Betty worked as a secretary for the Cleveland Housing Authority, and their children enrolled in Cleveland City Schools. From the perspective of the BIA, they looked like the relocation program's model family.

Raising a family with traditional Lakota values proved difficult in Cleveland during the late 1960s, however. In October of 1969, Means's daughter Michele came home from kindergarten and asked her father a troubling question: "Daddy, where were the Indians before Columbus discovered America?" Just a year before, as Means was preparing to leave Rosebud Indian Reservation, President Lyndon Johnson had signed legislation designating the second Monday in October as a federal holiday in honor of Christopher Columbus. Columbus Day was the culmination of efforts by the Italian American community to lay a claim deep in America's past at a time when they were confronting prejudice from the predominantly Protestant, "old-stock" Americans who had emigrated from Western and Northern Europe. Origins matter, especially for a society with a legal tradition from English Common Law that recognizes a right of possession upon the principle of "first in time, first in right."

Means was certainly familiar with Eurocentrism and historical myopia, much of it the product of cultural ignorance. He was once asked at a backyard barbecue in Shaker Heights how long Indians had lived in Cleveland. His response reflected the traditions of many Indigenous cultures: "We've been here from the time the Earth was formed, or soon thereafter."[3] Despite abundant evidence that Indigenous people had been on the continent for well over ten thousand years, many American history texts at the time began the country's story with the arrival of European colonists or the voyage of Columbus. Michele's question gave Means a mission. "That slapped me in the face," he later recalled. It was one of many events that propelled him to dedicate the rest of his life to advancing the cause of dignity for Indigenous communities. He belonged to a new generation of activists and historians who confronted the Columbus myth head-on by beginning American history with the story of the land's first inhabitants.

Ice

We don't know the names of the first people who stepped foot into what is today called northeast Ohio. Archaeologists and historians refer to them by the names of American towns where their tool kits were first discovered and cataloged, such as the Clovis or Folsom people. Sometimes scholars use the awkward moniker

"Paleoindians" as a catchall for the first inhabitants. Regardless of what they called themselves, these people carried with them a rich culture and powerful tools that would forever alter ecosystems throughout the continent.

Although there is accumulating archaeological evidence of human activity in the Americas as far back as twenty thousand years before present (BP), the scientific consensus identifies permanent, widespread human settlement of the North American continent at about 13,000 BP. These first humans entered a land in transition as a massive continental ice sheet was in full retreat. Interpreted somewhat creatively, the creation myth of Native peoples that Means shared at the Shaker Heights dinner party is dead-on. A two-mile-tall glacier had completely remade the North American landscape, and his ancestors settled in its shadow.

A defining characteristic of humanity has been our ability to populate new territories. Although anatomically modern humans first appeared about 300,000 BP, we had managed to explore and settle the continents of Asia, Europe, and Australia by 65,000 BP. Why did it take an additional fifty thousand years to reach North and South America? Part of the reason is that Europe, Asia, and even Australia were accessible by either foot or a short sea voyage (less than one hundred kilometers). Another reason is that exploration was a by-product of population density. Recent genetic research has demonstrated a clear link between Indigenous Americans and Native Siberian peoples. The oldest verified sites suggest humans didn't fully settle Siberia, Korea, and Japan until around 40,000 BP, long after human groups in the south had branched off and discovered Australia.

The other reason humans didn't arrive on the shores of Lake Erie until relatively recently in our historical journey has to do with climate. The earth rotates along an axis tilted about 23.4 degrees, which provides us with the yearly seasonal cycle. But the planet's angle of repose in its cosmic dance with the sun contains its own cycles: its axis wobbles between 22.1 degrees and 24.5 degrees once every forty-one thousand years, and the shape of its orbit fluctuates on a longer, one-hundred-thousand-year cycle.[4] On a planetary scale, a degree of difference here and a slight wobble there have massive effects at the continental and human scale. Around 33,000 BP, the winds changed as a result of these cycles. Summers became a bit cooler, and snowpack failed to melt and began to accumulate from one season to the next, eventually compacting into ice. It wouldn't relent for nearly ten thousand years.[5]

From its core in eastern Canada, the continental glacier was like a mountain range on the move in every direction, pulverizing everything in its path. Although most glaciers creep along at a pace of a few centimeters a day, scientists have recently observed "glacial earthquakes" on Greenland, when a glacier the size of Manhattan slid ten meters in less than a minute and produced a 5.0-magnitude earthquake.[6] At its peak, the continental glacier stood two miles high at its core in the province of Quebec and plunged south to cover about two-thirds of the state of Ohio. The ice advanced as far south as Canton and Youngstown in the east, another lobe pushed south of Columbus to Chillicothe, and ice engulfed Dayton before halting at the northern suburbs of Cincinnati. This most recent ice age, dubbed the Wisconsin, was only the latest of several glacial pulses, some reaching as far south as northern Kentucky and depositing massive hills of sediment and rock that give Cincinnati its sometimes dramatic geography (at least by Ohio standards).

Geologists estimate that the glacial ice over the Lake Erie Basin was a mile thick. As far south as Columbus, the ice would have been one thousand feet tall.[7] For some perspective, the largest building in the state, Key Tower, reaches only 947 feet into the sky. The weight of all that ice on the land left unmistakable signs. If you've ever traveled (or lived) north of the line connecting Cincinnati, Columbus, and Cleveland, you have the glaciers to thank for some of the monotony of the landscape. Just north of Sandusky are several locations where you can view deep tracks in the limestone bedrock created by the immense pressure of a mountain of ice. Just across the mouth of Sandusky Bay from Cedar Point, you can find the Marblehead Lighthouse, which is planted directly into the bedrock. Take a ferry to Kelleys Island about a mile to the north and you will find Glacial Grooves Geological Preserve. Four hundred feet long in places, the grooves left by the glaciers in limestone resemble the tracks left by a bus-sized sled in the snow. The pressure created by the sheer mass of ice was so great that it pushed the earth's crust into the squishy mantle. Parts of New York State have lifted up more than 150 feet in a process geologists describe as "glacial rebound" since the last of the ice melted away.[8] The ice was so heavy, the land is still recovering over ten thousand years after the glacier's retreat.

The first people to settle in Ohio would have faced a much different environment than the one we're accustomed to now. By the time they arrived, the ice would have pulled back into the northern reaches of the Great Lakes, but the average temperature would have been about eleven degrees colder than it is today.[9] Ocean levels would have been about four hundred feet lower as well, and the lakeshore would have been lapping at the escarpment that separates the heights from the rest of the city. This lake, which geologists refer to as Lake Maumee, swallowed much of the Maumee River Valley, the entire lakeshore in Michigan (including the area now occupied by Detroit and Toledo), and most of the Canadian province of Ontario. Around 12,000 BP, the location occupied by present-day Cleveland would have been the edge of the world. To the north sat the lake, and to the east, around present-day Buffalo, would have been the retreating ice wall. Even the night sky would have been different than our own, with the wobble in the earth's axis placing the star Vega, rather than Polaris, as the polestar around which the heavens turned each night.[10]

The continental glacier was also a blessing for Ohio. It created what would become Lake Erie, a rich ecosystem and freshwater source for millennia. The incredible pressure of the ice, and the melted water left in its wake, also deposited a thick layer of sediments known as glacial till. The till plains covering the northwestern two-thirds of the state provided a perfect substrate for plant communities to once again take root as the ice retreated. Although two centuries of intensive agriculture and development have eroded some of the best topsoil, the till plains remain the most fertile acres in the state. While the glaciers obliterated much of the landforms, they also filled in ancient riverbeds and valleys with a mixture of sand and gravel, producing subterranean aquifers throughout the state. Not all of these depressions were covered, however. Some pits, created by deep spears of ice, became kettle lakes that were sprinkled around the area. The climate and plant communities that greeted the first people to arrive in Ohio were somewhat similar to the interior of Alaska today. This boreal forest of spruce, tamarack, and pine would have been sprinkled with larch and hemlock. Cedar dominated the wetlands, such as the bogs and swamps created by glacial outwash, buried rivers, and kettle lakes. As the weather warmed, familiar hardwoods, like oak, chestnut, poplar, and willow, replaced the coniferous forests. These plant communities, in turn, provided a rich habitat for what ultimately attracted the first humans to Ohio: wildlife that ranged from the familiar to the fantastic.

Bones

We take for granted just how recent our understanding of natural history is. Our popular understanding of plate tectonics, for example, wasn't widely accepted until the 1960s. Although Darwin first proposed evolution by natural selection in 1859, one survey found that it wasn't accepted by a majority of adults in the United States until 2019.[11] Archaeology, history, and paleontology—the disciplines most focused on understanding the human past—didn't organize into professional, academic fields of study until the past 150 years. Before this, amateurs ranging from gentlemen scholars to laborers attempted to explain the bones, tools, and earthworks they unearthed in North America. In 1797, Thomas Jefferson reported on a set of strange bones originally thought to be discovered by workers in a West Virginia niter mine. The bones, which Jefferson believed to be those of a large lion he called "Megalonyx," actually belonged to an extinct giant sloth that stood nearly nine feet tall and weighed two thousand pounds.[12]

Cleveland's earliest white settlers found evidence of prehistoric monsters everywhere they turned a spade of dirt, it seems. Charles Whittlesey was just a child when his parents moved the family from Connecticut to the village of Tallmadge in 1813. He would witness a good deal of history in his own life. He served in the army during the Black Hawk War and even accompanied President Abraham Lincoln as an escort during the Civil War. He studied natural science at West Point Academy and put his knowledge to practical use, becoming one of Ohio's first field geologists. Although he used his knowledge to survey the subterranean resources that would fire the Industrial Revolution, his passion led him to help found the Western Reserve Historical Society and become its first president in 1867.

Through his network of neighbors and professional connections, Whittlesey gathered together every sighting of strange bones, earthworks, or artifacts and reported on them in a series of books. The early decades of white settlement were filled with puzzling reports. For example, while digging the coal vaults of the Merchants Bank at what is now the corner of West Ninth and Superior, workers were astonished to discover "elephant" bones. A tooth Whittlesey correctly attributed to "an extinct elephant" was unearthed near the present location of Terminal Tower. His field experience led to observations that would help guide future archaeologists. "Grinders of the elephant and mastodon are common in the superficial materials" just a few feet deep, he wrote.[13] When he published his *Early History of Cleveland, Ohio* in 1867, the American mastodon had been identified as a distinct species from modern elephants and had earned its own scientific name, *Mammut americanum.* America had its own elephants, and their bones were popping up across the landscape of northeast Ohio.

Bones, such as those belonging to Jefferson's Megalonyx, became curiosities for early settlers. Sometimes they made their way to amateur scholars, like Jefferson, who offered initial guesses at their origin. These bones would be featured in "cabinets of curiosity," precursors to today's museums of natural history, so locals could gawk at them in wonder for a small fee. One such place was the Firelands Historical Society, which was founded in Norwalk in 1857 to preserve documents and artifacts related to the region's early history. Sometime between 1857 and 1915, a farmer from Norwich Township, about twenty-five miles south of Sandusky, discovered bizarre bones in a bog on his farm and donated them to the museum. The ten bones collected dust for decades until 1998, when a member of the society discovered them in the attic and identified them as belonging to *Megalonyx jeffersonii*, the giant ground sloth the third president had first misidentified as a large cat. Curious to learn more, the museum turned to Dr. Brian Redmond, the current curator of archaeology at the Cleveland Museum of Natural History.

With the help of an international team of researchers, Dr. Redmond was able to confirm that not only did these bones belong to Megalonyx, but their size suggested the creature weighed over 2,800 pounds, or roughly the weight of a Kia Soul hatchback. Radiocarbon analysis revealed that the sloth lived and died sometime between 13,738 and 13,435 BP, the closing years of the Pleistocene Ice Age. The team also found microscopic traces of spruce, Douglas fir, and tamarack, all members of the boreal forest environment that replaced the retreating continental glacier.

The femur of the Megalonyx is perhaps the most significant bone in the entire state, and it challenges our sense of history as beginning with a few white folks from Connecticut who wore powdered wigs. In examining the femur, the team discovered forty-one marks that were consistent with butchery by stone tools. Under the microscope, the bone looks like a cutting board pitted with an array of marks, from fine cuts to deep chops. When the team finally published their research in 2012, they felt confident in reporting that these marks weren't made out of idle curiosity but by people who knew what they were doing: "The human butchers possessed previous experience with the anatomy of this creature as well as knowledge of the most efficient method of butchering the hind quarter of a sloth."[14] Here was the oldest evidence of human occupation of Ohio.

Archaeologists are usually a pretty reserved bunch, but when interviewed by local media, Dr. Redmond explained the significance of what has become known as the Firelands Ground Sloth. "What's rare in archaeology is to have something like this where you can see what is actually a moment in time," he said.[15] Few social scientists talk in terms of "proof," or the undeniable evidence linking a cause with an effect. Instead, you often read about probabilities, levels of uncertainty, or hypotheses. Although archaeologists had theorized about the arrival of humans in Ohio during the Ice Age, the Megalonyx bone is a rare trifecta of data: for a detective, it establishes a time, a place, and an activity. Professor Plum, in the library, with the candlestick. The chance discovery of the bones should also cause us to wonder how many more like it were crushed under plows or bulldozers and how many remain to be discovered in the future.

These bones are also evidence in a debate that has engulfed the field of archaeology for over fifty years concerning just what happened to all the large mammals (aka megafauna) that graced the continent when the first humans arrived. Although we don't know if these people actually killed this particular sloth or just took advantage of its death, the evidence of human butchery fits a pattern of behavior that some scholars argue pushed most North American megafauna to extinction in the centuries after the Ice Age. Dubbed at times the "Quaternary extinctions" or "overkill hypothesis," the idea that America's first humans quickly depopulated the largest land animals on the continent has gained support among scholars, despite provoking controversy.

The very concept of extinction is rather new and wrapped up in our notions of culture, science, and religion—cornerstones of identity. For Christian colonists from Europe, God's creation was too perfect to allow for such a disruption in the cosmic order. Even Enlightenment thinkers such as Thomas Jefferson were skeptical that any class of animals could vanish from the earth completely. In his report on the Megalonyx, he suggested further exploration of the continent would reveal living specimens associated with the strange bones piling up in the young country's cabinets of curiosity. "In the present interior of our continent," he wrote, "there is surely space and range enough for elephants and lions, if in that climate they could subsist; and for mammoths and megalonyxes who may subsist there. Our entire ignorance of the immense country to the West and North-West, and of its contents, does not authorise us to say what it does not contain."[16] At the time he penned these words, Ohio was firmly in the Northwest Territory, a land he believed might contain living populations of these creatures.

Indigenous communities eye the fields of archaeology and anthropology with suspicion, and with good cause. In North America, those two disciplines were founded by men who advanced theories of a rigid racial hierarchy that placed Indigenous people near the bottom and collected evidence by raiding Native burial grounds and ceremonial sites. The Philadelphia physician Samuel G. Morton spent much of the first half of the nineteenth century collecting and measuring the skulls of Indigenous people in order to establish a measurable basis for distinct racial categories. He employed multiple field collectors to procure samples, and many of them were ripped from mounds in Ohio. In his history of the racist origins of American ethnology, historian Robert E. Bieder notes, "the collecting of Indian crania appears to have been a cottage industry on the frontier."[17] Charles Whittlesey, now honored for his contributions to our understanding of Ohio's past, often interchanged the words "indian" and "savage" in his writing and was responsible for a long-standing misconception that most Indigenous earthworks were fortifications indicative of a culture committed to perpetual warfare.

Vine Deloria Jr., a twentieth-century Hunkpapa Lakota writer whose 1969 book, *Custer Died for Your Sins*, became a manifesto for the Red Power Movement, rejected most of the growing scientific understanding of Indigenous origins. Deloria mocked the "land bridge" theory of American settlement as a self-serving fantasy. "By making us immigrants to North America," he wrote, "they are able to deny the fact that we were the full, complete, and total owners of this continent." The "they" he refers to are white archaeologists and historians. He closely followed the emerging science and even celebrated archaeological discoveries that pushed back the time of human settlement of the Americas. As an intellectual pillar of the Indigenous fight for dignity, he also saw how opponents of the movement used science to undermine Native claims for sovereignty and respect. After delivering a speech at Stanford on the relationship between Indigenous people and the environment in 1990, he refused to answer any more questions after an audience member challenged him to address the wasteful nature of some Indigenous hunting practices. These experiences partly explain why Deloria dismissed the overkill hypothesis as just another example of mainstream science discrediting Indigenous culture. "Advocating the extinction theory," he wrote, "is a good way to support continued despoliation of the environment by suggesting that at no time were human beings careful of the lands upon which they lived."[18] For Deloria and many Indigenous activists, the emerging consensus about the first people to arrive on the continent was just one more hit job on their ancestors by academic disciplines founded on racist lies.

For all the above reasons, writing any ancient history of the Americas is inherently perilous. I'll also add another: At any moment, someone digging up a flower bed might just uncover artifacts that undermine conventional knowledge. That is exactly what happened over a period of five years beginning in 1988, when archaeologists working at four sites unearthed new clues about the behavior of Ohio's first peoples.

The Chert-Industrial Complex

If beasts like Jefferson's Megalonyx were the first economy to attract humans to Ohio, then chert became essential to rendering the creatures into meat, hides, and tools. Chert is a smooth sedimentary rock found in abundance throughout the Great Lakes. The raw stone has the appearance and feel of a fine-grained ceramic. When struck with another hard stone or bone tool, it produces conchoidal fractures that flake off, leaving a smooth surface and a razor-sharp edge. I once had the misfortune of witnessing the effects of such an edge firsthand when my wife dropped a ceramic casserole dish she was cleaning in the sink. She instinctively tried to catch the dish, which fractured into large shards. She pulled back her arms, ripped off her gloves, and revealed a surgical gash through her wrist that had severed four tendons and the median nerve.

Although we use "stone age" to colloquially refer to outdated ideas or technology, stone tools—in the shape of scrapers, axes, knives, and spearheads—gave ancient people extraordinary power over their environment. Archaeologists first associated these tools with early Americans at sites containing megafauna remains outside the small towns of Folsom and Clovis, New Mexico, in the 1920s and 1930s. Of most interest were the stone spearheads. Although stone scrapers and knives likely were employed for a variety of uses, the intricately crafted fluted spearpoints had one purpose—taking down large animals at short range. These paleo points have been discovered across North America, from the Arctic Circle in Alaska to the Chihuahuan Desert in Mexico. Ohio has an extraordinary concentration of them. Archaeologists have unearthed them in every county of the state, amassing over one thousand samples for analysis.[19]

One such site is located just outside Canton, about an hour's drive south of Cleveland. Near the edge of the glacial advance, the area in Stark County is dotted with hilly moraines, bogs, and kettle lakes. The soil, a rich loam deposited by glacial outwash, has been productive agricultural land. Plows unearthed stone tools near one kettle lake named Nobles Pond. In 1963, two amateur archaeologists began extracting artifacts from the field. Although the site attracted some scholarly interest, no systematic dig was conducted. That all changed in 1988, when the farmland drew the attention of real estate developers. Fearing a complete destruction of the site, archaeologists from Kent State University worked out a deal with the landowner to aggressively salvage as many artifacts as possible before the bulldozers arrived. Employing an army of volunteers, many of them KSU students, the team meticulously excavated and screened over 5,800 meters of land. By the time they finished in 1997, they had collected over seven thousand stone tools, including ninety-five paleo points.[20]

Nearly all of the tools recovered from the site originated from two locations about seventy miles to the south. Analysis found that about half of them had been quarried from a bed of Upper Mercer flint in Coshocton County. Most of the rest came from a nearly eight-mile-long vein called Flint Ridge, which runs through Licking and Muskingum Counties. Ohio is so rich in flint, a form of chert that forms in chalk or marl, that we made it the state's official gemstone. The rainbow-colored stone quarried from Flint Ridge looks like a kind of fantastic rock candy embedded with waves of aquamarine swirling around splashes of marigold, emerald, and blots of crimson. What surprised the archaeologists working at the Nobles Pond site is that the people who crafted these tools had abundant sources of chert in northeast Ohio, but they preferred the higher-quality stuff to the south. You may be asking yourself why these people expended so much energy to acquire a better version of something they already had access to. High-quality stones were easiest to work with; they allowed a flint knapper to create a consistently sharp edge, and they were easier to resharpen than stones from lower-quality quarries.[21] The added travel was apparently worth the effort.

Based on the evidence they've unearthed, archaeologists argue that people used the Nobles Pond site as a base camp to hunt, gather, and repair their tools. Archaeologists have identified cultural styles based on the size and shape of fluted points, just as iconic as modern artistic movements. The points from Nobles Pond match those of the Gainey style, a subgenre of the Clovis culture that predominated in the Great Lakes region around 11,000 BP. The site itself occupies an elevated ridge between the kettle lake to the east and the Jackson Bog State Nature Preserve to the west, ideal ecosystems to find large animals and forage-able

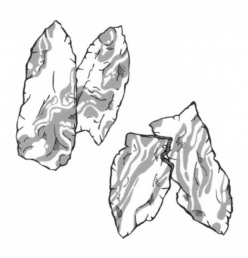

plants. Unfortunately, the area's acidic soil has destroyed all traces of bone, hide, plant fibers, and even wood. At Nobles Pond, we've found the cutlery, but the pantry is bare.

Fortunately, genetic science has advanced to a place where microscopic remains can flesh out our image of the location. Forensic analysis of proteins on 130 stone tools from the site returned forty-five positive results. Blood from the Cervidae family, which includes white-tailed deer, caribou, and elk, was the most abundant identification from the study, followed by rabbits. Proteins from bears were also discovered, which could have been from the common black bear or *Arctodus simus*, the giant short-faced bear. Larger than a grizzly or polar bear, the short-faced bear may have been the largest carnivore in North America when humans first arrived. Their remains have been found at other sites in Ohio, suggesting humans briefly shared the land with them in the closing years of the Ice Age. The researchers were surprised to find bison remains on the tools. A Pleistocene giant in its own right, *Bison antiquus* was about 20 percent larger than its modern, smaller descendants. Its remains are usually found in grassland environments to the south and west of the Ohio River. The tools also returned positive results for proteins of wildcats such as bobcat (*Lynx rufus*), fowl such as turkey and quail, and rodents such as squirrels, beaver, and porcupine. They also contained proteins from canines, which could include everything from wolves to the domesticated dogs the first Ohioans brought with them to the continent. Quite the menu.[22]

A year after the excavations at Nobles Pond were underway, a dragline operator named Phil Flowers was excavating peat from a former kettle lake at a golf course about five miles west of the Flint Ridge quarry when his equipment snagged on something heavy. They were bones of some kind, but Flowers wanted to check with the golf course owner before continuing with his

work. The owner, Sherm Byers, took one look at the bones and called his lawyer to see if his plans to add nine holes to the course were in jeopardy. Although the lawyer informed Byers that, short of human remains, his property rights extended to just about everything below the surface, Byers called both the local and state archaeological societies. The next morning, Dr. Bradley Lepper was standing over the pit, staring at the skull of a mastodon. Years later, he said he felt as though "a doorway into time opened before me."[23] Byers gave the archaeologist a single day to remove the skeleton so his expansion could continue without further delay. Lepper's hastily organized team managed the task in forty-eight hours of backbreaking labor, working in freezing temperatures and knee-deep muck. The dig site, captured in several photographs, was reminiscent of the cratered battlefields of World War I.

The remains of mastodons and their larger cousins, mammoths, have been found throughout Ohio, with sites in seventy of the state's eighty-eight counties. Cuyahoga County alone has seven sites containing prehistoric elephant remains, like those described by Whittlesey found in downtown Cleveland. Similar in size to modern Asian elephants, the American mastodon subsisted on tree and shrub branches as well as other fibrous plants. Like most large herbivores, they likely traveled in herds to protect their young. With an estimated life span of about sixty years, the American mastodon invested considerable energy in protecting their young. Based upon the size of their pelvic bones and our knowledge of the closely related Asian elephant, mastodons had a long gestation period—about twenty-two months—and they didn't reach maturity for a decade after birth. Females took about eight years to reach sexual maturity and would have nursed their young for four to five years, which would have delayed ovulation.[24] Although females would have remained in the matriarchal herd, fully grown males would have struck off on their own in search of mating partners. Modern male elephants experience a flood of hormones that literally ooze from their skin each year and lead them to aggressively challenge other males. This period, called musth, likely propelled mastodon mating patterns as well. The skeletons of male mastodons exhibit puncture wounds and broken tusks, signs that these mating competitions often left the loser gored and dying.[25] Enter a few bands of human hunters armed with deadly stone spears, and even light predation would have been difficult for these ponderous elephants to recover from.

As he unearthed the mastodon from the black peat, Dr. Lepper was surprised to discover a nearly complete skeleton. As the team's shovels and trowels reached the rib cage, he discovered a cylindrical mass of vegetation he hoped might be the remains of the animal's final meal. Years later, he still remembered the stench. "It smelled really bad," he recalled. "It smelled like a sewer."[26] He packed handfuls of the muck into plastic bags and continued to exhume the rest of the beast. The team carefully documented each bone and assembled them at a temporary laboratory in the laundry room of the former Licking County Tuberculosis Sanitarium. Once they were satisfied that no stray bones had been left behind, they carefully cleaned the skeleton and began shipping samples to colleagues throughout the United States. Using radiocarbon dating, a paleontologist at the University of Michigan determined the skeleton belonged to a young bull. Several bone fractures had healed by the time the animal died about 11,300 BP. This analysis also revealed the clear evidence of butchery by stone tools, as well as drag marks that had been made after the animal had died. Putting these puzzle pieces together, it's possible the mastodon was either killed or that its corpse was discovered by humans, who then dragged it to the shore of a kettle lake for initial butchery, then plunged it into the water, which served as a kind of Pleistocene refrigerator that would preserve the meat for later. This practice has been observed among diverse groups, and a similar mastodon skeleton discovered in central Michigan seems to have been anchored in place with rocks by Indigenous hunters.[27]

So why go through all the trouble and let the meat spoil? The researchers believe the carcass either sank to depths beyond the hunters' reach or the group never made it back to the site to complete their meal. Lepper sent samples of the gut contents to labs in Ohio, Pennsylvania, and Michigan. The results identified several wetland plants, such as naiad, pondweed, and water lily, as well as moss, grass, and woody branches. Based upon the seeds discovered in the gut contents, the team determined the mastodon died in late autumn. Dr. Lepper didn't have a smoking gun, but the preponderance of evidence left only a few suspects. "He was a big male, in the prime of life," he wrote, "who died with a full belly at a time of year when food was relatively plentiful and temperatures were not extreme. It is likely, therefore, that human hunters killed the animal."[28]

The Burning Tree Mastodon became a sensation. The laboratory analysis of the skeleton and gut contents deepened our understanding of a species that last haunted the forests of Ohio around 10,500 BP. Once samples were secured from the skeleton and casts were made, it was returned to the golf course owner, Sherm Byers. Byers wanted the archaeologists to either buy it or build a museum to exhibit it, but they declined. Ever the businessman, he put the skeleton up for auction, where it was sold and shipped off to Japan.[29] In a strange play of cosmic justice, the loss of the sustenance provided by the mastodon's flesh allowed us all to profit from the discovery of its remains.

Despite the evidence accumulating that the first people who arrived in northeast Ohio subsisted off the megafauna that would shortly go extinct, archaeologists couldn't rule out other theories. Although the paleo points excavated from Nobles Pond tested positive for the blood from deer, caribou, bear, and bison, all of the tools returned negative results for elephant antiserum. More puzzling was the fact that archaeologists couldn't locate a single stone point, scraper, or knife at the Burning Tree site, which was located only a few miles west of the Flint Ridge vein. Dr. Lepper believes that, with more time, the team may have been able to locate tools at the site (now a water hazard on the back nine). Finding both tools and bones together would offer the best evidence that the earliest people to settle in northeast Ohio subsisted off megafauna.

* * *

In 1993, Dr. Nigel Brush wasn't trying to crack Ohio's coldest case of what killed off the Pleistocene megafauna. He was leading a tour of glacial landscapes in Holmes County for the Killbuck Valley Museum of Natural History, pointing out ancient kettle lakes, moraines, and bogs left behind by the last continental glacier. He told the tourists that just fifty years earlier, a farmer had uncovered mastodon bones while digging a drainage ditch to clear a bog. Although a professor from the College of Wooster identified the bones as mastodon teeth and even wrote an article on them, nobody seems to have been interested enough to conduct a proper excavation. "The site passed into local legend as the mastodon that was never excavated," Dr. Brush wrote.

Retelling this yarn with his tour group, he was surprised when one of them piped up to inform him that, actually, he owned property next to the location and would be happy to host an expedition. Dr. Brush accepted the offer, but he called the dig off when it failed to turn up anything of interest. The effort, however, gained the attention of a neighbor, who had been a boy when his father unearthed the mastodon bones in 1938. The farmer showed Dr. Brush several of the teeth the family had collected, and the two men walked out to the exact location where they'd been found. Striking a deal with the family to conduct a full-fledged dig, Dr. Brush returned in the summer of 1993 with students from the University of Akron.[30]

The team located the remainder of the mastodon skeleton—first a pelvis, then a leg bone—resting on a thick layer of clay marl. Each night, the excavation pits would fill with a foot or more of water, a sign that the Ice Age bog had not entirely given way to human designs. The team also discovered deer bones scattered across the same layer as the mastodon remains. Like a crime scene detective, Dr. Brush constructed a clearer picture based on the clues his team unearthed. Still, he didn't have a perpetrator, and death by natural causes seemed the most likely fate of these ancient creatures. "The scavenging of Ice Age predators (such as dire wolves, sabertooth cats, and giant short-faced bears) could easily account for the highly disarticulated state of the skeletons," he later wrote. But on the ninth day, the team hit pay dirt. Scattered among the bones, the team unearthed flint scrapers as well as flakes that suggested intensive use and resharpening.[31]

Because the site was located so close to the surface (less than two feet in some places) and had been disturbed by previous excavations, it proved impossible to submit the artifacts for carbon dating. Dr. Brush mailed the flint tools off to the University of Calgary to test them for animal proteins. Two of the flakes that had been found near mastodon bones returned positive results for deer and elephant. In a short, two-page article published a year later, he summarized the results: "we conclude that both the mastodon and the deer at the Martins Creek site were likely butchered by Paleoindians."[32] When the paper appeared, flint tools had been found in association with mastodon bones in only three other excavations. The Martins Creek site firmly established that humans and mastodons not only shared Ohio's forests and swamps but also that humans preyed upon mastodon flesh when the opportunity arose.

The archaeological sites excavated in northeast Ohio in the late 1980s and early 1990s provide strong circumstantial evidence that the human newcomers were opportunistic hunters and gatherers. All three sites were edge habitats, landscapes where glacial bogs or kettle lakes intersected with forests or prairie. Twelve thousand years ago, the Martins Creek site was near a narrow peninsula, a spit of land that jutted out into a surrounding glacial lake. Although the subsequent years transformed it first into a bog and eventually into a muddy field with row crops, we can hazard an approximation of the site as it was in our mind's eye. We know from the excavation that the floor of the lake was a gooey clay marl that would have been an imposing hazard, especially for prehistoric elephants that weighed as much as ten thousand pounds. Dr. Brush suggests that the landscape created an ideal trap for Ohio's first people to herd, immobilize, and eventually kill deer and mastodons. We have ample evidence of similar "landscape" traps used by Indigenous people, such as the bison jumps at locations like Head-Smashed-In Buffalo Jump in the Canadian Rockies, and Bonfire Shelter located a few hundred feet from the Rio Grande River in Texas. We also know that hunting cultures throughout Africa, the Middle East, and central Asia built stone walls to funnel animals into "kill zones" if the landscape didn't cooperate. These "desert kites" illustrate a universal tendency among humans to plan and predict animal behavior.[33]

Our modern notions of hunting don't translate well into the past. Now, hunting in the United States is often an individualistic pastime, where the hunter tests their skills in pursuit of a prize beast. As recreation, it can have the appearance of a particularly bloody game. When it is your primary economic activity, however, the entire group is invested in its outcome. I experienced a taste of this when, at the age of ten or so, I woke up before dawn on Thanksgiving morning and piled into a car with my father and his five brothers. Our object was to secure a rabbit for the day's feast. With a twenty-gauge, break-action shotgun drooping over my forearm, I slowly marched through the late-autumn forest. My dad and uncles were fanned out on either side of me, forming a human wedge that, we hoped, would corral any critters into my sights ahead. This story doesn't end like most hunting tales, though; we went home empty-handed that day. There was so little excitement, in fact, I never even snapped the barrel into position in anticipation of a shot. But that day, I learned hunting could be a team sport.

All the evidence suggests Ohio's first people applied their generational knowledge to the collective task of surviving in a familiar but entirely new environment the moment they arrived. They carried a chert-based tool kit, perfected over generations, that allowed them to convert the protein, hides, and bones of the North American bestiary into food, clothing, and tools. They knew how to meticulously craft razor-sharp fluted points that, when attached to the end of a spear and thrown, could break the thick hide and layer of fat on an elephant or ancient bison, creating a mortal wound. Flint scrapers and knives efficiently cut through hides, sinew, and tendons and, in expert hands, could be knapped back to a sharp edge when dull. These tools were so critical that early settlers carried them, at times, hundreds of miles. One site between Akron and Medina, which archaeologists from the Cleveland Museum of Natural History excavated in the early 1990s, contained thousands of stone tools. After subjecting the artifacts to neutron activation, the scientists determined nearly all of them were composed of Wyandotte chert quarried from the Ohio River Valley in southern Indiana.[34] Having traveled at least three hundred miles, the tools showed signs of being heavily reworked, just like those from Nobles Pond. This culture invested significant time and effort into caring for these tools. They turned out to be the key to unlocking a new life in the land left in the glacier's wake.

Where the Mastodon Roam

For about seventeen million years, the land we now call Ohio was elephant country. The forests and swamps here were filled with the trumpeting sounds of mammoths and mastodons, and their grazing shaped dynamic ecosystems that, depending on the earth's wobble, seesawed between boreal forest, wetland, and ice. They evolved and branched out into a fantastic array of forms, from the American mastodon, which would have looked like a stockier version of elephants familiar in our own time, to the Columbian mammoth, which weighed over twenty thousand pounds and sported tusks sixteen feet long. Some elephants looked like Lovecraftian monsters; one species was equipped with four tusks, and another had a lower jaw that extended half the length of its trunk.

They persisted for so long in the region that they seemed to have coevolved with several plant species. Our forests are filled with their ghosts. If you've ever stumbled upon a patch of Osage oranges littering the ground like neon softballs in late autumn, you likely have Pleistocene megafauna to thank for dispersing them throughout the continent. Scholars have argued that avocados and even honey locust trees were prime fare for mastodons and Megalonyx. Honey locust trees may have evolved their extraordinary bark spikes to deter mastodons from getting carried away while they feasted on the tree's seedpods.[35] The plants have managed to find new, albeit awkward, bedfellows, but their fruit are best suited for the massive jaws of beasts that last walked Ohio's forests ten thousand years ago.

For a time, the prevailing theory for the megafauna's disappearance centered on climate change. The Ice Age must have scrambled ecosystems, the thinking went, creating new environments for disease and reducing forage. The megafauna were just too big for their own good, and dwarf variants, such as the American bison and tree sloths, survived due to their faster reproduction cycles. Climate scientists have identified at least eleven significant glacial periods, with the last three sending pulses of ice deep into southern Ohio. The megafauna found at archaeological sites throughout the state had survived all of these ice ages except the last. So what changed?

The most significant difference between the last ice age and all the previous ones was our arrival on the continent. When the first paleo points were unearthed at Folsom and Clovis, New Mexico, in the early twentieth century, the consensus view held that the first humans didn't arrive in the Americas until about one thousand years ago. Vine Deloria Jr. often encountered that mindset from opponents of Indigenous sovereignty. While taking a smoke break after testifying in the defense of the Oglala Lakota activists (Russell Means among them) who occupied Wounded Knee in 1973, a woman approached him and quipped, "Well, dearie, we are all immigrants from somewhere."[36]

Although Deloria would never admit it, the same archaeological evidence that associated Paleoindians with hunting Pleistocene megafauna also shattered the theory that Indigenous people had come to the continent recently. The discovery of a paleo point embedded between the ribs of an extinct bison species outside Folsom, New Mexico, in 1927 led to a paradigm shift in our understanding of the first people who settled on the continent. Every decade since, the evidence continues to pile up, linking early American hunters to butchered megafauna. To date, archaeologists have uncovered seventy mastodon or mammoth skeletons across the continent that exhibit the telltale signs of human hunters, such as the cut marks left by chert blades.[37]

Like many mammals, our species forms what ethologists call "fission-fusion societies." Our behavior is inextricably bound to group dynamics, and one of the key factors influencing our decisions is our ability to appraise our aptitude to access resources and amenities. If the prospects are good, we work to strengthen social bonds to ensure greater success. Otherwise, we venture out in small bands in search of undisturbed environments rich in wildlife. Evolutionary psychologists have dubbed this phenomenon "biophilia," a controversial scientific theory that locates the aphorism "the grass is always greener on the other side" in our DNA.[38] Whether or not you are willing to accept that notion, Ohio in the closing days of the Pleistocene would have offered curious bands of human hunters a veritable paradise filled with megafauna that had no evolutionary experience cohabitating with primates armed with stone-tipped javelins.

Just exactly when humans first arrived in the Americas remains hotly debated, and some sites suggest early pulses of migration as far back as 20,000 BP or earlier. In 2014, a global team of geneticists completed the sequencing of DNA from the remains of a child discovered in the only known Clovis-era burial site. Using advanced polymerase chain-reaction techniques, the team was able to compare the child's mitochondrial DNA markers with mutations found in remains from other populations. The geneticists discovered that this child unearthed in western Montana was part of a human lineage that separated from people in far eastern Siberia about 13,000 BP (give or take 2,600 years). Comparing samples, the team also determined that these Clovis-era people were direct ancestors to the overwhelming majority of Indigenous people found throughout the Americas.[39]

If you accept this direct lineage of America's first inhabitants through Siberia, their behavior in the new continents has historic roots. In 2012, a team of Russian archaeologists unearthed a carcass of a mammoth from the Siberian arctic. This wasn't just another pile of bones. As the team uncovered the remains, they found soft tissue, including skin and the distinctive hump of fat on its back, still attached to the skeleton. Other mammoths have been pulled from the permafrost with a full coat of fur, but this specimen provided evidence for our human proclivity for eating megafauna. Forensic analysis of the skeleton revealed a particularly violent end. The team's research, published in *Science* in 2016, reads like a crime scene report. One strong blow punctured the cheekbone, leaving the characteristic sign of a weapon with a flat, sharp point. Several of the mammoth's ribs had notches in them from similar blows, which likely targeted critical organs. Its left shoulder blade had been hit repeatedly by a weapon, and the spine of the scapula was fractured by a hard blow from a thrusting spear, suggesting a diverse arsenal of weapons. Finally, other evidence points to the butchering of the dead animal. The jawbone was broken, likely to extract the tongue, and the only remaining tusk revealed evidence of damage consistent with someone removing sharp ivory flakes for tools. Carbon 14 dating of the site and bones affirmed the kill happened around 44,650 BP, give or take a thousand years. This pushed back the arrival of humans in the Siberian arctic earlier than had been previously thought and firmly established that the ancestors of the first Americans knew how to kill megafauna.[40]

Whether or not earlier bands of humans had migrated before them, the Clovis people arrived with a tool kit that allowed them to thrive in every habitat on the continent. Within two thousand years, they had made their way from Beringia all the way to northeast Ohio, where they left their stone tools and the butchered remains of megafauna behind in places like Nobles Pond, Burning Tree Golf Course, and Martins Creek.

For geologists, the last glacial retreat marked the end of the Pleistocene and the beginning of the Holocene, an ancient Greek word for "entirely new," a fitting name for a time when humans spread across earth's last habitable continents. Humans and megafauna shared Ohio for little more than one thousand years before the beasts eventually disappeared from the archaeological record. For all our scientific and cultural sophistication, we know precious little about these first peoples. We refer to them as Paleoindians or the Clovis culture, but these names are rooted in the twentieth century. Surely they named the marvelous creatures that provided these earlier communities with nourishment. Surely their oral traditions invested them with significance. What names did they apply to the landforms, like Flint Ridge, or the kettle lakes and bogs they frequented?

The great human geographer Yi-Fu Tuan described the human relationship with the land with the following equation: Space + Culture = Place.[41] After the arrival of these first humans, we can begin to talk of Ohio as a place invested with meaning. The stories people tell themselves about their relationship with the land bind them to it. This is the root of indigeneity—binding your culture to a landscape and making a place you call home. Other than their chert tools, we have no other indication of how these people bonded with the land. There are no Chauvet caves adorned with art or burial sites from this time period in Ohio. And without more evidence, the past remains the province of our imaginations, biases, and beliefs rather than reality.

Deloria believed native oral traditions still contain "memories" of the deep past and that we can recover them through a process called "upstreaming." Many Indigenous oral traditions speak of ice and snow as barriers. For the Tlingit of southeast Alaska, that might be expected, considering they still have glaciers among their homelands, but for people who inhabit the Great Lakes region? Deloria recounts an Anishinaabe creation story that aligns rather well with how modern science understands it. "God tried four times to create the present world," it reads, "but the first three efforts were doomed to failure because there was too much ice. The fourth time the effort was successful."[42]

Although modern residents of northeast Ohio make a sport out of complaining about the weather, we do so from our heated homes while wearing synthetic fibers that envelop us like a second skin. The Indigenous experience could invest winter with malevolent spirits. Consider the wendigo, a terrifying legend among many Algonquian-speaking cultures that might be described as the Indigenous equivalent to Europe's grim reaper. Stinking of decay and motivated by a hunger for human flesh, the wendigo stalked the land like a zombie. It was composed entirely of ice and served as a portend of famine and hard winters. The gap in demeanor between the wendigo and Punxsutawney Phil says a lot about the relative stakes a bad winter could mean for the cultures that produced them.

Although many Americans take a literal interpretation of their own creation myths, Indigenous people understand their creation narratives as knowledge wrapped in the mystery of metaphor. In his famous interview with John Neihardt, Black Elk put it this way: "This they tell, and whether it happened so or not I do not know; but if you think about it, you can see that it is true."[43] In considering where to begin the human story in this land we call Ohio, we would do well to not form too concrete a picture of a world we know only through a precious few bones and stone tools scattered across the state. You may not want to leave room for a wendigo in the mind's eye, but you never know when a farm plow or construction backhoe will uncover something that completely rewrites our understanding of the past.

CHAPTER 2
Ground Rules

Summer is the season for forest mushrooms in Ohio. Wait a few days after a good, soaking rain, and fungi will explode from beneath damp leaf litter and rotting wood. With about ten thousand documented species, Ohio hosts a profusion of fungi. Mycologists do their best to sort them into broad categories with common traits: boletes are shaped like atomic bomb blasts, while polypores look like fins of coral. Identifying any individual species requires an understanding of multiple factors, including habitat, color, gill form, and the analysis of microscopic spores that give life to the next generation. Although guidebooks provide some help, there is no replacement for experience. That's why it's good to know a seasoned mycologist like Cleveland's own Jeremy Umansky.

It's a late July morning, and the temperature is already in the mideighties, but that hasn't deterred about twenty aspiring

foragers from joining Umansky for a two-hour class on identifying wild plants. We gather in the parking lot at Punderson
State Park, and Chef Umansky goes over the ground rules for the
day. Touching deadly mushrooms will not hurt you. Touching
some plants can hurt you. Be curious and ask questions. And,
most importantly, foraging for personal use is legal at state parks
in Ohio.[1] The group consists of an eclectic bunch: an engineer,
graduate students, and parents with small children looking for
an offbeat educational nature experience. When asked why she
took time on a Sunday morning to tromp around the forest, one
woman simply states, "I like to find things and eat them." Almost
everyone cracks a smile and nods in agreement.

Umansky is well-qualified to lead this group. He holds
a wild-foraged mushroom certification from the Michigan
Department of Agriculture and has been working with wild foods
for years. After attending culinary school in New York, he moved
back to his hometown with a passion for using local, often foraged ingredients to make Eastern European deli fare from scratch.
Walking into his delicatessen, Larder, in Ohio City's Hingetown
neighborhood, is a bit of a time warp. The kitchen is located in
the old Ohio City firehouse and was built when horses still pulled
the engines. Although most patrons focus on the delectable pas-
tries on display, a wall of shelves holds jars that hint at Umansky's
passion for transforming what most places would consider food
waste into delicacies. He specializes in the use of koji (*Aspergillus
oryzae*), a fungus responsible for the unique flavor of soy sauce,
miso paste, and sake. He uses it on nearly everything, imparting
its rich umami taste and complex floral and citrus notes.

Although he fills Larder's storeroom with local foods from
a network of small producers, Umansky is also a skilled forager,
and he often spends his weekends gathering ramps (*Allium tricoc-
cum*), apples, and even invasive Japanese knotweed to stock his

kitchen. At Larder, you can find chocolate infused with turkey tail mushrooms, pine needle-infused soda, and acorn-flour pasta. "Acquiring a lot of knowledge about microorganisms takes a long time, but today, comfortability is the goal," he says as he guides us further into the forest.

Umansky directs our attention to a patch of jewelweed (*Impatiens capensis*) speckled with bursts of orange flowers. Although jewelweed does have some culinary uses, its sap is high in saponins that bind to oils, making it a perfect remedy for irritants like the oily compound urushiol that makes poison ivy a nightmare during the summer. The buzz of a lawn mower and the metronomic blasts of a car alarm fade as we walk further into the damp forest.

Everyone is on the lookout for mushrooms, but Umansky tells us to pay attention to the tree species nearby. "Don't just go out looking for chanterelle mushrooms," he says, "go out looking for beech and oak trees." Because fungi lack chloroplasts, they can't make their own food through photosynthesis. Instead, they feed on organic matter using digestive enzymes. Some mushrooms break down decaying plant matter (sapotrophs), some form symbiotic relationships with trees (mycorrhizae), some parasitize plants, and some apply multiple survival strategies. Endoparasitoids like the Cordyceps fungi have even evolved to parasitize insects. The fungus converts the insect's body into mycelium and hijacks the animal's nervous system, compelling the bug to seek high ground, where spores bursts from its body, filling the air with a new generation. Although rare, local Ohio naturalists have discovered crickets infected with Cordyceps.[2]

Ohio hosts thousands of different fungi species, but only a handful are considered "choice" edibles. Giant puffballs, chicken of the woods, morels, oyster, and, of course, chanterelles are some of the most sought-after mushrooms in the state. The remaining fungi occupy dubious categories and require a trained eye to distinguish. "Toxicity is a sliding scale," Umansky cautions. "It isn't just die or not die, there's a lot of room in between. In the state of Ohio, there's only about seven mushrooms that are toxic enough to kill you by ingestion. Everything else is on this scale that goes down from there. There are mushrooms that will make you sick if you eat them, they'll make you wish you were dead, and the treatments are horrible, but you will live." He says that even our individual gut biomes determine our reactions to different species. *Boletus pallidus* is a great example—great to cook with, but half the people who try it get diarrhea. For some, even a choice mushroom like chicken of the woods will cause their lips to go numb and produce a red flush around the mouth that can last several hours. Umansky suggests inexperienced foragers first cook and eat a few ounces "to test for intolerance or other issues such as allergies." Start slow and wait twenty-four hours after eating to see how you digest a new mushroom before eating more, he cautions.

Otherwise safe mushrooms can also be dangerous if they're growing in toxic substrate. Because northeast Ohio lies in the heart of the rust belt, our industrial legacy makes urban foraging particularly fraught. "If it's an urban environment and looks like there's lots of industrial work being done, even if there's great plants growing and things seem like they're thriving, double check the area," Umansky warns. Mushrooms can thrive in even heavily polluted environments. That chanterelle you spy at the local park might have been soaking up heavy metals (or worse) as it absorbs the mistakes of our past. In the aftermath of the Chernobyl nuclear power plant disaster in 1986, wild mushrooms in the vicinity concentrated the radioactive isotope cesium-137 through the process of biomagnification. Although mushrooms are still able to survive, our thyroid glands mistake the isotope for iodine and unknowingly absorb the poison. With a half-life of thirty years, and destructive in even miniscule quantities, the cesium-137 released by our actions have foreclosed on foraging wild foods in some environments for centuries to come.[3] Umansky is far more concerned with more familiar pollutants, though. "The couple of feet on the edge of the trail," he cautions, "that's the dog pee zone."

As we fan out and scour the forest, it's difficult to get fully immersed in the setting. The roar of commercial planes periodically drowns out the sounds of the forest. Several times, my heart begins to race when I spot a splotch of white amid the forest litter only to discover a wayward golf ball from the course at the forest's edge. When describing the difference between chanterelles and their poisonous look-alike, the jack-o'-lantern mushroom (*Omphalotus olearius*), Umansky explains that white settlers were frightened by the green bioluminescent glow of *Omphalotus* species. Dubbed "foxfire," this phenomenon is endangered, he explains. "I've only seen it a couple times in our area because we have so much light pollution at night."

Public lands like Punderson State Park are guided by the principle of "multiple use," which affords consideration for the different ways people engage with nature. Although the principle is egalitarian on its surface, some uses foreclose on our ability to enjoy or even exercise others. Roderick Nash, an historian of American notions of wilderness, put it best: "Solitude is not easily shared."[4] This suggests that even a single use sought by too many people could destroy its enjoyment for all, a troubling thought for modern foragers.

Foraging has exploded in popularity in recent years. Based on Google trends data for North America, the search term "foraging" has doubled over the past two decades, usually spiking in late winter as the earth begins to wake up from its annual slumber.

Social media influencers and content creators have met the demand for knowledge of local plants and been rewarded with attention on par with celebrity chefs. Based out of Columbus, Alexis Nikole Nelson has over four million followers on TikTok, has appeared on *Jimmy Kimmel Live*, and is represented by United Talent Agency. She isn't bashful about including a heavy dose of history in her content. For her, foraging is not only a form of empowerment by gaining a small measure of independence from the marketplace, but it also connects her to her Black and Indigenous heritage.

In a 2021 interview with NPR, Nelson explained that it isn't easy or safe to be Black in public spaces, and that includes the forest. In May 2020, Christian Cooper was birdwatching in an area of Central Park known as the Ramble when a woman and an unleashed dog approached him. He asked her to leash the animal, and when she refused, Cooper attempted to befriend the dog, which caused the dogwalker to call 911 in distress. "There is an African American man—I am in Central Park—he is recording me and threatening myself and my dog," she said to the operator.[5] Video of the incident went viral and became a potent reminder that Americans don't leave behind their racial stereotypes when they venture out into nature.

Nelson's success has normalized the presence of an urban Black woman as an expert on spaces traditionally occupied by white suburbanites. She described the impact of Black representation in foraging. "One of the best days I think I've ever had in my life, I was out foraging and a girl who also happens to be Black—probably a teenager—she runs up to me and she's like, 'You are that girl from Tik Tok!'" she explained. "The way that her and her friends and her mom's face lit up, I went home and I cried....And the thing that stuck with me was she was just like, 'You're doing this for the culture.'"[6]

Nelson's story illustrates how intensely connected our relationship with nature is to our identity and place in society. The willingness of foragers like her and Umansky to share their knowledge with younger generations, and the rising popularity of foraging, suggests Ohioans are redefining their relationship with the land. In doing so, they are resurrecting a lifeway that defined the Indigenous relationship to these lands for millennia. Although most Ohioans have known no other system than industrial capitalism, it has only been engaged in shaping the land for about two hundred years. Compare that to the eleven thousand years of Indigenous occupation before it; our modern way of life represents less than 2 percent of the human experience living in Ohio. Seen another way, imagine a calendar representing the human story in Ohio. If the first people arrived on January 1, industrial capitalism didn't arrive until about noon on Christmas Day. Before white settlers arrived, Indigenous people sustained themselves and thrived for hundreds of generations in Ohio through hunting, foraging, and agriculture. As we struggle to strike a balance between material security, mental health, and environmental resilience today, we should take stock of history for some basic ground rules for living here.

Rule One: One Size Doesn't Fit All

The Clovis culture represents the first mass culture in North America. From the Arctic Circle to the deserts of Mexico, the Paleolithic tool kit the culture developed spread across the landscape for seven hundred years. No culture is a monolith, and Clovis was no different. When the first humans arrived in Ohio, their tools had been forged from local chert and would have been applied to local resources that required flexibility in their application, including large mammals, or megafauna. The extinction of the megafauna approximately ten thousand years ago necessitated additional cultural adaptation by Ohio's first settlers.

We do know for certain that their culture adapted to the absence of Pleistocene megafauna because the distinctive spear points that distinguish Clovis culture vanished along with the mastodons and Megalonyx. The ones that replaced them were smaller in dimension but equally deadly. The adaptation would have been a disruption, but it was one humans had a lot of practice with. In a way, our species was born with stone tools in our hands. Although scientists are fairly confident *Homo sapiens* branched off from our hominin ancestors no earlier than three hundred thousand years ago, evidence of stone tool use by hominins dates back over three million years. In January of 2023, an international team of archaeologists reported on a site in the upper Awash Valley of Ethiopia that contained over five hundred obsidian hand axes. Created through the same method of knapping that humans would employ to create paleo points in the Americas, the axes were razor-sharp. They were also 1.2 million years old. The archaeological team discovered the tools were crafted so uniformly that they described them as "standardized": "This was a stone-tool workshop." Their conclusion should make us rethink our ideas about our prehuman ancestors and our own relationship to tools in general, be it a paleo point or an iPhone.[7]

In the millennia after the megafauna's extinction, paleo points began to shrink significantly. In Ohio, archaeologists have identified a fracturing of the Clovis style of tools into a mosaic of different traditions with names like Kirk, Palmer, Thebes, and Gainey. One reason likely has to do with the size of the quarry. Bison, even the larger *B. antiquus* of the late Pleistocene, weighed only one thousand pounds, compared to the mammoths and mastodons that could approach fifteen thousand pounds or more in adulthood. Another reason has to do with a troubling aspect of how other animals respond to us. Biologists sometimes use the term "island tameness" or "ecological naivete" to describe the tendency for animals to disregard humans as a threat at first contact. After the settlement of the continent and the extinction of the megafauna, the species remaining had clocked humans as a threat and didn't allow them to approach and stick a stone point in their ribs. As a result, the first Americans designed weapons that could extend their reach. Propelled by atlatl launchers, chert-tipped darts remained the primary hunting tool until the bow and arrow arrived from the Arctic around two thousand years ago. Facing a transformed environment, early Americans adapted their culture to new realities.

Ohio had plenty of amenities to sustain modest human populations committed to a hunting and gathering lifestyle. By ten thousand years ago, the boreal forest was pushed north by a warming climate. Beech, oak, hickory, and chestnut trees replaced the conifer-dominated forests of the Pleistocene, providing significant forage opportunities. All of these tree species exhibit a boom-bust reproduction strategy called "masting." Walk through a hardwood forest in autumn and you will know whether you are in a mast year by how many nuts you find on the ground. Oak species, in general, produce relatively few acorns in off years. But every two to three years, they drop an unbelievable abundance of acorns, carpeting the forest floor (or your neighborhood sidewalk) with seeds. Unlike fruit trees, which want animals to eat their indigestible seeds, mast trees want to avoid hungry animals gobbling up their next generation. Masting evolved to limit the number of animals an ecosystem could support in off years and then overwhelm the environment in mast years with more nuts than the animal population could possibly eat, ensuring the germination of a new generation.

High in fat, and rich in protein and vitamins A and C, tree nuts challenge modern strains of domesticated cereal crops in terms of their nutritional density. Unlike domesticated crops, however, tree nuts like acorns are often loaded with bitter tannins that require significant labor to remove through pulverizing and washing the nutmeat. In the centuries following the megafauna's extinction, early Ohioans began to experiment with stone tools designed to process tree nuts. Hammerstones, pestles, and anvils from this time period, which archaeologists describe as the Early Archaic, give us a clue as to how people adapted to the changing landscape.

In 2008, archaeologists from the Cleveland Museum of Natural History excavated a Late Archaic (5,700 to 2,800 years ago) site just across the Black River from the massive US Steel mill in Lorain. Located near the French Creek Reservation, the site has witnessed dramatic swings in human land-use patterns. Although today it is part of the Lorain County Metroparks, it served as a farm and apple orchard for nearly 150 years before becoming parkland. Surveys from the time of white settlement identify beech and hickory trees along with red, white, and pin oak trees on the site, all mast trees. The 2008 excavation revealed an archaic settlement occupied sometime between 3,500 to 4,000 years ago. (Some evidence from the site suggests continued occupation after that.) Using hand tools and sifters, the archaeologists discovered multiple middens, or waste pits, containing worn-down tools, broken stone points, and animal bones. Although the midden layers contained raccoon, turtle, catfish, and wild turkey bones, the remains of one species predominated. "The relatively large sample of deer leg bone and antler fragments," the archaeological research report reads, "indicate that the hunting and processing of this animal was a primary activity of the pre-contact occupants."[8] Several burn and smudge pits excavated at the site were likely used to dry and process deerskins that would have clothed and sheltered the population from the elements.

Excavations also revealed twelve tools made of ground, not knapped, stone. These were designed for heavy-duty usage that would have shattered chert implements. Polished smooth from years of use, these stones were used to hammer, mash, and pulverize food, shape wood, and sharpen bone tools. Littered with mast, the middens revealed another essential component of Archaic culture. "The large quantities of burned nutshell reveal that gathering of mast from hickory, walnut, and possibly acorn was also an important subsistence activity," the report notes. The French Creek Reservation site was likely a seasonal camp, occupied in the autumn, just as deer and mast would have been most abundant. This transient settlement pattern is consistent with historical descriptions of hunting and gathering societies who move through the landscape according to the seasonal availability of food. Thousands of years from now, what stories will our trash tell about us? Will it tell the story of a people adapting to or fighting against a changing environment? Will there even be anyone around to excavate it?

Rule Two: Celebrate Your Environment

The camp at French Creek Reservation likely supported a population of not more than a few dozen people who would have been related through kinship ties. How they understood their relationship to the surrounding environment has been mostly lost, but there are important clues that indicate their deep bond to the creatures that sustained them. The archaeologists at the site found much more than just waste pits. They discovered a floor, complete with postholes, made from clay that had been meticulously cleansed of sediment and laid out to create a plat-form for ritual activities. The deliberate deposit of several ban-nerstones—used as weights for atlatl launchers—and deer bones suggests a ceremonial recognition of the significance of the deer and the tools used to hunt them to sustain the life of the village. In his published article on the deposits, Dr. Brian Redmond ad-mits the limitations of our analysis. "The specific nature of these rituals is unclear," he concludes.[9]

Although we will likely never know exactly how these tools were used or the meaning they held, they, along with the ani-mal remains, were deliberately placed and interred here. A small fire had been made and, either when it burned out or was ex-tinguished as part of a ceremony, the deer bones were carefully placed in the charred clay. Unlike the bones in the midden pits, these were not disarticulated or smashed to extract marrow. At three different locations, a deer shoulder blade was paired with an antler. The midden pits revealed rough sketches of the settle-ment's economy, but these ritual deposits suggest much more was going on than just hunting and gathering.

The tradition of animal sacrifice appears in nearly every culture, and almost every holy book contains instructions for the proper way to do it. Although the practice serves multiple purposes, from sanctifying a life event to offering basic instruc-tions for sanitation, the human fascination with animal sacrifice acknowledges the dependence of any hunting or herding peo-ple on the death of their fellow animals. Thanks to our modern economy and its ability to alienate consumers from the land, few of us have to witness the slaughter necessary to sustain us. Even for those who say grace before digging into a meal, I doubt your thoughts wander to the killing room floor. Hunting and herding people had no such buffers, so they created them in the form of rituals tied to stories. Based on the quantity of deer remains and signs of rendering hides, the people who occupied the camp at the French Creek Reservation site likely constructed rituals to understand, sanctify, and celebrate the animal so central to their existence.

Although we have no records of this group, Indigenous cultures throughout the Midwest understood animals largely through stories and ritual. These traditions employ animals, or human-animal hybrids, to impart valuable life lessons. Sometimes tragic, comedic, romantic, or downright vulgar, these stories provide models of behavior both good and bad. Ella Cara Deloria (Vine Deloria Jr.'s aunt) preserved dozens of these tales in 1932 when she published *Dakota Texts*. A Yankton Dakota, Ella was born in 1888 on the nation's reservation just two years before the Wounded Knee Massacre. A brilliant student, she earned a scholarship to Oberlin College, where she studied before transferring to Columbia. Her education in northeast Ohio would serve as a springboard directly into the heart of a brewing academic revolution.

At Columbia, she met Franz Boas, a pioneering figure in the study of the human past and cultural differences. Boas believed anthropology and ethnology had been corrupted by racist assumptions that placed Western civilization at the vanguard of human history and judged every other culture against its model. To counter this, he argued scholars could only understand a culture by living among its people and adhering to a dispassionate, objective perspective. When interpreting fieldwork data, he advanced the idea of cultural relativism, an admission that every observer holds cultural biases that distort their perspective.

Ella was a natural study and fell in with some of Boas's most brilliant graduate students, Margaret Mead and Ruth Benedict. Growing up in the shadow of genocide, both literal and cultural, Ella now found herself in a community dedicated to understanding and cataloging Indigenous culture. After she graduated, she returned to the Lakota reservations on the northern plains and recorded her people's stories, dances, and rituals. And in *Dakota Texts*, she published two stories that may help us better understand the culture of the people at the French Creek Reservation site. In the story of Elk Man, a handsome lothario who can seduce any woman upsets the sexual norms of the community and earns a death sentence from the elders. After promising the Elk Man's brother horses, a home, and a wife in exchange for his permission, the elders hatch a plot to assassinate the man at the upcoming village games. The story emphasizes the disruption caused by the Elk Man's sexual appetite. As the games approach, the story notes, "he outdid even himself, by eloping with all the remaining women with good reputations; and ruined their names." Sensing his demise, the Elk Man instructs his sister-in-law to perform a ritual sacrifice of his remains after he is killed. "Cut off my head, and sever my right arm at the shoulder-joint," he tells her. "Then run with the head and arm to the thick wood and leave them there."[10]

The assassination plays out as expected, and the man's sister-in-law follows his instructions. The villagers bury his body and burn a fire over it. The elders renege on their promise of wealth to the brother, who is startled by the cry of an elk later that night. His assassinated brother appears before him "whole and well." When confronted by the man they had just murdered, the village elders finally grasp the lesson. "And then it was clear that the young man was really an elk, and so it was beyond their power to subdue him by killing him," the story continues, "neither could they put a stop to his attraction for women." The story of the Elk Man contains a familiar trope in Indigenous narratives that ascribe to animals a supernatural power to regenerate so long as one observes, in this case, a ritual sacrifice. The significance of the shoulder and head to regeneration is a tantalizing detail given the pairing of antler and scapula in the ritual burials at the French Creek Reservation site. As for the narrative elements concerning betrayal and the ability of sexual promiscuity to disrupt a community, I'll allow the reader to draw their own lessons about human nature from this story.

Ella Deloria was clear about how the Lakota understood these stories. In the introduction to the narrative, she writes, "They are intended to amuse and entertain, but not to be believed." The stories of Elk Men, Deer Women, and warriors who became snakes were not to be taken literally but rather as allegories about the relationship between humans and the land. They were never considered the final word on the nature of life; instead, they invite the listener to contemplate the great mystery of existence and understand it on their own terms.

Although the tale of the Elk Man leaves plenty of room for interpretation and reveals a complex culture struggling to make sense of their place in the world, other stories contain unambiguous lessons born of past mistakes. Few are as explicit as the Blackfeet story of the Buffalo Wife. It begins with a village on the verge of starvation because the bison refuse to be scared over a nearby cliff. Spying the herd mingling near the jump, a young woman cries out to the bison and promises to marry one if the herd will throw their bodies over the cliff. To her surprise, the bison begin to jump willingly. A large bull approaches her to make good on the deal and carries her away in horror. After butchering the bison herd, the woman's father sets out to locate his daughter. With the help of a magpie (corvids are powerful figures in many Indigenous traditions), the father locates and sends a message to his daughter to meet him at a nearby wallow. Before they can escape, the herd discovers the plot and tramples the father to death "until not even a small piece of him could be seen."

Shocked with grief, the woman receives a powerful rebuke from the bison bull. "Ah!…you mourn for your father. Now you see how it is with us. We have seen our mothers, fathers, and many of our relatives hurled over the rocky walls and killed for food for your people." Having imparted the lesson, the bison offers the woman a chance to return to her people if she can resurrect her dead father. With the help of the magpie, she locates a vertebra from her father, covers it with her robe, and literally sings him back to life. Before she leaves, the bison teach her their dance and song and encourage her to carry its wisdom to her people: "through which the animals slain each year are returned to life."[11]

This story provides the origin of a critical cultural practice and situates it in the context of environmental limits. The story also drives home a point present in many Indigenous traditions: the blurring of the boundary between humans and animals. The Salmon Boy story of the Tlingit, somewhat similar in construction to the Buffalo Wife narrative, describes each species of salmon as a "people" with their own identity.[12] The ritual dances and songs reinforced the lesson for each generation, embedding it into the culture's very identity.

A span of over a thousand miles and several thousand years separates these Lakota, Blackfeet, and Tlingit stories from the people who lived off the deer and mast at the French Creek Reservation site. Reconstructing the richness of their culture from a few broken tools and bones is a hopeless endeavor. We may as well hand over a crushed plastic water bottle and a broken keyboard to a group of aliens and expect them to understand the complexity of our own civilization. When paired with the narratives of historical Indigenous cultures, however, the archaeological evidence suggests an acknowledgment of the dependence these people had on the wild animals that survived the

Pleistocene extinctions. This is different from viewing Indigenous people as America's first "environmentalists" who lived in balance with the land. Rooted in the racist myth of the "noble savage," the twentieth-century attempts to assign contemporary ethics to ancient people ignored plenty of evidence to the contrary. Cautionary tales such as the story of the Buffalo Wife describe a culture struggling and, at times, failing to navigate a complex relationship with their environment.

Culture is always in a feedback loop with its environment, and Indigenous people were able to occupy the land we now call Ohio for over ten thousand years because their culture had been shaped by hard lessons about what worked. Some elements, like the stories above, are tied closely to particular locations or animals that make life possible. How would you describe your own culture's relationship with the environment? What stories does our modern culture tell us about the land beneath our feet or the resources essential to our lives? If our culture becomes unmoored from the land, how far can we distance ourselves from it before nature will remind us of our body's reliance on pure food, water, and oxygen?

Rule Three: Not All Progress Is Good

All children are curious about the world around them, but the Goslin brothers took it to extremes. Robert and John Goslin became Boy Scouts and explored every creek and rock ledge around their hometown of Lancaster, about thirty miles southeast of Columbus. Although most children participate in the Scouts to learn skills that modern industry is in the process of making obsolete, the Goslin brothers went well beyond the usually modest requirements of earning merit badges. By age eleven, Robert had uncovered so many Indigenous artifacts that he opened his own museum. The brothers became so proficient at it, that in February of 1927, they began excavating a local rock shelter known as Kettle Hill Cave. When their hand trowels uncovered a human skeleton, meticulously wrapped in woven reeds, their efforts would gain the attention of Dr. H. C. Shetrone, an archaeologist at Ohio State University and director of the university's museum. The brothers instantly became local celebrities. The *Columbus Dispatch* reported on their find, and an accompanying photo of them, decked out in Boy Scout uniforms and standing over the burial, appeared in the paper.

When Dr. Shetrone arrived, he assisted the brothers in excavating the site. Although it would receive far less attention, the plant remains this odd crew unearthed would show that life in Ohio began to change about three thousand years ago. The refuse pits contained the familiar forage of tree nuts, but they also held the remains of plants such as maize, squash, and rice that would be the foundation of a new way of life.[13] For nearly eight thousand years, people living in Ohio had relied on animals for the vast majority of their diet. Evidence from multiple sites throughout the Midwest have led archaeologists to argue that as recently as three thousand years ago, hunting accounted for as much as 80 percent of the subsistence needs for people throughout the Great Lakes region.[14] What could make a society change their way of life after such a long period of time? Was the change for the better? How scholars have answered those questions has often come down to what they value in the present.

Western notions of progress have changed over time, but they are often tied to measurements of material wealth as defined by macroeconomic forces such as productivity metrics, education levels, and infant mortality rates. For centuries, critics have challenged this value system and pointed out that less quantifiable metrics, such as happiness, freedom, and altruism, serve as better standards of progress. The entire science fiction genre plays on the juxtaposition of worlds overflowing with fantastical material wealth, scientific knowledge, and technological power, all made possible through brutal exploitation and violence. Although we have been raised in a world filled with these cautionary tales, we still struggle to imagine how too much of a good thing could be so bad. By these standards, the people inhabiting Ohio didn't make much "progress" from the end of the last ice age until the arrival of Europeans, despite the fact that they had managed to survive for over ten thousand years.

The fluted chert points of the Clovis tool kit represented progress in this older, material definition. They propelled humans across the North American continent, but this success came at a price. Armed with the sharp, leaf-shaped Clovis points, early Americans wielded a tool that could kill the largest land animals on the planet. The megafaunal extinction event at the close of the Pleistocene may represent the first time in our species' history that our power to change the environment exceeded our understanding of nature. Ronald Wright has described this event as the first example of what he termed a "progress trap." "Paleolithic hunters who learnt how to kill two mammoths instead of one had made progress," he wrote. "Those who learnt how to kill 200…had made too much."[15] Although the inhabitants of Ohio would adapt their tool kit to the new reality, the future would hold similar progress traps that would test their ability to change their way of life.

Wright represents a school of thought that emerged in the mid-twentieth century following the fieldwork of Boas and his students, including Ella Deloria. This generation of scholars described several advantages of a hunting and gathering lifestyle over one rooted in an industrial economy organized around wage labor. After all, who wouldn't want a more diverse, healthier diet, heaps of leisure time, and an egalitarian social structure? Although valorizing hunting and gathering lifestyles was a necessary corrective to the ethnocentric views at the time, some modern writers reduced the broad spectrum of cultures practicing these lifeways into a monolith that would serve as an antidote for all our modern ills. Before he won a Pulitzer Prize for *Guns, Germs, and Steel*, popular science writer Jared Diamond described agriculture as "The Worst Mistake in the History of the Human Race."[16]

The more extreme iterations of these ideas haven't aged well. At their worst, they exoticized hunting and gathering cultures to serve as a rhetorical escape from the problems of the modern world, a rich tradition you can find in the art of Picasso and Gauguin or the writing of Herman Melville (*Typee*) and Edgar Rice Burroughs (*Tarzan of the Apes*). This romanticization links back to the myth of the noble savage that captured the imagination of colonial writers such as Jean-Jacques Rousseau and James Fenimore Cooper. Despite its exaggerations and rhetorical excesses, the tradition forced scholars to confront the very real evidence that hunting and gathering cultures created complex and even desirable civilizations worth inhabiting. Notwithstanding the efforts of Boas and others to unmask our modern biases, some of the most respectable archaeologists and anthropologists continued to disregard ancient life throughout their careers. The University of Chicago archaeologist Robert John Braidwood, a founder of the field of scientific archaeology, for example, described hunting and gathering people as "savages." "A man who spends his whole life following animals just to kill them to eat, or moving from one berry patch to another," he wrote, "is really living just like an animal himself."[17]

Although multiple studies have concluded that hunter-gatherer cultures lived quite well, there is no denying it was an active life. Through forensic analysis of human bones, anthropologists from Ohio State University determined that the people living in Ohio about three thousand years ago had "robust skeletal health...with few cases of infectious disease, dietary deficiency, and disease stress." Most of the skeletons, however, showed evidence of degenerative joint disease (DJD). Half of the population in the study exhibited signs of arthritis or other DJD by the age of thirty. The disease manifested differently in male and female bodies, heavily suggesting gender divisions of labor.[18] If you were to ask a doctor of osteopathic medicine, they would tell you DJD is the result of "mechanical stress," repetitive and sometimes intensive action. Tennis elbow, turf toe, and carpal tunnel syndrome are types of DJD that come when our bodies intersect with the demands (and, sometimes, the pleasures) of modern life.

Mechanical stress was a necessary part of life for our species throughout history. It remains so today. The Centers for Disease Control and Prevention (CDC) estimate that a quarter of the US's adult population has some form of arthritis.[19] Repetitive stress injuries have been a focus for organized labor since the birth of the Industrial Revolution. When the Smithsonian Folkways released an anthology of classic labor songs in 2006, included on the album was the song "Carpal Tunnel" by labor organizer John O'Connor, with a chorus that illustrated the inhuman demands of factory labor:

> I got that old carpal tunnel and my hands won't move
> But the foreman tells me to stay in the groove
> You cut that cattle as fast as I do
> You'll get that carpal tunnel too.[20]

Ohio's prehistoric people didn't have foremen driving them at work, but they did have to shape the environment to survive. Although we use the term "hunting and gathering" to describe these cultures, most of the labor involved creating tools and rendering raw plant and animal parts for consumption and materials. The repetitive actions of knapping chert, processing animal hides, pounding seeds, and shaping wood would have been enough to produce the types of joint disease observed in the skeletons of hunting and gathering peoples. Outfitting a single person with pants and a shirt required the skins of at least five deer and eighty hours of labor to transform the dead animal into wearable clothes.[21] Much of that labor required repetition, such as scraping the flesh off the hide and massaging the leather for hours on end. To our modern sensibilities, this seems like drudgery, but for the men and women who transformed the bodies of animals into tools for survival, it was an expressive art form that conferred social status as well. Our culture valorizes hunters as breadwinners and for "bringing home the bacon," but hide workers created wealth for the community by transforming raw materials into goods that held value both for their utility and as currency they could exchange for other goods.[22]

The stone grinders discovered at the French Creek Reservation archaeological site illustrate how processing plants also created a great deal of labor. When the colonial naturalist William Bartram traveled among the Creek Nation in the 1770s, he reported how tree nuts remained a staple for these people thousands of years after the advent of agriculture. "I have seen above an hundred bushels of these [hickory] nuts belonging to one family. They pound them to pieces, and then cast them into boiling water, which, after passing through fine drainers, preserves the most oily part of the liquid: this they call by a name which signifies hiccory [*sic*] milk; it is as sweet and rich as fresh cream, and is an ingredient in most of their cookery."[23]

Although stone points, scrapers, and grinders were central to the hunting and gathering economy, the manipulation of fire may have been even more important to maintaining a way of life. For most of us born into technologically advanced cultures, we consider fire in just a few contexts: as a source of heat in the hearth or furnace, as a form of entertainment, and in the process of refining materials in a kiln, refinery, or mill. Nearly all other forms of fire fall under the "wild" category and are considered destructive. Although early Ohioans clearly used fire in these same contexts, they also employed it to shape their environment.

We are able to reconstruct some of these prehistoric ecosystems because scientists have developed the ability to read the past by analyzing the layers of sediment deposited on the bed of ancient lakes. Just as climate scientists can measure the levels of CO_2 by drilling deep into the cores of glaciers and examining a thin cross section under a microscope, we can identify and measure the pollen and charcoal present with remarkable accuracy. In the late 1990s, paleobotantists working on cores from a lake on the Cumberland Plateau in eastern Kentucky not only traced the replacement of the Pleistocene boreal forest with hardwood mast in microscopic pollen levels, they also found a jump in the prevalence of charcoal in lake sediment beginning about three thousand years ago.[24] Just like the rings on a tree, the land has a way of recording its own history, and the story at Cliff Palace Pond was shaped heavily by fire three millennia ago. When hemlock trees retreated northward around 4,800 years ago, it made room for eastern red cedar, which crowded out the oaks, walnuts, and chestnuts. Although invasive, red cedar is so intolerant to fire that the US Forest Service advises that "a single fire may remove eastern red cedar from a site."[25] Mast trees, in contrast, can survive periodic, low-intensity blazes. Somewhere along the way, prehistoric peoples discovered the connection and used fire to favor the trees that could feed them. The strategy was extremely effective. In his history of precolonial America, Charles C. Mann estimates that by the time white settlers arrived, "as many as one out of every four trees in between southeastern Canada and Georgia was a chestnut."[26]

By changing forest ecosystems through fire, the people who occupied Ohio three thousand years ago created a cascading effect through the environment. By encouraging forests filled with mast, Indigenous people also created the perfect environment for both turkey and passenger pigeons. Considered a semidomesticate, turkeys coevolved with Indigenous cultures. Both bird species gobbled up tree nuts whole, but the passenger pigeon was nothing short of a biological hurricane. Somewhere in size between a mourning dove and a rock pigeon that you can find in most urban areas today, passenger pigeons flew low to the ground at speeds reaching sixty miles per hour. White colonists called the bird the "blue meteor" due to its speed and gray-blue body feathers punctuated by a blaze of iridescent throat feathers that reflected shades of copper, purple, and green. Despite a somewhat restricted range that included the Great Lakes and Appalachia, the passenger pigeon was likely the most populous bird on the planet when Europeans arrived in North America. Their numbers defy the ability of words to communicate. Their flocks, often described as waves or even rivers of birds, chased mast through the forests of the Great Lakes. When they located a carpet of tree nuts, they would create roosts so thick that multiple historical sources report how their combined weight could tear the limbs off a mature tree.[27] Despite competition for the same foods, people and pigeons coexisted in the forests of Ohio for over ten thousand years.

Based on data collected from sites across Ohio, archaeologists determined that the human population began to significantly increase around three thousand years ago.[28] Although we still aren't sure the exact trigger for this change in the relationship between people and their environment, it would lead to the most significant revolution in human life in the region since the extinction of the megafauna. Whether as a result of better understanding ecological rhythms, the relaxation of family planning practices such as abortion and infanticide, or another, unknown cause, population growth necessitated changes in the way people lived on the land. It likely accelerated the use of fire to shape forest environments and perhaps led to the discovery of new sources of forage. Anthropogenic (human-created) fires remove dense brush and understory bushes, leaving an ideal habitat for opportunistic perennial plants. And perhaps feeling the pressure of a growing population on their subsistence practices, people in Ohio began to experiment more intently with several native plant species around three thousand years ago.

Seeds from the amaranth family of plants have been found at archaeological sites throughout Ohio dated to this time period.[29] Known by common names such as lamb's quarters or goosefoot (due to the shape of its leaves), *Chenopodium berlandieri* pops up in early spring and grows a foot or so before flowering and developing thick seed clusters. Nutritionally, chenopods and other plants in the amaranth family are packed with protein and calories. Quinoa, a close relative of *C. berlandieri*, packs 222 calories into a single cup, which equals or surpasses most other domesticated whole grains.[30] The problem is that the seeds are no bigger than a match head and would have required tremendous labor to harvest meaningful amounts.

The remains of sunflowers (*Helianthus annuus*) also begin to appear at this time. With seeds twice the size of chenopods, sunflowers are dense in protein, fiber, and fat. Although they are easier to harvest than goosefoot seeds, you will need to compete with the American goldfinch, which can be found fluttering around drooping sunflower heads in late summer. I've seen a flock of goldfinches pick clean the head of a sunflower the size of a dinner platter in a single day. The plants produce such prodigious amounts of seed because each generation must survive the foraging habits of animals. Cultivation is never guaranteed. Last spring, I confidently sowed over one thousand sunflower seeds in my yard only to watch chipmunks devour them, stuffing dozens in their cheeks until they looked like a band of jazz trumpeters. No amount of bitter coffee grounds, cayenne powder, or even physical shielding deterred them. They consumed every seed.

The people living in the valleys and ridges of Ohio also cultivated squash (*Cucurbita pepo*) at this time. Archaeological sites throughout Ohio dating back thousands of years are littered with easily identifiable squash seeds. Even rinds have survived, buried generations ago in refuse pits.[31] Containing a rich variety of subspecies, from hardy acorn and butternut to soft-skinned zucchini, the squash family may have been the first plant domesticated in North America. Cultivated primarily for its seeds and its use as gourds, squash would have provided the people living in Ohio with another source of calories packed with protein and oils.

Taken together, these experiments represent a cultural revolution, introducing low-scale horticulture into their hunting and gathering economy. In the mid-twentieth century, scholars identified the Ohio River Valley and Mississippi Bottoms as one of only a handful of locations where humans had pursued plant domestication. Known as the Eastern Agricultural Complex (EAC), the domestication of plants provided Indigenous communities with insurance against uncertainty.[32] With periods ranging from two to ten years, when and where mast might fall always varied. This reality required a complex decision-making process that balanced the risks of moving a community against the possible rewards of seasonal (or annual) abundance. EAC crops helped alleviate some of the opportunity costs of staying put. Although they couldn't compete with a forest floor carpeted with mast, the plant seeds from the EAC offered a reliable source of calories that didn't put the heavy burden of relocation on the bodies of the community.

The growth of populations and their experimentation with plant cultivation also coincides with several cultural elaborations discovered at archaeological sites throughout Ohio. Although we have evidence of human and even Neanderthal ceremonial burials in Europe and Asia dating to one hundred thousand years ago (or earlier), burials didn't become prevalent in Ohio's archae-ological record until about three thousand years ago. Some of the older sites dedicated exclusively to burial have been found in glacial landforms such as kames and moraines.

Death, and the way people respond to it through ceremony, tells you much about a culture. A corpse, of course, presents a practical problem for a community that becomes apparent af-ter a few hours. Just as important, though, is the destruction of the social role filled by the dead individual within the com-munity. Addressing the grief created by the passing of a loved one is at the heart of every mortuary ritual in human cultures spanning the globe. One of the most universal methods of hon-oring the dead is the deposition of grave goods along with the deceased's physical remains. Grave goods represent a form of sacrifice intended to do one of three things: aid the deceased in the afterlife (if such a thing exists for a culture), celebrate the deceased through a meaningful object from their life, or signify the connection between the mourners and the dead. Among the most powerful emotions in the human experience, grief drives people, even those living seemingly modern, rational lives, to sometimes strange behaviors. In my community, Cleveland's Slavic Village, the sites of violent auto accidents or murders are clearly demarcated by elaborate shrines that often involve im-ages of the deceased, along with stuffed animals and a dizzying number of empty liquor bottles, indicating a celebration of the dead. Decorating the graves of loved ones—whether it takes the form of flowers or a simple stone resting on a grave marker—is a practice that transcends boundaries of faith. When the actor and northeast Ohio native Ryan Dunn died in an auto accident in 2011, the staff at La Cave du Vin in Coventry Village set out a glass of his favorite drink at the bar to await a patron who would never return again.

Although we will never know exactly how the prehistoric people of Ohio celebrated their dead, they left plenty of graves behind to show us they had developed complex ideas about the end of life. Interred with the bodies were an array of tools such as awls, projectile points, and bannerstones that likely belonged to the individual. Tobacco pipes also appear in grave sites dated to this time, indicating that the cultivation and use of tobacco had been enmeshed into the culture.

Many burials were also adorned with items best described as decorative or even sacred. When two teenage boys discovered skeletal remains along the Little Darby Creek just west of Columbus in 2009, they reported it to the police, who called in the Ohio Bureau of Criminal Investigation. It didn't take long for detectives to determine that this cold case was better handled by archaeologists at Ohio State University. The skeleton, along with a cache of grave goods, had been laid to rest about 1,445 years ago (give or take a decade or two) and covered with a layer of red ocher, a pigment derived from iron-rich clays.[33] The Little Darby Creek was familiar ground for archaeologists, who have found dozens of similar caches, including copper beads likely mined from ore veins far to the north along the shores of Lake Superior.[34]

These discoveries suggest that the people living in Ohio had established an elaborate, national trade network. A burial site on the Marblehead Peninsula near Sandusky Bay, which was excavated by a team from the Cleveland Museum of Natural History, uncovered the shells of lightning whelks and cotton fibers, both native to the Gulf of Mexico.[35] This trade network wasn't some kind of prehistoric superhighway between Lake Erie and Texas; instead, it would have been a decentralized distribution system capable of transporting nonperishable goods over long distances through an overlapping web of political, economic, and familial connections. The networks distributed extraordinary items that could have bonded families, settled disputes, or served as a medium of exchange for a range of resources. To the astonishment of archaeologists, several burial mounds in the state even contained meteorites, either as fragments or shaped into ornamental beads.[36]

Sometime around 1,500 years ago, Indigenous communities began constructing their own earthen burial mounds that have amazed and befuddled visitors since the earliest days of white settlement. Many of these mounds are hidden in plain sight. Archaeologists estimate that there were once ten thousand or more burial mounds in the Ohio River Valley. Today, a combination of ignorance, grave robbers, and the desire for real estate has destroyed most of the sacred grounds of prehistoric Ohio. The largest burial mound in the state is located in Miamisburg, just south of Dayton. At sixty-eight feet tall, it offers a commanding view of the Great Miami River's floodplain. The city manages the site but does so poorly. The mound is the central feature of the ninth hole at Mound Golf Course, where you can take a flight of stairs to its pinnacle, a grotesque profanity of a sacred place. (Modern burial sites have plenty of visitors who walk over graves, but at least the graves are clearly demarcated, communicating a clear expectation of behavior.) Across the street is a mound of another sort. Mound Laboratories created detonators and other components for nuclear weapons during the Cold War until the company was decommissioned in 2006. Entombed below are enough traces of plutonium-238, thorium-232, polonium-210, cesium-137, and tritium that—even after a cleanup costing more than a billion dollars—the Environmental Protection Agency (EPA) prohibits any residential development on the site.[37] The juxtaposition of the two mounds unmasks the hubris behind our traditional notions of "progress."

The construction of these mounds required the organization of labor on a scale that suggests the formation of a social hierarchy. Miamisburg Mound contains perhaps 1.5 million cubic feet of earth and stone, a monumental undertaking for a people wielding stone tools and carrying baskets made of deer hide or woven fiber.[38] Historians and anthropologists have hypothesized that hierarchies predate settled communities, and if research on our closest living primate relatives is anything to go by, the practice predates even our own species. The hunter-gatherer economy, however, placed important limitations on the accumulation of wealth and power. Scarcity of labor demanded forms of mutual aid that would have quickly ostracized "selfish" individualism. The necessity to move through the landscape also limited personal "property" to the tools or resources that a single individual could create or refine with their own skills and easily transport across large distances. Only with the establishment of a sedentary agricultural lifestyle would the creation of the traditional instruments of wealth accumulation (the collection of rents and taxes or the accumulation of personal property) have even been possible.[39]

The people living in Ohio began to commit to the path of sedentary agriculture with the arrival of cold-tolerant varieties of maize and beans around two thousand years ago. For the next thousand years, Ohio became a cultural incubator, spawning intricate cultural complexes known to modern scholars by the names Adena, Hopewell, and Fort Ancient. Villages clustered around river valleys and were surrounded by garden plots filled with plants from the EAC, as well as maize and beans. Although hunting and gathering remained important, domesticated plants overtook foraged foods as a growing percentage of the diet. Five hundred years before the arrival of Europeans in North America, archaeological evidence suggests that maize alone made up as much as 75 percent of the diet for some villages in Ohio.[40] Populations increased as well. Although hunter-gatherer camps supported no more than two dozen souls, agricultural villages in Ohio could support over one hundred people. Grave goods, including masks and fetishes in the form of forest animals, suggest a profound ritual connection hinted at by the oral traditions, such as the Buffalo Wife and the Elk Man, recorded during this period.

These people also employed their labor to construct mounds for purposes other than human burial. Stretching over 1,300 feet long, Serpent Mound in Adams County is the largest representation of a snake on the planet. Despite multiple excavations, archaeologists have failed to discover any artifacts within, suggesting the mound's sole purpose was to serve as an effigy, likely for ceremonial purposes. Dozens of these earthworks have been discovered throughout the region, including an alligator in Granville. Unfortunately, few have survived the centuries as well

as Serpent Mound. Similar earthworks appear throughout northeast Ohio, often perched above river valleys. The most accessible site for Clevelanders is the Fort Hill Earthworks in Rocky River Metropark. Beyond the nature center, take a flight of 155 steps up the escarpment to one of the best views in all of Cuyahoga County. In the summer, you can make out the shadowy shapes of fish in Rocky River and—with the exception of a road and passing air traffic—be transported to another time. The stairs will deliver you to the hilltop's narrowest point, a spit of land that widens to cover five acres of hardwood forest. Bisecting the point from the rest of the hill are three earthen walls that emerge from the forest floor like waves. In 2018, a research team from Cleveland State University discovered charcoal from a firepit at the site dated to around 2,250 BP, a time when Rome was at war with Carthage and the Mauryan Emperor Ashoka was promoting the teachings of Siddhartha Gautama, the Buddha. The team also discovered two mounds that have since been eroded, which served as a gateway to the site and marked the spring and autumn equinoxes through the centerline of the entire earthworks.[41]

People living in Ohio had also developed a sophisticated understanding of astronomy and likely employed it for both ceremonial and practical purposes. A site known as SunWatch just south of downtown Dayton offers perhaps the clearest picture yet of the lives of Indigenous people in the centuries before colonization. Excavations in the 1960s and 1970s revealed the postholes and foundations of an entire village on the banks of the Great Miami River. Arranged in a circular pattern, the village likely used the rich floodplain soils for an agricultural complex consisting of sunflowers and the "three sisters" of maize, beans, and squash. Archaeologists were able to reconstruct the village from the ground up with the help of an unlikely source: mud dauber wasp nests. Imprinted on the nests are exquisite details of the construction materials from the village, including smooth clay walls, wood roof beams, and even the plants used for the thatch roof based upon seeds that clung to the mud. The central plaza—at the center of which stood a fifty-foot-tall red cedar post that served as a solar calendar—was likely swept clean for use in dances or other ceremonies. Eight other posts were arranged around the pole that cast shadows on observation stations to signal dates in April and August, marking the start and finish of the growing season for maize. One building dubbed Solstice House II was positioned so that the rising sun would perfectly eclipse the center pole on the winter solstice.[42]

SunWatch reached a population of nearly 250 people before it was abandoned around eight hundred years ago. The "Mound Builder" civilizations vanished so thoroughly that by the time Europeans arrived, many of the ancient earthworks were already overgrown or in a state of ruin. Although the Indigenous cultures that occupied Ohio into the historical period continued many of the traditions from these earlier eras, they had forsaken large settlements that had been the hallmark of the Adena, Hopewell,

and Fort Ancient periods. The influence of these cultures born out of Ohio's river valleys spread as far north as New Brunswick and reached all the way to the Gulf Coast, where people who had never seen a glacial kame constructed ceremonial and burial mounds throughout the Mississippi Valley modeled on those in Ohio. If progress is an escalator from the material poverty of hunting and gathering to the excesses of modern consumer capitalism, why would a people, such as those who inhabited SunWatch, choose to go backward to a life that was more reliant on hunting and gathering?

One answer rests in a dirty secret about the agricultural revolution from archaeological sites around the world. Compared to their hunting and gathering neighbors and ancestors, agriculturalists were consistently shorter, experienced more malnutrition, were riddled with more disease, and lived shorter lives. Skeletal remains from Ohio confirm this trend.[43] The move to permanent settlements and an increased reliance on domesticated plants presented our ancestors with a devil's bargain: you could replace the *quality* of each individual life with a greater *quantity* of people. City life didn't have to be a better choice, it just had to outcompete the alternative, which is what happened in most environments through history. Burial sites throughout the Ohio and Mississippi Valleys from this time period suggest a growing social inequality. The set piece for the climax of this riverine, "Mound Building" culture can be found just across the Mississippi River from the city of St. Louis. Known today as Cahokia, the settlement peaked about nine hundred years ago. Supporting at least fifteen thousand people, it was not only the largest city in North America but likely matched the size of London at the same time.[44] For comparison, New York City didn't surpass Cahokia's population high-water mark until a decade prior to the American Revolution.

But that size came at a cost. Cahokia's burial mounds challenge some of those in Egypt's Valley of Kings for their exhibition of rigid class boundaries. At one site, archaeologists discovered ornately decorated remains of a few high-status individuals. Adorned with copper, mica, and shells from hundreds of miles away, and deposits of newly made tools, these skeletons show signs of eating a diet richer in animal proteins—and that contained less maize—and overall better health than the background population. These few, high-status graves are surrounded by the bodies of over one hundred people whose skeletons bear the typical signs of a low-status agricultural diet composed primarily of maize. Likely offered as a sacrifice, the bodies of these low-status individuals, almost all of them young women, show signs of violent ends, including blunt trauma, decapitation, and being pierced by projectile points. Dental remains from the mass grave determined that these young women were distantly related to the high-class individuals and were likely either levied from surrounding settlements, perhaps as a form of tribute, or taken as war captives.[45] The arrangement of some of the skeletons suggests that many of the dead had been lined up at the pit's edge, bludgeoned on the back of the head, and thrown in. Some of those sacrificed were still alive when they were buried, their arms and fingers digging at the sand, trying to climb out of the mass of bodies at the time of their death.[46]

Cahokia would eventually collapse under its own weight, with a helping hand from the types of climate cycles that have undermined many civilizations that made the mistake of calibrating their population levels to boom years. Tree-ring data shows the cultures inhabiting the Ohio River Valley endured a dry spell nearly 1,600 years ago that continued for the better part of a century and could have driven some incipient agriculturalists back to a low-intensity, hunting and gathering lifestyle. The great filter came in the thirteenth century, with the arrival of what paleo-climatologists have termed the "Little Ice Age." When Cahokia was abandoned in the late fourteenth century, the region was experiencing one of the worst droughts of the past two thousand years, a death sentence for a culture dependent on maize for over half of its calories.[47]

Feedback Loops

The richness and complexity of Indigenous cultures that emerged, flourished, and sometimes died in Ohio is beyond the ability of any single book to convey. The fragmentary evidence available describes a curious, inventive, and adaptable people who were also able to make some familiar mistakes from the human story. The existing evidence is scarce. SunWatch, for its intricate celestial geography, was occupied for no more than twenty years: shorter than the basketball career of LeBron James or even the life of the recreated village that stands in its footprint today. How representative was it of the people who occupied Ohio at the time? Where did the villagers relocate to and under what conditions? For all our knowledge, we will likely never answer these questions.

What we do know is that the people occupying the bluffs and valleys of Ohio understood their relationship to the land through ceremony, ritual, and narratives that tied them to the animals and plants that sustained them. Today, modern chemistry describes the benefits of planting nitrogen-fixing beans in association with a nitrogen-hungry grass like maize. Somewhere along the way, ancient Americans discovered the connection and reinforced it through narratives, such as the Haudenosaunee tale of the Weeping Maize, Bean, and Squash People. Occupying traditional homelands in upstate New York, the Haudenosaunee carried on some of the traditions of the Mound Builder cultures, including the cultivation of the Three Sisters.

Maintaining a complex agricultural system wasn't easy, and there is no replacement for gardening instructions in the form of a story. The tale begins much like that of the Buffalo Wife, with a village on the edge of starvation. An old chief walks among her garden, worried about the future of her people, when she hears the sound of weeping. She is surprised to discover that the plants themselves are crying out to her, and she questions them to discover the source of their grief. In a turn that may hit a bit close to home for many gardeners (or keepers of houseplants), the plants inform her they are suffering from neglect. "You place us in the ground to grow, but you do not perform your further duties," they tell her. The village convenes a council to address the complaints, stipulating the proper way to hill up earth around maize, sufficiently water, and periodically weed so, as the plants say, their "enemies" will not "come and strangle us to death." When the next planting season arrives, the villagers perform every task as instructed, but they are shocked to discover evidence of "something damaging and destroying the plants": "Some sort of people, it seemed, were coming unseen and taking away the maize and beans and leaving only shells of the squash." What to do?

A group of warriors stood watch over the garden and discovered "a number of persons tearing off the ears of maize and gathering bean pods." The warriors captured the thieves and brought them before the village, where they were beaten by the assembled crowd, who "whipped the maize thieves so severely during their captivity that their faces became striped and their tails ringed from the blows that they received." For their part, the squash thieves "had their upper lips split, so that they should not be able again to eat squashes."[48] Thus, the origin story of racoons and rabbits is tied to a cautionary tale about proper gardening. Usually a task assigned to children, defending crops from the depredation of racoons or rabbits became essential to Indigenous communities that relied on the bounty of the Three Sisters.

Our feedback loops today have little connection to the land under our feet. For years, I pulled at the weeds that crowded my garden plots. I had identified many, such as dead nettle, cleavers, and bindweed, that always seemed to get a jump start on my lethargic domesticates, including mounds sown with the Three Sisters. One weed species in particular seemed to come up amid my rows without fail. Glaucous in color, and at times nearly white at the stem, the weed popped up every year, despite my efforts to eliminate unwanted plants. Seemingly indestructible, it persisted in the soil seed bank year after year. It wasn't until the COVID pandemic drove me to explore botany as a hobby that I identified it. Unmistakable in appearance, I had been pulling goosefoot from my garden, a plant Indigenous cultures had cultivated in these valleys for thousands of years. In my ignorance, my attempts to grow a garden of "native" plants had excluded a cultivar with a deep history of tying people to this land. When the weather warms and you head out on your adventures, keep your eyes peeled. Punching up through sidewalk cracks, abandoned lots, and the land at the edge of forests are a few inconspicuous plants that carry the legacy of generations of Indigenous Ohioans who carefully collected and planted the best seed year after year.

In 2023, UNESCO designated eight mound complexes in Ohio as the newest World Heritage Site, describing them as "the most representative surviving expressions of the Indigenous tradition now referred to as the Hopewell culture."[49] It is the only UNESCO site located in Ohio and just the twenty-fifth site within the United States. When adopted in 1972, the World

Heritage Convention sought to identify and preserve "cultural and natural heritage of outstanding universal value." Which of our modern efforts might meet that standard? Our culture is equipped with indescribable power and a hunger for ever more control over the natural world. Although we have vanquished the deprivations of early agricultural life, our moment in the sun has been short-lived. The culture that brought us the motto of "Move fast and break things" might learn something from the hard-earned lessons of Ohio's past. Can we build an egalitarian society that sustains itself over millennia, or will we fall into the same progress traps that ensnared the people at Cahokia?

CHAPTER 3
Apocalypse

The world changed on March 11, 2020. In the weeks leading up to that day, increasingly urgent news trickled out of China about a mysterious new virus that was quickly spreading in the city of Wuhan. Originally identified as a form of pneumonia, by early January, public health officials in China identified the disease as a novel coronavirus, and within days, both the CDC and the World Health Organization introduced the world to a new name in our disease lexicon: severe acute respiratory syndrome coronavirus 2 (SARS-CoV-2). By March 11, the word "pandemic" had eclipsed the cluster of names for the new disease as schools, universities, international borders, and much of the economy locked down to halt the virus's spread.

I was teaching mostly pre-med students at Michigan State University's Lyman Briggs College at the time, and the virus became a topic of discussion from the very start of the semester in January. On January 28, I brought a box of surgical masks to class and challenged students to wear one throughout the discussion on the emergence of a new disease environment following the domestication of animals during the Neolithic period. I taught the entirety of my classes that day while wearing an N-95 respirator, and we discussed the efficacy of masks as a public health intervention and how different cultures experience health and sickness. It all seems so innocent in retrospect. That spring, several of my students became sick and recovered. Many were pressed into service on the pandemic's front lines as hospitals struggled to field a staff that could support an avalanche of people struggling to breathe as the virus took hold of their lungs. For public health workers, it felt like a war.

Essential supplies vanished within days, sometimes only hours. On March 13, President Trump declared a national emergency, and fear gripped communities throughout the country. I was astonished to discover that the twenty-four-hour Giant Eagle grocery store located on West 117th Street had to close overnight to simply restock empty shelves. On March 15, I queued up with a group of about a hundred people at 6:00 a.m. just so we could be sure to get supplies before they eventually ran out. Many folks loaded up on groceries, but several stockpiled mountains of toilet paper. Rumors of panic-buying leading to shortfalls became a self-fulfilling prophecy. One man waited in line with me for an hour to buy nothing more than a shopping cart overflowing with two-liter bottles of Pepsi. A day later, Governor Mike DeWine declared a state of emergency for Ohio that would persist for over a year.

During that time, all of our technological achievements that we had heralded as signs that we are the most advanced civilization in world history seemed to work against us. The virus, which can begin shedding as soon as three days after infection, spread across the planet via our commercial jet aircraft. Health officials in Thailand announced the first confirmed case of the virus outside of China on January 13. A few days later it popped up in Japan. A week later it was in South Korea and had arrived in the United States in the body of a thirtysomething-year-old man who was returning from a family gathering in Wuhan. Although antibody tests suggested the virus was already in the US in late December 2019, by the time the CDC began implementing public health screenings at major airports, it was too late. By the end of February, the virus had hopped on flights and begun circulating among population centers in every continent on earth except Antarctica, which would eventually identify its first case in December 2020.

Part of the problem in containing the virus was the fact that it replicated far faster than it killed people. Although different variants have been more or less infectious, the basic reproduction number for SARS-CoV-2 is somewhere between two and three. This means, on average, someone sick with the virus is likely to spread the disease to two or three other people, who will themselves do the same. Like a wildfire, a virus will eventually run out of fuel no matter how quickly it spreads, but with over seven billion souls on the planet, it found purchase in every forum of public life. The Cleveland Public Library, all of the art and natural history museums, and many schools throughout northeast Ohio canceled in-person events and services, some for the remainder of the year. Governor DeWine ordered the closing of all bars and restaurants for three months before growing fears of economic collapse pushed him to permit indoor dining again. The Major League Baseball season did not begin until July 23, with teams playing only sixty games out of a typical 162-game schedule. Without fans in attendance, Progressive Field covered large sections of the stands with tarps featuring the logos of sponsors to try and make up for the loss of revenue. Piped-in crowd noise was used to fill the eerie silence in a space that was accustomed to hosting over thirty-five thousand fans.

Many families found themselves locked inside and wholly dependent on internet service to access school, work, and entertainment. As our world seemed to shrink to fit inside the walls of our houses and apartments, many people turned to the Cleveland Metroparks for relief from cabin fever. At over five thousand acres, Rocky River Reservation covers nearly thirteen miles of river valley from Lake Erie south to Strongsville. In the spring and summer of 2020, it became apparent that a century of planning by Cleveland's Metroparks never anticipated a world where nature would become the primary amenity for the city's population. Hoping to take a walk and get some fresh air amid the chaos, at times I would find the valley full of people, cars overflowing parking lots and crowding the shoulders on the edge of the road. The Metroparks system notched record-breaking attendance in 2020 with 19.7 million visits, a trend that held nationwide as people poured into the only spaces that felt safe amid a global pandemic.[1] These numbers are particularly staggering because they occurred despite a three-month closure of the Cleveland Metroparks Zoo and the cancellation of all organized sports and outdoor education programs. Some parks saw attendance rise by 130 percent over previous seasons.[2]

The pandemic also revealed deep inequalities in access to open space for Clevelanders. Fearful that the virus might spread via long-lasting droplets, Governor DeWine ordered the closure of all public playgrounds on March 22, 2020. Although many reopened in July, the city of Cleveland didn't fully reopen its public pools, basketball courts, and playgrounds until the summer of 2021, more than a year after the initial lockdown. Playgrounds had the appearance of a crime scene, with loud signs announcing their closure and yellow caution tape draped over swing sets and

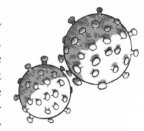

slides. SARS-CoV-2 spreads primarily via aerosol particles, the microscopic, lighter-than-air mist produced when we talk, sing, or even breathe, but it took public health officials time to eliminate fomite infection as a possible vector in the pandemic's panic-stricken early days.[3] As some of us wiped down our groceries and delivery boxes with sanitizing wipes and sprays, the playgrounds that serve as the few patches of greenspace for many inner-city communities closed across the country. By examining datasets created by location-based web services, like those used by Google and Instagram, a team of researchers found that closed parks and playgrounds saw attendance drop by 76 percent, while larger parks enjoyed a 63 percent increase in use.[4] Wealth also determined our exposure rates. An analysis of cell phone location data by the *New York Times* found that people living in the richest metropolitan areas were able to cut their movement significantly more (and sooner) than residents of the poorest neighborhoods during the pandemic. The data revealed a deep divide between those who could transition to a relatively safe, work-from-home environment and those who could not. People living in the highest-income neighborhoods, as the analysis revealed, "have essentially halted movement," while location data for poor neighborhoods "shows an uptick in their movements…coinciding with the start of another workweek."[5]

Although our access to information allowed for the instantaneous transmission of critical updates and guidance, it also quickly politicized public health decisions and even the science behind our medical interventions, such as masks, vaccines, and even the threat posed by the virus. With Ohioans trending conservative in their politics, vaccine rates lagged at 65 percent compared to a national average of 81 percent. And while people are still getting sick and dying from COVID as I write this, the danger posed by the virus has waned, and life for many has returned to normal. Three years after the first Ohioan died from the disease, the COVID pandemic claimed over forty-one thousand lives, a loss roughly equivalent to the combined populations of Shaker Heights and Beechwood.

For all the chaos the pandemic created, it could have been much, much worse. The nearly instantaneous adoption of public health measures by governments and businesses, and the rapid development of several vaccines, significantly reduced the stress on our hospitals. One study found that the vaccines alone averted over eighteen million hospitalizations and saved the lives of over three million people nationwide.[6] Changing the behavior patterns of over seven billion humans produced some startling effects on our environment as well. Climate scientists at the Jet Propulsion Laboratory in Southern California discovered that the combined effect of lockdowns, the rise of remote labor, school, and fitness, and changes in consumer behavior led to a 5.4 percent reduction in CO_2 emissions in 2020.[7] Despite all our interventions, nearly everyone became infected at some point. By 2022, data collected from blood donors by the CDC showed that 77 percent of the population had been infected at least once.[8] We were fortunate that the case fatality rate was so low for a virus that excelled at finding us.

Over the course of the pandemic, Ohio lost .3 percent of its population. Each life lost diminished communities, robbed families of their loved ones, and deprived all of us of the accumulated wisdom and skills unique to each individual. Sickness and death visited every community. For me, the disease cut short my Uncle Don's life in August of 2020. Growing up in rural Ohio, I remember how my uncle had showed me how he raised pigs, how to safely handle firearms, and the best places to hunt squirrels on his working farm. He spent the last days of his life gasping for air, beyond the help of even our most advanced medical technology.

SARS-CoV-2 is only the most recent "virgin soil" epidemic, an epidemiological term for a disease that encounters vulnerable populations for the first time. Although we are still searching for the source, the virus is also zoonotic in origin, endemic in the population of one animal species before a chance mutation allows it to infect humans. Virgin soil epidemics have shaped human history, redirecting the trajectory of entire continents. In the fourteenth century, the black death arrived in Europe and exterminated a third of the continent's population. Some cities lost half their population in a matter of months. The staggering losses threw Europe into spasms of violence, religious experimentation, and labor shortages that began to unravel the logic of feudalism.[9] Rather impressive for a bacterium that spends the majority of its life in the gut of a flea. Human immunodeficiency virus (HIV), responsible for the cluster of symptoms described as acquired immunodeficiency syndrome (AIDS), is another zoonosis responsible for one of the deadliest virgin soil epidemics of recent history. Making the jump from chimpanzees to humans sometime in the early twentieth century, HIV blazed a path through human populations, killing forty million people over the course of the last century.[10]

Although we haven't eliminated disease as a driver of historical change, modern medical science has spared us from the ravages of virgin soil epidemics. We sometimes forget just how recently we developed our current medical knowledge. The scientific community did not even coalesce around the germ theory of disease until the last decades of the nineteenth century. Nearly all of our knowledge of viruses, bacteria, and modern epidemiology has been developed in the past 150 years, or the span of two human lifetimes. Just over five hundred years ago, the Pacific and Atlantic Oceans had been sufficient to isolate the Americas as a distinct disease environment. That all came crashing down for the people living in Ohio when strange new immigrants crossed the seas and brought with them the legacy of over ten thousand years of disease history within a few generations.

Human cultural traditions the world over have a grim fascination with the end of the world. Our species, endowed with conscience and aware of its own mortality, has created elaborate hellscapes in countless oral traditions, books, plays, and cinema. The consequences for the people and land in Ohio in the centuries after the first contact with people from Europe, Asia, and Africa were truly apocalyptic. The first historical documents to describe the land and people of Ohio describe the destruction of a way of life that had persisted since the end of the last ice age. What was created in its wake is the landscape we now inhabit: a world of machines, fossil fuels, and concrete that has replaced forests to make way for all of us.

The First Horseman

By the late fifteenth century, the people living in Ohio had forged a mixed economy that blended an ancestral hunting and gathering tradition with horticulture organized around maize, beans, and the plants domesticated in the Eastern Agricultural Complex. Although they no longer constructed elaborate ceremonial or burial mounds, their reliance on agriculture anchored them to particular landscapes, especially fertile river valleys, for long stretches of the year. Communities such as SunWatch village, with garden plots and permanent structures assigned to different purposes, would have been typical of this time period.

Many villages from this time period also show signs of social and environmental stress. SunWatch was abandoned after a generation, perhaps due to depleted soils, and was ringed by a defensive palisade, suggesting that conflict between settlements became a necessary element of community planning.

At the time, Ohio was a borderland shared by two distinct linguistic traditions. In the east, the Haudenosaunee people (who the French called Iroquois) forged a confederacy centered on Lake Ontario and shared cultural ties with the Wyandot and Erie people who occupied the shores of Lake Erie. To the west were Algonquian speakers, like the Fox, Miami, and Shawnee people. Our conception of history is often shaped by mental maps, such as those in textbooks, that demarcate territories with clean boundary lines. Attempting to do so for the people of Ohio prior to contact with Europeans (and a good time after) is a fool's errand, however. The Wyandot people, who became the last sovereign Indigenous nation to occupy Ohio after statehood, in the span of two hundred years occupied homelands in the St. Lawrence River Valley and were pushed throughout the Great Lakes region by war, disease, and opportunity before the US government's colonial policies forcibly resettled them in Oklahoma. The Shawnee, identified with territory stretching from Indiana, through Ohio, and into Kentucky, may have arrived in these lands after fleeing homelands on the Atlantic Coast imperiled by European colonialism.

Whoever occupied Ohio lands likely first encountered the consequences of European colonialism in the form of disease, perhaps as early as the sixteenth, but no later than the mid-seventeenth, century. Long before cattle, swine, or even "old-world" weeds like dandelions arrived in Ohio, the smallpox virus (*Variola major*) infiltrated Indigenous communities throughout the Great Lakes region before many people had even set eyes upon the strange, white-skinned people establishing trading posts and settlements along the Atlantic Coast. The historian Alfred Crosby, who established disease as a central actor on the stage of American history, described smallpox as "a disease with seven-league boots."[11] Although the virus did not have the magical boots from European folklore that allowed the wearer to travel the span of a marathon in a single stride, the latency between infection and symptoms, coupled with a basic reproduction number two to three times higher than even SARS-CoV-2, endowed it with a terrifying potential to spread across vast distances. Smallpox spreads via airborne water droplets that we expel when we cough, sneeze, or talk, and through fomites, such as the clothes and bedding of an infected individual.

It could take two weeks from the time of infection until the unmistakable symptoms emerged in a sick individual—enough time for the virus to travel extensively. Although not contagious during the incubation period, an infected person could expect to come down with fever and vomiting sometime in the second week. After a couple days of deep chills and fluid loss, a rash would develop into sores on the inside of the mouth and surface of the tongue. In the span of a day or two, the rash would spread to the rest of the body and blossom into dimpled blisters. Concentrating at the extremities, the pustules were hard to the touch and could even appear on the eyes, permanently scarring the cornea and blinding those lucky enough to survive. After another week or two, the pox blisters would weep, form a crust, and scab over. Once every scab fell from the skin, the disease would have run its course and the individual would no longer be contagious, leaving the survivor scarred with the telltale pockmarks of the disease.[12]

Although it varies in severity depending on the clinical manifestation, smallpox has about a 30 percent case fatality rate.

CHAPTER 3: APOCALYPSE

Because viral particles break down with time, forensic investigations of human remains have failed to isolate exactly when and where the virus first emerged. The preserved flesh of several Egyptian mummies, including the body of Pharaoh Ramses V, exhibit pockmarks consistent with a smallpox infection. In 2004, a team of archaeologists exhumed a graveyard in eastern Siberia and were surprised to discover viral DNA fragments of smallpox in the lung tissue of one body that had been preserved in permafrost for three hundred years.[13] What we do know is that it emerged in Asia sometime soon after the rise of the first agricultural civilizations and blazed a path through human history for thousands of years, killing perhaps as many as a billion people before the World Health Organization declared it eradicated in 1980.[14]

The virus arrived in the Americas in the bodies of Europeans and enslaved Africans during the fifteenth and sixteenth centuries. The Spanish brought smallpox with them during the conquest of Mexico in 1520. Over the next decade, the disease had burned through the Isthmus of Panama and struck the heart of the Inca Empire, killing its ruler, Huayna Capac, his appointed heir, and perhaps hundreds of thousands of Andean people. The epidemic destabilized the empire and led to a bloody war of succession. The Spanish conquistador Francisco Pizarro led two expeditions to subjugate the empire in the 1520s but was repelled each time. After a decade of war and disease, the Inca Empire, perhaps the largest on the planet at the time, fell in the early 1530s during Pizarro's third attempt.[15]

Although Europeans explored the coast of North America soon after Columbus's first voyage, there were few opportunities for their diseases to reach Indigenous people living in the Great Lakes region until the mid-1500s. The earliest expedition into the continent occurred in 1539, when Hernando de Soto landed near

Tampa Bay. Over the next two years, he explored the southeast before dying of fever on the banks of the Mississippi River. In his attempts to recreate the conquests in Central and South America, de Soto captured and tortured anyone in his path. In the spring of 1540, he was traveling through present-day South Carolina when his company discovered four men in a village. A Portuguese knight known as the "gentleman from Elvas" served on the expedition and chronicled the brutality of the conquistador with an almost banal detachment. "There four Indians were captured, and no one of them would say anything else than they did not know any other village. The governor ordered one of them to be burned. Thereupon, another said that two days' journey thence was a province called Cutifachiqui." When he arrived, de Soto was greeted graciously and adorned with gifts of animal skins, blankets, and pearls, but he was also informed that much of the surrounding region was unoccupied: "The Indians said that two years ago there had been a plague in that land and they had moved to other towns." The party traveled to and raided the abandoned settlement, looting a cache of pearls from the graves.[16] Although it is impossible to surmise exactly what the gentleman from Elvas meant when he used the word "plague," less still what the woman from Cutifachiqui actually communicated to the translator, with smallpox already tearing through empires in Central and South America, it is probable that a pathogen introduced by Europeans had preceded them deep into the North American continent.

Communicable disease bounced through Indigenous settlements beginning with the first contact with Europeans. Viruses such as smallpox and measles certainly had the potential to wend their way into the continent and visit villages throughout Ohio, sometimes burning out in one community only to leapfrog through trade routes a year later and spread further. In every case, the results would have been devastating. Scholars, including

Crosby, have argued that the general 30 percent case fatality rate would have been higher among populations without prior experience with a disease like smallpox. Anyone afflicted with smallpox who survives the ordeal benefits from lifelong immunity, which eventually limits the potential effects of future outbreaks. At the beginning of the sixteenth century, the people of Ohio could be described by epidemiologists as immunologically naive. Therefore, when smallpox or any other pathogen arrived on the shores of Lake Erie and the banks of the Cuyahoga, Ohio, and Tuscarawas Rivers, everyone living there had the potential to fall ill simultaneously. At times, the ability to strike an entire community at once pushed the case fatality rate of diseases like smallpox up to as much as 90 percent or more.

Movies and television shows portray a heroic image of modern medicine driven by spectacular technology and brilliant physicians. To be sure, that is part of the story, but what often makes the difference between whether a patient suffering from a viral infection survives or not is simple bedside care. Vaccines only work prior to infection, and while antiviral drugs can improve health outcomes, there is no existing cure for a patient presenting with a virus. Without the infrastructure to care for them, even Europeans living in the modern period have suffered catastrophic mortality rates. A generation of scholarship highlighting the destructive effects on Indigenous populations has fueled a misconception that the Native people of the Americas were almost genetically predisposed to perish following the arrival of old-world pathogens. In his pathbreaking essay on virgin soil epidemics, Crosby carefully described how the context of disease, and not genetics, determined health outcomes. After all, during the American Civil War, 38 percent of white Union soldiers who contracted smallpox died of the disease, despite generations of ancestors who had prior immunological experience with the virus.

Crosby chillingly explained how the basic care necessary to survive and gain lifelong immunity was made impossible when an entire community fell ill. "The fire goes out and the cold creeps in; the sick, whom a bit of food and a cup of water might save, die of hunger and the dehydration of fever; the seed remains above the ground as the best season for planting passes, or there is no one well enough to harvest the crop before the frost." Survival, in short, was determined far more by a community's ability to provide basic care for the sick than any other factor.[17]

Whether or not smallpox arrived in the Great Lakes from the Spanish in the sixteenth century is still up for debate, but we are certain the French brought it with them in the seventeenth century. In 1608, they set up a permanent settlement in the St. Lawrence River Valley with the founding of Québec. Disease followed them in short order. Fur traders and the Jesuit religious order established contact with Indigenous communities deep in the heart of the Great Lakes within a decade. From 1632 to 1673, the Jesuits compiled annual reports from their posts throughout the region for their superior based in Québec. Although colored by their own worldview, these reports offer us the first record of day-to-day life during this crucial period. One Jesuit, Père Jerome Lalemant, described a smallpox outbreak among the Wyandot in 1639 and 1640. "The Hurons," he wrote, "no matter what plague or contagion they may have—live in the midst of their sick.... In fact, in a few days, almost all those in the cabin of the deceased found themselves infected; then the evil spread from house to house, from village to village, and finally became scattered throughout the country."[18]

When Indigenous communities quickly figured out disease vectors, Lalemant assigned their understanding to supernatural forces. "They observed," he noted, "with some sort of reason, that, since our arrival in these lands, those who had been the nearest to us, had happened to be the most ruined by the diseases, and that the whole villages of those who had received us now appeared utterly exterminated." Then later, "the devil did not fail to seize his opportunity for reawakening all the old imaginations, and causing the former complaints of us…as if it were the sole cause of all of their misfortunes, and especially of the sick. They no longer speak of aught else, they cry aloud that the French must be massacred." The Jesuits were able to stave off calls for their murder, in part due to their own immunity conferred by past exposure to the disease. When a village fell sick, sometimes only the Jesuit fathers were capable of performing the simple care necessary to nurse the infected person back to health, a quality the Indigenous communities did not fail to recognize. Lalemant wrote, "they [the Wyandot people] said, it must needs be that we had a secret understanding with the disease (for they believe that it is a demon), since we alone were all full of life and health, although we constantly breathed nothing but a totally infected air,—staying whole days close by the side of the most foul-smelling patients, for whom every one felt horror." Lalemant admits, "we were dreaded as the greatest sorcerers on earth."[19] Under such circumstances, one can begin to appreciate how enduring a dread illness under the care of such "sorcerers" could profoundly influence a survivor.

Although the people living in the Great Lakes region had no way of knowing it, the coming decades would be the most calamitous of the past thirteen thousand years. Disease outbreaks would ricochet across the landscape, followed by wars marked by unimaginable brutality. Our best estimates place the entire Indigenous population between the Mississippi and Ohio River Valleys, from the Great Lakes east to the Atlantic, at around 715,000 people prior to European contact; about the same size as Cleveland in the 1970s.[20] In the span of two centuries, from the arrival of the French to Ohio statehood, the land south of Lake Erie and north of the Ohio River would lose 99 percent of its Indigenous population.

The Second Horseman

In the prologue to *The Canterbury Tales*, Geoffrey Chaucer describes various characters about to embark on a pilgrimage. Although written in Middle English, I think you can parse the prose. Among the pilgrims, Chaucer describes a merchant "with a forkéd berd, In mottéleye, and hye on horse he sat; Upon his heed a Flaundryssh bevere hat."[21] Writing in the decades after the black death, Chaucer was keen to identify the emerging fashion of wearing beaver hats and associate it with an expanding merchant class. The hairs on beaver pelts could bind to one another easily and withstand harsh chemical baths that made them strong yet flexible, the perfect material for hat-making. No doubt you have seen beaver hats, or depictions of them, through various media. The tricorn hats of the seventeenth century adorned revolutionary armies in America and France as well as pirates (real and fictional) such as Blackbeard and Captain Jack Sparrow. The tall capotain hats worn by the pilgrims of Plymouth Colony never had buckles, despite our popular imagination, but they were made of beaver skin. The wide-brimmed "wideawake" hats that sit on the heads of figures in paintings by Rembrandt, Vermeer, and the Quaker Oats mascot were all made of felted beaver fur. In the nineteenth century, hatters modified these older styles and developed a multitude of forms our modern eyes would recognize as "top hats," staples for any prop department in a theater that regularly produced the plays of Charles Dickens or Jane Austen.

By the mid-nineteenth century, the popularity of beaver hats nearly drove the species to extinction and pushed the price of the material beyond the reach of all but the very wealthy. When Abraham Lincoln left the White House to attend a production of *Our American Cousin* at Ford's Theatre, his signature top hat was made of silk, not beaver.[22] In Chaucer's time, the animal was still abundant in Europe, but over-trapping soon extinguished local populations. In the sixteenth century, trappers had to travel to Scandinavia to find healthy populations and then to Siberia when the market drove European beavers to oblivion. When Samuel de Champlain founded Québec in 1608, he hoped it would secure access to the region's beaver pelts, which he would supply to Parisian hatters. He arrived in the midst of a veritable rush of colonization. A year earlier, the Virginia Company of London had succeeded in establishing a permanent settlement at Jamestown, and in the coming decades, Swedish, Dutch, and English companies would settle the Atlantic Coast of North America in the hopes of gaining a steady supply of beaver pelts and other trade goods.[23]

Both the Eurasian (*Castor fiber*) and North American (*Castor canadensis*) species of beaver occupy a unique ecological niche. Aside from the capybara, beavers are the largest member of the order Rodentia and have evolved to exploit riverine environments.

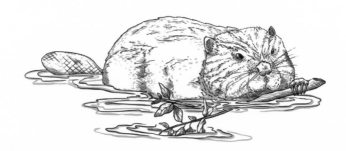

Their heads are a powerhouse of muscle and bone, designed to chew wood and even pull logs. Their long incisors grow continuously throughout their lives to keep pace with the wear created from a diet of tree pulp and fibrous reeds. Although the animal's front paws resemble those of a racoon, its hind feet are webbed to propel it through water. Its flat, paddle-like tail stabilizes the animal underwater and also serves as fat storage for winter months. Its coat of fur, so prized by European merchants, protected it from both the elements and offered a layer of protection from predators. Through dam building, beavers create extensive wetland environments that serve as habitat for a range of plants and animals. Indigenous people certainly hunted them as food and for their pelts; some of the stone tools unearthed at the Nobles Pond site tested positive for beaver DNA. The animal never became a primary target for Indigenous populations, however. Archaeological sites throughout Ohio show that cervids such as deer and elk were preferred over a rodent that was much smaller and far more elusive. It was only with the arrival of Europeans, and the incentives they offered for beaver pelts, that the ten-thousand-year-old relationship between Indigenous people and beaver populations became imperiled.

European trading outposts could be both a threat and an opportunity for Indigenous communities. As the writing of Père Lalemant makes abundantly clear, the Wyandot people understood the origin of the pestilence that periodically carried away whole communities. Removing an entire village from the sphere of influence of a European power would seem prudent, but that would have to be balanced against an equally dangerous threat: new weapons in the hands of your neighbors. Each spring, Wyandot men gathered the pelts of every beaver they had trapped the preceding year, often amounting to twelve or fifteen thousand skins per year (and sometimes as many as twenty-two thousand), at the French fort at Québec.[24] In exchange, they received metalware such as axes, knives, and awls, as well as protection from the Haudenosaunee confederacy to the east. The French, however, refused to arm the Wyandot with firearms until the 1640s. The Dutch traders arrayed along the Hudson River Valley had no such prohibitions and happily exchanged muskets for beaver pelts to the Haudenosaunee, creating a power imbalance between members of the confederacy, such as the Mohawk and Seneca and their neighbors who still relied on stone, primarily flint points and knives.

As early as 1634, Père Paul Le Jeune urged his compatriots to convert the Indigenous communities surrounding Québec to a sedentary life so they could be made into better Christians and so "that the beaver might thus be kept from extermination."[25] By then, Indigenous communities throughout the Great Lakes and St. Lawrence Valley had seized the opportunity to empower themselves by sacrificing beaver. In one letter, Le Jeune relates just how fully one Innu man had adopted the logic of the market by reducing beaver to literal commodities. "The Beaver does everything perfectly well, it makes kettles, hatchets, swords, knives, bread; and, in short, it makes everything." Le Jeune's

Innu host, who traded with both the French and English, clearly felt as though he got the better of Europeans. Flashing a knife at Le Jeune, he said, "The English have no sense; they give us twenty knives like this for one Beaver skin."[26]

The international market for beaver didn't transform all Indigenous people into capitalists overnight, however. Many participated on their own terms and viewed "trade" as an opportunity to exchange gifts and cement communal ties. At the annual rendezvous in Québec, the market price for beaver pelts was of little concern to the assembled hunters who were most interested in securing goods for their communities and affirming their connection to the French, who promised to patrol their borderlands and protect them from Haudenosaunee raiding parties. But the very need for protection reflected a practice among some Indigenous communities of using newly acquired European firearms to exert control over their neighbors.[27]

The uneasy patchwork of Algonquian- and Iroquoian-speaking communities throughout Ohio was torn apart by the arrival of the market. Access to trade goods divided the territory. Although there were notable exceptions, in general, the Algonquian-speaking people accessed goods through the French centered in Québec, while the Iroquoian-speaking communities relied on the Dutch traders at locations like Fort Orange (present-day Albany). Sensing a power imbalance in the 1640s, Iroquoian-speaking communities throughout the Great Lakes launched full-scale attacks against Wyandot villages in the St. Lawrence Valley and along the shores of Lake Erie. Although raiding supply caches and gaining access to river valleys full of beaver were the primary motivations, documents from the era suggest war was also motivated by the need to replace community members who'd been lost in epidemics. Disease robbed Indigenous communities not just of individuals but also the roles they played in communal life. Whether you call it slavery or nonconsensual adoption, the practice of replacing lost family members seems universal to the human experience and has been codified in the Bible and the Code of Hammurabi. For the Haudenosaunee, though, the number of captives acquired through violence never kept pace with the combined effects of disease and the very war intended to revitalize the community. The captives of what have been labeled the "Mourning Wars" would be ritually accepted into the community, sometimes into the very roles once filled by dead husbands, wives, and children. Although the tradition was rooted in the deep past, and though it shared some similarities to marriage ceremonies the world over, the rapid depopulation of Indigenous communities drove it to a scale that had never been seen before.[28]

After the Haudenosaunee sent war parties as far west as the Wisconsin River Valley to crush their Algonquian-speaking neighbors and secure the beaver trade throughout the Great Lakes, they turned on their own Iroquoian-speaking neighbors and former allies. The Erie people, whose homelands encompassed the south shore of the lake that bears their name, became the target of a full-scale war from the Haudenosaunee confederacy to their east in the 1650s. Although contemporary accounts suggest the two cultures were fairly equivalent in population, the Haudenosaunee benefited from their proximity to European merchants, especially the Dutch, in ways that were impossible for the more distant Erie at that time. Two years of war shattered the Erie nation. The survivors were either adopted into Haudenosaunee villages or scattered westward, eventually joining other refugees fleeing the bloodshed. Victory over the Erie was purchased with beaver skins that pushed the Haudenosaunee into closer cultural contact with European traders and missionaries. Upon the defeat of the Erie, a Jesuit missionary reported that several Onondaga men and women, "coming in great number to our cabin...confessed that they indeed believed at heart." Somewhat surprised by the rush of neophytes, the missionary reported that "what made them believe was partly their last victory over the Cat Nation [Erie]." Apparently, "they had promised, before the battle, to embrace the Faith if they returned victorious," he wrote, "they could not now retract after so successful a triumph." The victory celebrations included the ritual torture of men and children as young as ten, who were brutalized in ways that make crucifixion seem almost merciful in comparison. Despite bearing witness to these acts, the Jesuit missionary practiced prayer in the French language with the assembled mass until he felt satisfied in their grasp of the pronunciation of—if not the meaning behind—the words uttered in French by Onondaga tongues. In the end, the defeat of the Erie people was sealed with a Christian blessing.[29]

The Widowed Land

For much of the next century, the land between Lake Erie and the Ohio River became a no-man's-land patrolled by Haudenosaunee war parties and beaver expeditions. Without people to tend them, the fields of maize, beans, squash, sunflowers, and all the domesticated plants of the Eastern Agricultural Complex would have been overrun by competing plants. Without people to clear the forest understory with periodic burns, the forest would have reclaimed the sites of former villages and fields, drastically changing the ecosystem in Ohio. By the end of the seventeenth century, much of the beaver that had helped shape Ohio's river environments had been trapped, skinned, and traded to European merchants for manufactured goods. By the first decade of the eighteenth century, the beaver frontier had already moved on to the upper Great Lakes, north of the Wisconsin River.[30] Plants, rather than people, were shaping the environment for the first time since the Ice Age.

What happened in Ohio was only one chapter in the overall story of a continent-wide destruction of Indigenous America by the combined forces of disease, war, religion, and market incentives, all initiated by Europeans. The impact was so great that climate scientists can see it in the record of historic CO_2 levels. We are accustomed to seeing charts of the dramatic rise in CO_2, but in the centuries after contact, the concentration of carbon dioxide in the atmosphere actually decreased by seven to ten parts per million (ppm), resulting in a slight *drop* in surface air temperatures. Like a bank account, atmospheric carbon concentrations are the by-product of inflows and outflows. For the centuries preceding European contact with the Americas, the carbon budget remained stable—that is, as much carbon was removed from the atmosphere as was created, creating an equilibrium of steady CO_2 readings. But what had removed so much CO_2 from the atmosphere following the colonization of the Americas that it appears as a dip in the record? The answer, in short, is plants.

Following years of analysis, a team of climate scientists from the United Kingdom discovered two surprises. The first explained the reduction of global CO_2. "The global carbon budget of the 1500s cannot be balanced until large-scale vegetation regeneration in the Americas is included," they wrote. The second hints at the scale of Indigenous land use in Ohio and throughout the Americas. The centuries after contact resulted in a loss of 90 percent of the population of Indigenous communities, or about fifty-five million people. We tend to think of the Industrial Revolution as the beginning of human impacts capable of changing ecosystems on a global scale. The Anthropocene, a proposed geological epoch that demarcates the time when humans become the driving force for environmental change, is often associated with the rise of global CO_2 levels brought on by industry. But for Ohio and many other landscapes, the Anthropocene began much earlier. "These changes," the climate scientists concluded, "show that human actions had global impacts on the Earth system in the centuries prior to the Industrial Revolution."[31]

The French stepped in to profit off these conditions by establishing forts and trading posts throughout the Great Lakes at places like Detroit, Presque Isle (Erie, Pennsylvania), Duquesne (Pittsburgh), and Miami (Fort Wayne, Indiana). One French trader known only by his honorific, Sieur de Saguin, established trading posts on both the Cuyahoga and Chagrin Rivers (the latter likely reflecting Indigenous attempts to pronounce the Frenchman's name).[32] Although the presence of French merchants and missionaries would, in the long run, destroy Indigenous communities, in the short-term, French forts served as a foil to British forces clamoring for land in the middle ground between the two colonial empires.

Of course, the narrative of white colonists replacing Indigenous communities comes with a warning: Indigenous people and their cultures survived these world-ending forces. Pockets of refugees occupied Ohio throughout this period, although they were often in a precarious state of flux. The sometimes-blended communities they built would form an Indigenous resurgence that asserted power even after Ohio statehood in 1803. The Shawnee, Miami, and Lenni Lenape people rebuilt a vital Indigenous presence throughout Ohio, especially as the Haudenosaunee were ground down by periodic epidemics and colonial wars on their borders.

Great leaders emerged in Ohio, some with radical ideas about how to live in this new land born out of catastrophe. Prophets such as Neolin and Tenskwatawa, who grew up in this postapocalyptic Ohio, both experienced visions that included visits from the Spirit of Life. For the Lenni Lenape prophet Neolin, the British represented a diabolical force that needed to be expelled from Indigenous life. "If you suffer the English among you," Neolin warned, "you are dead men. Sickness, smallpox, and their poison will destroy you entirely."[33] Similarly, the Shawnee prophet Tenskwatawa had turned to alcohol to cope with the trauma of disease and war. In a daze, he experienced a vision worthy of Dante's *Inferno* that included a revelation of paradise that seems to describe the precontact state of Ohio. He described "a rich, fertile country, abounding in game, fish, pleasant hunting grounds and fine corn fields."[34] Sinful Shawnee, according to this prophecy, would endure fiery torture until their sins had been cleansed from their flesh. Tenskwatawa offered a new social order that would allow adherents to avoid the worst torments. Like Neolin, the Shawnee prophet equated alcohol to poison and encouraged the community to throw out their steel implements and relight their lodge fires in the traditional manner as a symbol of their new path. Tenskwatawa also reinforced authority in tribal leaders at a time when the market and European religions were pulling apart the center of community life.

Inspired by these visions and the religious awakening that followed, Indigenous military leaders created powerful alliances to protect their homelands. Despite a 1763 proclamation from King George III that forbade settlement west of the Appalachian ridge to quell Indigenous concerns of colonial expansion, settlers took their chances throughout the region. The expulsion of the French from North America during the worldwide conflict known as the Seven Years' War created a vacuum filled by leaders inspired by the prophets living in Ohio. The Odawa chief Pontiac organized attacks on British forts along Lake Erie in an attempt to preserve Indigenous sovereignty against the colonial power.

Failing to capture Detroit, the Odawa succeeded in capturing Fort Sandusky and burned it to the ground in 1763. Pontiac's war raged for three years and resulted in several massacres and the destruction of several British forts, and it ended with a frustrating return to the previous status quo. The British promised to restrain colonists, and Indigenous nations acknowledged the growing colonial presence throughout the vast territory between the Mississippi River and Appalachian Mountains.

The war revealed a bitter colonial hatred of Indigenous communities. Jeffrey Amherst, the commander-in-chief of British forces in North America, articulated an unequivocal desire for outright genocide to achieve peace. During the siege of Fort Pitt in the summer of 1763, in a letter written to William Johnson, an imperial superintendent of Indian affairs, Amherst described a desire for "Measures to be taken as would Bring about the Total Extirpation of those Indian Nations."[35] In the days before the siege, a Lenni Lenape delegation arrived at Fort Pitt to both warn the British of the coming conflict and to urge them to flee and avoid bloodshed. William Trent, a leader of the Pittsburgh militia, thanked the delegation and initiated the most well-documented case of germ warfare in American history. Trent detailed the events in his private journal. "Out of our regard to them," he wrote, "we gave them two Blankets and an Handkerchief out of the Small Pox Hospital. I hope it will have the desired effect."[36] Having rebounded from the first wave of epidemics and the devastation of the Beaver War, the Indigenous communities of Ohio found themselves the subject of an explicit campaign of ethnic cleansing that would continue unabated.

Whether they were a stratagem or a reflection of long-term imperial interests, the British attempts to contain colonial settlements to the Atlantic Seaboard would perish during the American Revolution. Although most of us are more familiar with the soaring language that opens the Declaration of Independence, the text later lists a total of twenty-seven grievances. The final grievance reveals how the new colonial power viewed Indigenous nations. Directed at King George III, it states, "He has excited domestic insurrections amongst us, and has endeavoured to bring on the inhabitants of our frontiers, the merciless Indian Savages, whose known rule of warfare, is an undistinguished destruction of all ages, sexes and conditions."

In the Treaty of Paris of 1783, the British Empire relinquished all claims to the land south of the Great Lakes, opening the door that had been closed by the Proclamation of 1763. A year after the war, the newly independent United States enacted the Ordinance of 1784, announcing that Ohio country would become a territory in a new empire, administered by a governor until it reached a population of sixty thousand "free inhabitants": "Therein, such State shall be admitted, by its delegates, into the Congress of the United States, on an equal footing with the original States in all respects whatever, and shall be at liberty to form a permanent constitution and State government."[37] The path had been cleared to transform the entire Great Lakes region into an extension of the settler-colonial world, where the market would determine the relationship between people and the land. Ohio lands were quickly divided up by different interests. Lands along the Scioto River Valley were given away to war veterans as payment for their service. Others, such as Connecticut's Western Reserve along Lake Erie, were claimed by states, and they would be used to line the pockets of land company investors (Cleveland and the east bank of the Cuyahoga) or pay war debts (the Firelands).

The following years became the final, desperate stand of Indigenous communities throughout Ohio. Leaders like Little Turtle, Blue Jacket, and Tecumseh (Tenskwatawa's older brother) followed the steps of Pontiac and gathered coalitions to defend their homelands. For a time, they appeared on the verge of securing a stalemate and enlisting the support of the British. Arthur St. Clair, the first territorial governor of the Northwest Territories, formed an army of around 1,400 soldiers to crush Indigenous resistance to US designs on Ohio. While encamped on the Wabash River, St. Clair's army came under attack by a force that reflected the polyglot communities throughout Ohio. Old enemies, Wyandots and Haudenosaunee, joined warriors representing Shawnee, Miami, Lenni Lenape, Odawa, Ojibwe, and Potawatomi communities. The battle was a masterstroke of Indigenous strategy. If not for a desperate bayonet charge to clear a lane of retreat, the entire force would have been destroyed. Having three horses shot from under him, St. Clair was fortunate to have made it back to Fort Washington in Cincinnati. From there, he delivered a report of the battle to Secretary of War Henry Knox. Over six hundred of his soldiers had been killed and half of his 124 officers had been killed or wounded. Only twenty-four men returned unharmed. Now largely forgotten, "St. Clair's Defeat" would be the high-water point of Indigenous resistance in American history. In terms of lives lost, the coalition forces inflicted a greater defeat on US forces than any suffered during the American Revolution, and more than twice the number killed at the Battle of the Little Bighorn eighty-five years later.[38]

The Indigenous coalition could not sustain a larger campaign, however. Furious at the defeat, President Washington forced St. Clair to resign his army commission and poured men and resources into Ohio to shatter Indigenous sovereignty. In the subsequent months and years, a series of treaty concessions followed a punishing military campaign. The 1795 Treaty of Greenville identified the Cuyahoga River as the boundary between Indigenous lands to the west and US territory to the east. With a southern boundary roughly following the divide between rivers flowing north to Lake Erie and those running south to the Ohio River, the treaty line ceded most of the state of Ohio to the young republic. Although leaders such as Tecumseh continued to engage the British in Canada to counterbalance the spread of US colonists throughout the Great Lakes, many Indigenous communities fled to the west after centuries of disease, war, and chaos.

Holy Ghosts

1812 was an ominous year. A series of massive earthquakes centered around New Madrid, Missouri, could be felt on the shores of Lake Erie, portending trouble ahead. The United States officially declared war for the first time in its history, sparking the War of 1812. At the literal edge of "Indian Country," the tiny village of Cleaveland wouldn't be officially incorporated for another two years. Despite a series of treaty concessions, the white settlers felt as though their grip on the east bank of the Cuyahoga was precarious. Indigenous camps along the Rocky River brought unsettling news from the interior.

The first public execution in northeast Ohio occurred on June 26 that year. Nearly the entire community assembled on Public Square to witness it. Many people sat on a pile of recently cut timbers that would be assembled into the village's first courthouse in the following days. The gallows had been erected on the northwest corner of the square, just south from where the Old Stone Church stands today. John O'Mic, a young Ojibwe man, had been convicted of murdering two fur trappers near Sandusky. With fear of war with the British in the air, and with rumors of Tecumseh rallying allies to attack settlements, the death of a couple Americans, which many saw as an affront to the authority of the new state government, demanded frontier justice.

Mingling in the crowd that day was Juliana Walworth. Still a teenager, she had grown up with O'Mic in Painesville, where they had played along the Grand River as children. By all accounts, O'Mic did not meet his fate easily. He clung to the gallows posts and twice asked for alcohol to calm his nerves. In the middle of the ordeal, Walworth grew upset, wondering, "why should I wish to see my old play-fellow die?" Years later she recalled, "I got out of the crowd as quick as possible and went home." What she missed was a bookend of sorts to two eras.[39]

When O'Mic's body dropped from the gallows, breaking his neck, a summer storm approached from the west, dispersing the spectators. Had he died a generation earlier, his kin would have performed funeral rites and returned his body to the Ohio soil. A new age had dawned on Ohio, however. That night, a group of doctors from the region (including some whose family names grace buildings throughout the state) dissected his corpse. By one account, his skeleton stayed in the possession of the physicians who were desperate for anatomy specimens to study.[40] O'Mic's remains have never been located.

Of course, even if he had received a proper burial, that was still no guarantee of a dignified rest. Although immigration to Ohio was slow at first, the opening of the Ohio and Erie Canal between Cleveland and Akron in the summer of 1827 connected Ohio to faraway markets in ways that the colonial French, British, and Dutch traders never could have imagined. At times, entire communities transplanted from settlements back east to northeast Ohio. A religious community from upstate New York arrived in Kirtland, about twenty miles east of Cleveland, in 1831. Their leader, a charismatic twenty-five-year-old, Joseph Smith, who called himself "the Prophet," had been troubled by the inability of the Bible to account for the Indigenous people of the Americas or the ruins of their civilizations that dotted the landscape. Before immigrating to Ohio, Smith had been transfixed by a glacial kame rising from the earth in Manchester, New York. He announced that an angel named Moroni had revealed to him the locations of divine texts that would rectify the biblical omission of Indigenous people. The first text had been buried in a vault on the kame, which Smith named Cumorah, and was accompanied by artifacts of the lost civilizations.

Organized as the "stake of Zion," the community of "saints" in Kirtland would become the headquarters of the Latter-Day Saints Movement, whose adherents were known as Mormons. In Kirtland, the Mormons organized schools, ran a publishing business, and built the Kirtland Temple, which still stands today. Smith also began collecting artifacts that would aid him in his quest to reconcile the Bible with the American experience. He studied mummies and papyrus from ancient Egypt and also engaged in what had become a growing pastime among colonists: raiding Indigenous burial mounds.[41]

Smith's days in Kirtland were numbered. His radical religious visions, combined with the power he held over nearly two thousand followers, threatened the community. In March of 1832, a mob attacked him, tarred and feathered his body, and left him, in the words of one biographer, "naked, bruised, covered with tar, and nearly unconscious."[42] He would continue to endure the scorn of the outsiders so long as he could rely on his community of saints. He finally fled Kirtland in 1838 after a bank he had organized and promoted collapsed and caused many depositors to break from him.

Mormonism was an early attempt to create a framework for understanding pre-Columbian civilizations that challenged some core, "old-world" beliefs. Other settlers treated the earthworks and burial mounds with a more utilitarian spirit. One mound at the corner of East Ninth and Euclid was cleared during the early expansion of the city. Today, a Heinen's grocery store occupies its approximate location.[43] Local rumors, likely apocryphal, suggest that early settlers chose their cemeteries by simply plotting them over Indigenous burial mounds. Mounds at cemeteries in both Avon and Boston suggest it was at least plausible.

Death has a power to strip away much of what distinguishes us in life, which is why cultures throughout the world celebrate and mourn the dead in elaborate ceremonies—to reinvest a bit of that meaning. Not all of us have been able to experience it the same way, however. Like John O'Mic, the remains of many Indigenous people are sitting in cabinets and collection trays at museums and universities throughout Ohio. According to a database maintained by ProPublica, as of this writing, Oberlin College has made available for return the remains of four Indigenous people in their collection. The Department of Anthropology at Cleveland State University possesses the remains of thirty-five individuals who have not been made available for repatriation. The Western Reserve Historical Society, where I completed much of the research for my first book, has the remains of ninety-nine bodies within their archives. The Cleveland Museum of Natural History, whose archaeologists I have cited throughout this text, has the remains of four hundred people. By far the largest collection of Indigenous remains in the state is held by Ohio History Connection, formerly known as the Ohio Historical Society. Of the 7,167 human remains in their collection, only seventeen have been made available for return.[44] Nearly all of these institutions have articulated a land acknowledgment, but their failure to move more swiftly (or at all) to repatriate human remains for a proper burial have frustrated Indigenous communities.

Nancy Kelsey, a journalist and Anishinaabe activist living in Cleveland's Slavic Village, recognizes it isn't always easy to repatriate Indigenous remains or artifacts. As she writes, "because tribal infrastructures are often underfunded as it is, the expectation that tribes take on the responsibility of repatriating remains and sacred objects is unrealistic." History and US policy hasn't made that process easy. Despite a rich history stretching back to the last ice age, there are zero federally recognized tribes in Ohio. But just because federal policy denied Ohio's Indigenous people legal recognition doesn't mean the people vanished. "We, Native people, are modern, resilient and thriving people, who still live in Northeast Ohio," Kelsey says. Indigenous communities in Ohio are looking for institutions to do the hard work of bridging the divide. Kelsey says those relationships "are still salvageable and absolutely worth pursuing."[45]

An essential element in processing grief is the acknowledgment of community loss. During the SARS-CoV-2 pandemic, psychologists described a phenomenon known as "disenfranchised grief," where the bereaved are robbed of the acknowledgment necessary to process a profound loss.[46] Disenfranchised grief may be the most generous way to describe the failure to repatriate Indigenous remains. For many settlers, Indigenous earthworks and human remains were either an impediment to "progress" or a specimen to be studied in the service of science. Returning ancestors to the land with the dignity that has been denied them for generations would be the beginning of an acknowledgment of the world created and maintained by Indigenous people in Ohio for over ten thousand years. The destruction of that world over the course of two centuries would forever alter the relationship between the people of Ohio and their environment. This apocalypse for Native people stripped the land of cultures that had coevolved with the plants and animals of the region. And as white settlers asserted control over Ohio at the dawn of the nineteenth century, a war against nature commenced that would undermine the ability of the land, air, and water to support life.

CHAPTER 4
The War on Nature

Every year since 1996, the Cleveland Rowing Foundation has hosted the Head of the Cuyahoga Regatta on the Cuyahoga River. The event draws thousands of rowers and spectators, cultivating a hope that the river can break free from negative associations linked to its industrial past. The 2016 regatta began as usual, with rowers dipping their oars into the cool water and spectators crowding the banks of the river as though awaiting a parade. A morning rainstorm soaked the participants as they wove their way along the dramatic bends of the navigation channel. By midday, however, the skies broke on a beautiful summer day.

Out of sight of the regatta, the rain from the morning storm fell on a landscape that two hundred years of white settlement had altered dramatically. The eastern woodland that had once dominated the countryside had been nearly eliminated and replaced with concrete, asphalt, buildings, and turfgrass. Trees, even recently planted ones, can intercept 50 percent or more of rainfall, depending on their age and species.[1] Rather than flowing into the thirsty forest soil, the rain on this summer day fell on land covered with impermeable surfaces that shed 90 percent of the water that falls upon them, splashing toward the nearest intercepting sewer. Rowers are accustomed to struggling against currents and obstacles, but this day offered a new feature to the course that was a consequence of a two-hundred-year-long war against nature that began with white settlement.

As rowers made their way through the crooked river, the collected rainfall of over 4,300 acres in Ohio City and Tremont flowed off roofs, driveways, sidewalks, parking lots, and lawns into the largest combined sewer overflow on Cleveland's west side. There, it mixed with raw sewage and was delivered through a sixteen-foot-diameter tunnel directly to the Cuyahoga River at Scranton Flats. The discharge was so powerful it pushed the crews in their sleek shells as if they were mere pool noodles. A day celebrating the rebirth of the Cuyahoga as a recreational amenity confronted the legacy of a centuries-old war against nature that sought to control every element of the environment. Past decisions made it literally shit on the city's parade that day. How else are we held captive by a legacy of fighting nature instead of working with it? What would the land say if it could speak for itself?

Ghost Maps

Ohio is haunted by its past, and even the names we use for the land and water have either disputed or unknown origins. Take the Cuyahoga River, for example. Historians feel pretty confident that it originates in an Iroquoian word, but depending on the particular language, it could mean "crooked" or "jawbone." Indigenous place-names can seem timeless, but the Haudenosaunee people who applied that name to the river had themselves arrived only recently, having fought a war of conquest against their western neighbors. We seek authority in longevity and forget that the victors often erase the past or rewrite it to suit their own needs. Names can also adapt to different uses. We all know how our own names can feel quite different when spoken by a parent, a friend, a lover, or a police officer. Place-names provide only the illusion of stability to a land governed by its own logic that prefigures our own designs and expectations for it.

For many, the name "Cuyahoga" likely invokes images from the past two hundred years. Like many rivers bearing Indigenous names, the past has been paneled over by new associations. Although it was born out of the Ice Age, the Cuyahoga's identity is irrevocably bound to what happened along its banks over the last two centuries. A short walk from Wendy Park, you can stand at the mouth of the river and witness the end journey of water that began in places like Hambden Orchard Wildlife Area in Geauga County. When Cleveland was first surveyed in the last decade of the eighteenth century, the mouth of the Cuyahoga was several thousand feet to the west, near where Edgewater Park meets the Westerly Wastewater Treatment Plant. Viewed across a long enough timescale, most rivers whipsaw over the land like an untethered, high-pressure water hose, settling into a channel one century, or millennia, only to eventually dig a new path, reshaping the land in the process. Soon after white settlers arrived, the Cuyahoga became a force to be harnessed, domesticated, and controlled. The river's dance across the landscape would be too destructive for a culture wedded to notions of property predicated on stability over time. If the boundaries described in land deeds shift over time, the entire legal apparatus for capitalism breaks down.

Early attempts to describe property boundaries used a system known as "metes and bounds," which identified natural landmarks to distinguish the edges of a land deed. Rocks, shorelines, trees, and rivers were all common boundary markers. But what happens when a tree dies, a river changes course, or a landslide carries stones away? Time and nature made a mockery of such attempts to describe and possess landscapes. Although parts of Ohio were surveyed along this older system, Ohio territory became a testing ground for a new system of organizing land: the public land survey.

Viewed from a commercial aircraft today, the state looks like a crazy quilt of different systems. The land parcels of the Virginia Military District look like a jigsaw puzzle of trapezoids because they were organized according to the metes and bounds system between the Little Miami and Scioto Rivers. Fly north of Dayton toward Toledo and the land there resembles the township and range pattern colloquially known as "the grid." Founded by settlers from Connecticut, Cleveland retains a mixed system of circles common to New England, along with the angular lines of the cadastral grid. The first surveyors celebrated the organization of what they viewed as wild lands into an abstraction by naming a street and village for the Greek mathematician Euclid. Public Square, the four squares at the heart of the city, first appeared as a mathematical abstraction on paper before it ever emerged on the land. It is the epicenter of the American way of organizing land with little regard for the geography, plants, or animals that inhabit it. And though it has changed over the past two centuries, Cleveland's Public Square remains a park set off from the surrounding blocks dedicated to commercial and residential activities. It is a contradiction: Here at the center of it all is the thing that we are not.

One of the markers of agricultural civilizations is their ability to control water systems through irrigation, aqueducts, canals, reservoirs, levees, and dams. If you walk down to the Flats, the Cuyahoga River you see today in the five miles of navigation channel maintained by the US Army Corps of Engineers looks very different after two hundred years of engineering. At the time of white settlement, the river fit into a narrower channel. Heavy rains or melting snow caused floods that frequently spilled into the floodplain we know today. One such flood occurred in February of 1883. Heavy rain fell on the city and funneled into the Flats, swallowing entire industries. The *Cleveland Leader* described the river valley as "an immense lake."[2] It was as if Lake Erie had swallowed the lower Cuyahoga Valley and transformed it into a bay. The flooding was so intense it engulfed the river's two major tributaries: the Walworth Run on the west bank near I-90, and the Kingsbury Run on the east bank just north of where I-490 crosses the river. You need a map and a little historical knowledge to locate these tributaries today because the city chose to sacrifice them to a new idea of "progress."

The Walworth Run roughly followed the course of present-day Train Avenue, wending a way between the bluffs that mark the boundaries of Ohio City to the north and Tremont to the south, carving out the Scranton Flats over millennia. During a December rainstorm in 1859, the Walworth Run swelled with rainwater, washing away four bridges, a flouring mill dam, and part of a cattle yard. The demands of early settlement situated infrastructure in close proximity to running water that, at times, reclaimed the real estate located on floodplains. Unwilling to regulate or ban the dumping of pollution into waterways, the city opted to sacrifice multiple tributaries of the Cuyahoga, transforming them into subterranean sewers in the late nineteenth and early twentieth centuries.

You can still see where the old stream empties into the Cuyahoga at the Scranton Flats park along the Towpath Trail. Instead of the gentle, spring-fed creek it once was, you are greeted by the gaping maw of a concrete culvert maintained by the Northeast Ohio Regional Sewer District. Quiet on most days, the culvert serves as a combined sewage overflow during heavy rain events, belching storm runoff and raw sewage directly into the Cuyahoga around forty times each year, sometimes splashing sewage on rowing crews racing through the river. A sad fate for a stream that defined the landscape on the near west side.

Such is the destiny of many of the landscapes we live in. Shaped by millennia of natural forces, they proved incompatible with industry and consumer capitalism. In the end, the land will win. Remember that. The drops of rain that fall on Geauga County will, with time, crash through every dam, levee, and culvert we construct to control its flow. For how insurmountable our present environmental crises seem, how invincible our technology appears, every time humans fight a river, it is always a battle we lose in the end. Unfortunately, not every member of nature's community is as resilient as rock. Many of the plants and animals that coevolved with the land and water in Ohio for millions of years couldn't survive a landscape reorganized to serve a global market. The war on nature in Ohio has been a self-inflicted wound that every child in the state inherits without knowing it. Our wetlands are no longer shaped by the diligence of beavers. Automobiles have replaced wolves as the primary predator of our deer population. Our skies are no longer darkened by ribbons of passenger pigeons each year. Even the night sky, a reminder of an infinite cosmos that challenges our sense of importance, has been vanquished by a flood of artificial light, much of it wasted in pursuit of the appearance of security and prosperity. If the price of progress was the disenchantment of the world, what are we hoping will replace the paradise that sustained us since the end of the last ice age? The answers are not reassuring.

Wilderness as Obstacle

Although many historians have gone to great pains to dispel the notion that white settlers met a "wilderness" when they arrived in the Americas, Ohio country was a more complex story than one people and culture replacing another in quick succession. Henry David Thoreau described the role human perception plays in our overall understanding of the world. "Generally speaking," he wrote, "a howling wilderness does not howl: it is the imagination of the traveler that does the howling."[3] White settlers arrived with a culture that assigned Indigenous people to a subhuman category. Documents from the time are filled with the word "savage" to describe Indigenous people, cultures, and behaviors. When you denigrate a people into the category of animals, it isn't that difficult to view the landscape as uninhabited, despite the presence of entire nations.

All cultures undertake visions of utopia to guide their relationship with the land and the other civilizations upon it. Sovereignty is at the core of every culture's vision for its future: the power to demarcate itself from what it is not and be secure in that sphere. Many Indigenous cultures defined their own cultural horizons in familiar ways—by a sacred geography rooted in a particular landscape, by language, and by kinship. These visions were shattered by the process of colonization. Europeans introduced new elements—disease, firearms, and a market economy—that upset the balance of power and divorced animals, plants, and even inorganic minerals from their role in the community of life central to Indigenous notions of identity. The mass graves at Cahokia reveal that Indigenous cultures had the ability to advance their own visions of dominion and violence over neighbors, but hierarchical cultures with a ken for empire were the exception, not the rule, in Ohio's human history prior to the arrival of white settlers. Much of that history, such as the Haudenosaunee Beaver and Mourning Wars, was a direct response to white colonial policies. The end result created a landscape that confirmed the utopian vision of settler-colonialism. A landscape sparsely inhabited by Indigenous communities that, for the most part, had arrived as refugees from elsewhere confirmed ideas of Native inferiority and the need to "improve" the territory for "progress."

Historian Roxanne Dunbar-Ortiz has argued that the purpose of settler-colonialism in the American context was "to terminate Indigenous peoples as nations and communities with land bases in order to make the land available to European settlers."[4] Whether annihilated as people or a culture, Indigenous communities were seen as incompatible with American democracy. Although reformers sought either the assimilation of Native peoples or their separation and confinement on reservations, many Americans viewed Indigenous people as subhuman impediments to progress.

Scholars who study the genocides of the twentieth century have identified how the process of extermination always begins in the mind. Stripping people of their identity, their sovereign nationality, are necessary steps in the dehumanizing process that creates a permission structure for racial violence, ethnic cleansing, and programmatic genocide. The Nazi motto of "*Blut und Boden*," or "blood and soil," was a very old concept when it emerged in the 1930s, and it borrowed many ideas from the North American colonial experience. The tenuous state of Indigenous communities in Ohio following the American Revolution seemed to confirm settler notions of the territory as a lawless jumble awaiting the benevolent care of Christian, capitalist culture.

The land, too, seemed in a state of disarray. The wars of the seventeenth century depopulated Ohio to such an extent that it altered the land's animal and plant populations. Kathryn M. Flinn, an ecologist at Baldwin Wallace University, found that forests in Cuyahoga County bear evidence of massive disruption prior to white settlement. Flinn set out to better understand a chasm in the archaeological and historic record, and what she discovered seems almost scandalous to print: From 1640 until 1742, there is no evidence of permanent human settlement in northeastern Ohio. Scholars have demonstrated how the Indigenous use of fire altered landscapes and how the replacement of Indigenous land-use patterns with those of white settlers could, at times, lead to a process termed "mesophication." The cessation of widespread human-created fires in the seventeenth century favored forests where fire-sensitive, shade-tolerant tree species would thrive in ways that were impossible under intensive Indigenous fire-management regimes.

By 1800, when the first ecological survey data was collected in Ohio, the land had been bereft of intense management for nearly 150 years. Flinn found "no evidence for the hypothesis that the vegetation of northeast Ohio was shaped predominantly by frequent fire and subsequent fire suppression" during this time. To the contrary, survey data from 1800 show that the fire-intolerant American beech tree covered 46.5 percent of the land in northeast Ohio. The most successful species following white colonization, according to Flinn, were those with what ecologists call a ruderal strategy, "a combination of adaptations to

frequent disturbance including fast growth, short time to repro-
ductive maturity, large allocation to reproduction, and effective
seed dispersal." That is, settlers created an environment in Ohio
that favored trees that bounced back quickly from the damage
done by axes, plows, and foraging livestock.[5] Although beech
trees flourished in the absence of human intervention during the
seventeenth and eighteenth centuries, the settler-colonial experience selected for maple trees, which made up over 50 percent of
all tree species by the early twenty-first century.

Our forests tell stories if we know how to listen to them.
But for colonial minds of the eighteenth century, they existed,
at best, as springboards to white settlement and, at worst, as barriers in need of removal. Although he never set foot in Ohio,
Benjamin Franklin already had designs on the land decades before the Revolutionary War. In the 1750s, he advanced a scheme
to settle colonies in Ohio "for the extreme richness and fertility
of the land." Franklin held a utilitarian view of nature as a tool
for advancing human desires, and he was clear in articulating his
vision of a future utopia along the shores of Lake Erie. "From
these natural advantages," he wrote of Ohio, "it must undoubt-
edly (perhaps in less than another century) become a populous
and powerful dominion, and a great accession of power, either
to England or France."[6] The American expression of "blood and
soil," as proclaimed by thinkers such as Franklin, was clearly
rooted in the environment's potential to give birth to a new,
white nation on Indigenous soil. Transforming the Ohio "wilderness" into fertile soil for American utopian visions would require
a level of violence against the environment that represents the
most profound shift in the human relationship with the land
since the retreat of the great continental glaciers.

Reconstructing historic tree populations is far easier than
doing the same for animals. All indications are that the human

depopulation of Ohio in the seventeenth century initiated significant changes to animal populations. The most momentous seems to have been what ecologists call an "ecological release," an event that occurs when a limiting factor—in this case, Indigenous hunters—are removed from the landscape, allowing another species to flourish. Without the intensity of predation from human hunters, all manner of wildlife exploded into their ecological niches in the 150 years prior to white settlement.

At the same time Franklin was dreaming of a new American empire fixed on the shores of Lake Erie, an eighteen-year-old kid from Pennsylvania named James Smith was realizing Ohio was still very much Indigenous land. While working on a road through the Cumberland Valley in Pennsylvania in 1755, Smith was captured by a French-allied Indigenous war party at the beginning of the French and Indian War. While under French custody at Fort Duquesne (modern-day Pittsburgh), he was adopted by a Piscataway family who traveled with him west into Ohio territory. For four years, he lived among the Piscataway people until he escaped in 1759. His experience was published years later, one of many "captivity narratives" that document Indigenous life through colonial eyes. Although many captivity narratives contain gross exaggerations, distortions, and outright lies, Smith's provides a rare description of Ohio territory in the years just prior to white settlement.

Smith and his adopted family traveled the banks of the Black River between the present-day cities of Elyria and Lorain. He describes a land covered by black walnut, maple, ash, buckeye, honey locust, hickory, and oak trees. Every day, his companions hunted deer, racoons, and bears in abundance, often only taking choice cuts of meat and stripping the animals of their valuable furs for market. He describes a Wyandot village where he ate potatoes dipped in racoon fat. "In this route deer, bear, turkeys, and racoons, appeared plenty," he notes, "but no buffalo, and very little sign of elks." Smith accounts for only a few beavers during his journey, a sign perhaps of their scarcity after a century of intense fur trapping. He described racoons "remarkably large and fat" and of foraging for mast among stands of chestnut. When the party reached Lake Erie, he describes bald eagles devouring small pools of fish left at low tide along the shore. Over the course of a two-week time span, the party killed a total of four bears, three deer, "several turkeys, and a number of racoons," all within walking distance of camp.[7]

Smith, who reflexively reduced animals to resources, received important lessons in an Indigenous understanding of reciprocity and mutual aid. When a Wyandot man visited his camp, Smith "gave him a shoulder of venison which I had by the fire well roasted." When his adoptive brother, Tontileaugo, returned to camp, Smith shared the details happily. When Tontileaugo learned that Smith had not offered sugar and bear's oil to the guest to accompany the meal, he scolded him. "You have behaved just like a Dutchman," Tontileaugo admonished. "When strangers come to our camp, we ought always to give them the best that we have." Tontileaugo forgave Smith for his misstep but informed him that he must "learn to behave like a warrior, and do great things, and never be found in any such little actions."

Smith soon traveled along the Cuyahoga with another adopted brother and described a land filled with fat deer, wolves, racoons, geese, and cranberries. He learned how fur trappers used steel traps to catch and drown beaver, and he even dissected one to verify that they did not, in fact, eat fish as one of his books suggested. His Indigenous brother laughed: "He said the man that wrote that book knew nothing about the beaver." Smith and his adopted family didn't know it, but they were enjoying the last years of Indigenous sovereignty in Ohio territory. Within a decade, the French would abdicate their claims on the continent and propel white settlers on a crash course with colonial authorities over Indigenous lands in the Great Lakes. The coming conflicts, spasms of violence, and treaties stripped Indigenous people of their connection to the land in Ohio and also signaled doom for the animals Smith described as being in such abundance during the 1750s.

John Milton Holley visited the Cuyahoga River in September of 1796. A surveyor for Moses Cleaveland, Holley represented the first wave of white settlement. Immediately upon arriving at the mouth of the river, he spied a campfire on the far shore, and the surveyors greeted an Indigenous hunting party. Holley spotted a bear swimming across the river and hastily jumped in a canoe to pursue it. "But there was such a noise and hallooing," he wrote in his journal, "that the bear swam back and escaped."[8] Once he and the surveying party laid out an imaginary grid over the land, the process of realizing the new utopia began. He had little appetite for an adventurous life hacking a living out of the forests of Ohio. When winter hit, he joined his fellow surveyors in a near mutiny that forced Cleaveland to return home to Connecticut earlier than planned. The two men never returned to Ohio, content to make a living in the thoroughly domesticated lands back East.

The few settlers who were drawn to northeast Ohio in the following decades described a sense of contempt for the hardships they endured. James Kingsbury and his family, for example, had followed one of the first surveying parties to the Western Reserve in 1796. The Kingsburys settled the banks of the Cuyahoga, perhaps the first white settlers of what would become the city of Cleveland, and built a log cabin in the hopes of making a life there. The first winter nearly ruined them. With the family on the brink of starvation, Kingsbury ventured out and shot a passenger pigeon, which helped him nurse his wife back to health.[9]

It was a poetic microcosm of how the next century would play out: the exchange of wildlife for settlers.

Kingsbury and his family left the new settlement almost immediately, abandoning their homestead. The river valley, then languid and marshy, harbored swarms of mosquitoes responsible for frequent outbreaks of malaria. Within a year, they had created a new settlement a few miles to the south, which was appropriately named Newburgh. Located on higher ground far from the marshy flats, it seemed far more promising than the location organized around Public Square at the mouth of the Cuyahoga River in the first decades of white settlement. Charles Whittlesey, in one of the earliest histories of Cleveland, described the year of 1797 as "so sickly about the mouth of the Cuyahoga, that the settlers sought the highlands to escape remittent fevers."[10] "What is now Newburg [*sic*]," Whittlesey wrote, "was then much the largest settlement."[11] Kingsbury preferred the heights above the river so much that he lived out the remainder of his life there until his death in 1847, long after the city of Cleveland had grown into its own.

Kingsbury wasn't alone in his experience. Samuel Huntington arrived in the spring of 1801 and built a home on the banks of the Cuyahoga near Public Square. Huntington, who would go on to be the second chief justice of the Ohio Supreme Court and the state's third governor, did not find the site designated for settlement by the original surveyors to his liking. A year after arriving, he was returning home from Painesville. At about the present-day location of the Agora Theater at Euclid Avenue and East Fifty-Fifth Street was a swamp. Night had fallen, and navigating on horseback was no easy task. According to an account shared by Nathaniel Doan, Huntington was attacked by "a gang of hungry wolves" and survived only because he was able to fight them off with the aid of an umbrella "with which he charged them right and left."[12] By 1805, he followed in Kingsbury's footsteps and abandoned his Cleveland home for the falls at Mill Creek, near Newburgh. The combination of wild animals and "the prevalence here of the detestable ague" drove him, like many early settlers, to the heights.[13] In the first decades, the settlement remained a rough-hewn promise more than a reality. In 1802, a man near the present-day location of the river's mouth at West Ninth Street fended off and killed a bear with a garden hoe.[14] If Cleveland would fulfill the promise that men like Ben Franklin envisioned, it would need to wage a campaign against the wildlife that already called it home.

Scorched Earth

The global market arrived before white settlers and prepared the way for the conversion of the land from a biological community into an array of resources ripe for the taking. By the early nineteenth century, the few remaining beavers James Smith had sighted in the 1750s had vanished. Although the fur trade transformed their bodies into fashionable hats for posh Europeans, the animal's role in shaping the Ohio landscape carried on for several generations. Their dams and lodges haunted the landscape like ruins of a fallen civilization. As late as 1881, historians of Medina County reported the presence of a beaver dam on the River Styx, even though "no beaver was ever known to have been caught in this region."[15]

Other animals required more intentional effort to eradicate. Although Indigenous civilizations nurtured dogs as animal companions, the absence of good candidates for livestock domestication in the Americas meant that cultures evolved a sense of respect and understanding for the role predators played in the larger ecosystem.[16] It would seem it is more difficult to revere animals that eat your food. Europeans brought with them vulnerable livestock that engendered an adversarial posture toward "wild" animals. In the words of environmental historian Dan Flores, bounties "were the Old Worlders' first wildlife laws in America and by the twentieth century every state but one had them."[17] Wolves roamed the forests near downtown Cleveland into the 1820s and made easy meals out of the livestock vital to the success of early settlers. State bounties paid out of public taxes provided an incentive and permission structure for an all-out war on predators. Hunters could cash in on such bounties by returning a pair of ears or, in the case of Ohio, a scalp. In the 1820s, the going rate for the scalp of an adult wolf was three dollars, while the scalp of a juvenile returned a bounty of $1.50.[18] Not bad for a time when the purchasing power of a single dollar translated into roughly twenty-five dollars today and the hunter could still sell the remaining fur on the market. As late as 1833, the Cuyahoga County treasurer reported payment of twenty-four dollars over the calendar year for wolf scalps, an amount that would dwindle to nothing by mid-century, as the combined forces of human hunters and landscape change pushed wolves out of northeast Ohio.[19]

Both market and government incentives drove individuals to exterminate predators in Ohio following the first wave of white settlement, but organized communal action demonstrated the culture's commitment to the project of wildlife eradication. For European peasants, holidays have long been communal events organized around feasts. Communal hunts in the early years of white settlement served dual purposes: to provide meat for the long Ohio winter and to create a landscape more amenable to domesticated livestock. Settlers in Hinckley, Ohio, had struggled to pacify the land into a pastoral utopia. Shepherds there awoke one morning to the massacre of over one hundred sheep, torn apart by rampaging wolf packs.[20] In the autumn of 1818, farmers from Medina, Summit, and Cuyahoga Counties assembled in Strongsville, in the words of one historian, "to resolve on a war of extermination against these beasts." The result was an announcement of a great hunt to commence on Christmas Eve day. The plan had a brutal simplicity: "the farmers gather by early daybreak, armed with rifles, guns, pitchforks, flails, clubs, and every available implement of war; form a continuous line on the four sides of the township, and, at a given signal advance towards its center, killing, shooting, and slaughtering all game that came within reach."[21]

When the day arrived, each battle line was composed of approximately one hundred men. A "long-drawn blast" from a bugle signaled the order to march, and the assembled men advanced, their feet crunching on a brittle crust of snow. Soon the sound of musket fire and barking dogs rose into the air, causing animals to flee toward the center of the township, the designated kill zone for the day's hunt. When the lines converged on the center, the distance between each man shrank until they were marching shoulder to shoulder, becoming "almost a solid phalanx of men." The terrified animals, cornered and surrounded on all sides, made desperate attempts to escape. With no place else to turn, the deer dashed toward the line of men where many were shot, "forked and clubbed, and some, the larger and fleeter, escape—bounding over the heads of the hunters." In the melee, opportunities for friendly fire increased rapidly. One group of deer attempted to rush the northern line of men, where Lathrop Seymour stood ready. He was hit by buckshot across the left side of his body and pulled off the formation to receive medical treatment.[22]

William Coggswell, a hunter from Bath, Ohio, barely escaped injury. Having already shot and killed several wolves and bears, he and his dog found themselves confronted with, as he described it, "a monstrous bear—I think the largest I ever saw of that species." Although the bear had been wounded twice by gunfire, Coggswell found himself caught in the line of fire as several men attempted to finish off the animal. "There were probably 100 guns fired within a very short space of time, and the bullets sounded to me very much like a hail-storm." Having killed the bear, Coggswell nonchalantly described his brush with death: "as it happened, neither myself nor dog were hurt."[23]

As the gunfire died down, a "rousing big fire" was built and a party of men were dispatched to Richfield to use the bounty money from the day's hunt to procure a barrel of whiskey, which they returned with on a sled pulled by a team of oxen. As cups were passed around, a roll call returned the names of 454 men, the largest hunt ever organized in American history at the time. The men also took a census of the day's slaughter, which revealed a grim toll. All told, the hunt had killed seventeen wolves, twenty-one bears, over three hundred deer, and countless racoons, possums, turkeys, and foxes. A bear was roasted over the fire and passed around to warm the bellies of the tired men. The furs of some animals were removed, and everyone gathered as much meat as they could carry, but the carcasses of most of the animals were left to freeze in the Ohio winter air. This hunt had the sole purpose of reshaping the ecosystem of Hinckley Township—any food or furs harvested were merely by-products of the greater cause—and it worked. The following year, the township was surveyed and divided into one hundred lots, each 160 acres in size, and placed on the market at three dollars per acre. In a single day, the tricounty effort made the land safe (or safer) for agriculture and broke the relationship between humans and wildlife that had been forged since the end of the last ice age.[24]

Today, Hinckley is still rooted to its rural, agricultural past. If anyone outside of Medina County knows about the area, it's for the buzzards (actually turkey vultures) that flock to the township every spring from as far south as Peru, drawing birders from miles away to marvel as the birds wing over their roost in Hinckley Reservation Metropark. Local legend ties the two identities of this landscape together. As the story goes, the buzzards never caught anyone's attention until the spring of 1819, when the hundreds of frozen carcasses abandoned by the Christmas Eve hunt thawed and attracted the scavenging birds. They've returned ever since, an echo from the thunderclap announcing the end of an ecological era.

Sporting Fun

Although the Great Hinckley Hunt in 1818 would be the largest, it was by no means the only organized campaign to eradicate wildlife in northeast Ohio. A year later, another holiday hunt was organized in Willoughby that killed two elk, ten turkeys, seventeen wolves, twenty-three bears, and seventy-five deer.[25] To the west, a hunt organized in southeast Lorain County near Liverpool Township in the summer of 1819 pulled together approximately three hundred men in an effort to recreate the success at Hinckley. This hunt was organized in a circle rather than a square, which replicated the same danger of cross fire. When the frightened deer tried to escape the closing ring, one hunter shot another through the heart, killing him instantly. As word spread among the hunters, they all ran to the scene to inquire about the identity of the man, allowing hundreds of deer, wolves, and bears to flee unscathed.[26] The era of assembling small armies to destroy wildlife came to an end nearly as soon as it began. Ultimately, the swirling mix of excitement, inexperience, and whiskey proved too dangerous to participants. Bounty hunters and private hunting clubs would eat away at the remaining wildlife in northeast Ohio for the rest of the century.

In November of 1830, the Nimrod Association of Cleveland sponsored their first hunt, but the years of warfare had made game harder to come by. The club announced a modest haul of ten deer, six turkeys, and a single bear over the course of a two-day hunt.[27] One signal that the war against wildlife was coming to an end was the transformation of animals from dangerous threats into mere playthings. In the 1830s, two brothers, Alexander and Abner McIlrath, opened a tavern and general store at the northwest corner of Euclid and Superior Avenues in Cleveland. Abner organized hunts and shooting contests from the tavern and assembled the first wildlife menagerie or zoo to demonstrate his hunting prowess and attract patrons. Visitors came to see a bear, wolf, and eagle tied to trees outside the tavern, curiosities of a vanishing era.[28]

As larger wildlife withered under the combined assault of hunting and habitat loss, northeast Ohio residents still marveled at the seemingly infinite bounty of wild birds and fish. Although the commercial fishery on the American side of Lake Erie has been all but closed for decades, it was once the most productive fishery on the Great Lakes. As the eleventh-largest freshwater lake on earth, Lake Erie has enormous biological potential. Its relatively shallow waters and major river systems allow it to host a diverse array of species. Commercial records indicate at least nineteen different species throughout its history with economic value, including blue pike, white fish, yellow perch, and walleye. The Lake Erie fishery was so productive that, in some years, it equaled the total landings of all the other Great Lakes combined.[29] When white settlements reached Rocky River in 1813, the *Cleveland Leader* reported fish were so abundant that "one man fishing would catch with a spear as many as 50 or 60 large pike in one night."[30]

The early commercial fishery employed large seines, either cast across rivers like the Maumee or dropped from boats near shore on the lake. Ice fishing was also productive during the frigid winter months, when ice closed the lake to boat traffic. Lake trout (*Salvelinus namaycush*) remained active in the winter and could be caught by drilling holes through the ice and dropping lines in the water. With some adults reaching over fifty pounds, a full-grown lake trout would require a heroic struggle to land. No doubt many fish were caught for subsistence, but the logic of the market also ensnared Lake Erie. In February of 1839, the *Cleveland Herald* announced that the fish market at Buffalo was stocked with "an abundance of white trout, three to four feet long!"[31]

Lake whitefish (*Coregonus clupeaformis*) appear in many accounts from this period as well. Smaller than trout, they feast on bottom-dwelling shellfish, snails, and larvae, a perfect niche to inhabit in Lake Erie's shallow waters. The waters off Vermillion were teeming with lake whitefish according to newspaper accounts from the 1830s.[32] Cleveland's growing population created a market for fish from all over the Lake Erie basin. In the winter of 1840, a fishmonger on Superior Avenue announced in a local newspaper a stock of "100 barrels whitefish and trout" for sale.[33] In the decade leading up to the Civil War, the industrial logic that would transform the country had already arrived on the lakeshore as permanent pound nets dotted the coast, filtering adult fish into catch basins that would be emptied into a vessel's hold on a regular schedule and shipped to market. The lake's seemingly infinite bounty had been remade into an organic machine to feed a booming population.

Birds, too, got pulled into the well of market relations. Snowy owls once ranged to the Great Lakes' southern shores. Although climate change has steadily pushed their range northward, in the nineteenth century, they could be spotted as far south as Cleveland. In January of 1847, the *Cleveland Herald* reported that "white or Arctic owls have appeared in this vicinity in unusual numbers the present winter." The newspaper also noted how enterprising boys had been "hawking them about our streets at half a dollar a head since the start of winter."[34] Just like the eagle on display at McIlrath's tavern, this arctic visitor learned the hard way that northeast Ohio was no longer friendly territory.

No other animal fell under the sporting gaze as much as the passenger pigeon, however. With some flocks estimated to contain billions of birds, residents of northeast Ohio marveled at the dark, swift clouds of birds as they flew overhead. York Township in Medina County regularly hosted such large roosts that hunters were warned not to venture into the forest with torches or lanterns; the flame could startle the pigeons, who "would instantly dart for the light and dash it to the ground, and endanger the eyes and face of the reckless hunter." The flocks remade entire ecosystems. After an old-growth forest had been removed for farmland, the settlers of York Township discovered a layer of guano six inches deep.[35] In the spring of 1833, a large flock of passenger pigeons roosted in Medina County. Each day from sunrise until 9:00 a.m., "the sun was obscured by them as they rose and flew in a northern direction," only to return near the end of the day and blot out the sun as they returned to their roosts. Once settlers understood the scale of the roost, they hurried to arrive before the chicks could fly of their own accord. One historian related how "people came in wagons from all over the country, and carried the squabs away in bagfuls." The roosts of northeast Ohio gained such notoriety that commercial hunters organized a rendezvous at Lodi in 1850. From their headquarters, they would venture out to kill thousands of pigeons at a time, pack them in barrels, and ship them to markets in the East. By 1881, local historians wrote that "these birds have abandoned this territory as a nesting-ground," and "though they stop here now occasionally for feeding purposes," they do so "in greatly diminished numbers."[36]

Often arriving as winter stores wore thin, passenger pigeons became a centerpiece of settler cuisine. The great naturalist Alexander Wilson dined on them so frequently that he remarked, "the very name becomes sickening." Cookbooks of the time suggested preparing the bird in stews and potpies, and hunters would preserve packed barrels full of pigeon meat with salt or congealed lard to prevent decay. The biological abundance also led to wasteful practices. Settlers fed pigeons to livestock, especially pigs, and a traveler leaving Cleveland for the Ohio River reported, "We saw many carcasses of these birds outside the villages, such numbers having been destroyed, that the inhabitants could not consume them, and they were accordingly thrown out as refuse."[37]

Perhaps the most wasteful practice was reducing the bird to sport for shooting competitions. Long before video game arcades, Americans entertained themselves by slaughtering hundreds of pigeons in competitive matches. Abner McIlrath organized pigeon shooting competitions from his tavern, where the stakes could attract considerable attention. As news of the bloody Battle of Antietam was circulating through the city in the autumn of 1862, the *Cleveland Leader* dedicated precious column inches to a description of a pigeon shooting contest between William King of Cleveland and Robert Newall of Buffalo with a $1,000 purse. For scale, Abraham Lincoln earned a salary of $25,000 that same year. Although King killed seventy-nine of the ninety birds he shot at, Newall bested him with a score of eighty-two to claim the prize.[38] By 1875, competitive shoots became organized nationally when the first Grand National Pigeon Shooting Tournament was held at the Northern Ohio Fairgrounds. Drawing 139 sportsmen from across the country, the tournament awarded cash prizes amounting to $4,100 and garnered the attention of the *New York Times*.[39] Passenger pigeons, the most numerous bird species on the continent (and likely the earth), held marginal value only as either "poor-man's food" or as violent entertainment.

If passenger pigeons had been simply entertainment and cheap protein, they may have survived into our lifetimes. But like predators, they also frustrated white settlers' plans to domesticate the land. Although they had coevolved with hardwood trees to forage on mast, as settlers replaced Ohio's forests with farmland and orchards, the birds adapted. In autumn, pigeons fed happily on cultivated cherry trees in Cleveland. Birds killed at a swamp thirty miles south of the city in 1857 were found with bellies full of rice from southern plantations.[40] Pigeons had been known to feed on the wild rice that grew in abundance in the wetlands bordering the Great Lakes and easily transitioned to other cultivated grains when these wetlands were drained and replaced with farmland. In his history of the bird, A. W. Schorger stated simply, "All the cultivated grains were eaten." He described how farmers grew so accustomed to driving pigeons from their wheat fields that they began using the grain as bait to attract and shoot as many birds as possible to reduce the nuisance. Barley, rye, oats, maize, and peas were all gobbled up by flocks of pigeons. Schorger even found reports of passenger pigeons feeding on lettuce greens and hemp seeds to the dismay of farmers. The birds created so much damage to crops that the Bishop of Québec excommunicated the species "more than once."[41]

As the pigeons became a threat to settlement, Americans grew increasingly hostile toward the bird, and the fact that the pigeons took little heed of humans further antagonized them. On windy days, pigeons flew only a few feet off the ground, treetops, or rooftops. Throughout the mid-1800s, residents of northern Ohio reported large flocks that would roost near Cleveland or Cedar Point, wake to feed, and fly over settlements at great speed, only to return, startling residents on each leg of their trip. One flock performed this dive-bombing action on East 105th Street in Cleveland, scaring residents who shot guns into the air in the hopes of scattering the mass of birds. The blasts confused the pigeons to such an extent that they perched on trees and even the backs of horses traveling on the street.[42] One flock buzzing the city in 1860 was met not only by gunfire but also a volley of fireworks in a desperate attempt to shoo them from the area.[43] In late December 1869, the *Cleveland Leader* reported that "persons residing near the courthouse were aroused at an early hour by the sounds of musketry." Terrified that a riot was afoot, they ventured into the street only to discover "a number of persons shooting the pigeons on the court house."[44]

Forty-five years later, the last passenger pigeon in the state of Ohio died at 1:00 p.m. on September 1, 1914. Given the name Martha, the bird's death signaled the extinction of a species that had filled the forests of the land for the past fifteen million years. With an estimated population somewhere between three and ten billion at the start of European colonization, the passenger pigeon had survived multiple ice ages, the birth of the Great Lakes, and the arrival of Indigenous hunters. The advent of the combined forces of a global market and intensive agriculture proved too much for a species that dropped only a single egg a year, roosted communally, and abandoned defenseless squabs at the first sign of disturbance. Evolution had adapted the passenger pigeon to simply outproduce the losses incurred by predators and variations in the environment, but the land-use patterns of white settlers would prove too far-reaching and sustained for the species to adapt.

Although bounties and the fur market served as shock troops for wildlife eradication, the death knell for many species in Ohio accompanied the habitat destruction resulting from white settlement. Many sources state the last wild wolf in Ohio died in 1842, but not all sources agree. A history of Sandusky County published in 1882 identifies an N. P. Hathaway as killing the last wolf in the county in 1858. The publisher's brief remark elicits not even a hint of conqueror's remorse, stating the local extinction "marked the beginning of safety for sheep and other weak domestic animals."[45] Black bears were driven from the state around the same time. Ohio's forests, once rich with the sounds of wildlife, withered from the onslaught of progress. From the vast bison herds on the plains to the dizzying flocks of passenger pigeons on the Great Lakes—all succumbed to American notions of progress in the nineteenth century. For historians Dan Flores and Sara Dant, Americans at that time would bring about "the largest destruction of wildlife anywhere in world history."[46]

Artificial Moonlight

As the American mission to replace wildlife habitat with dense settlements was well on its way, enterprising minds in Cleveland turned to freeing civilization from other limits imposed by the environment. Charles Brush and John D. Rockefeller had a lot in common. Born a decade apart in the first half of the nineteenth century, the two men spent their formative years in Cleveland, both attending Central High School, the first public high school in the city at a time when free public education only extended to elementary school. For a week, the two even shared the same room in a boarding house, though neither knew of the changes the other would eventually bring to the world. Brush would follow a path to higher learning, earning a bachelor's from the University of Michigan and a PhD from Western Reserve University. Rockefeller, meanwhile, dove headfirst into business, earning a name for himself as a merchant's clerk and discovering profits by eliminating unnecessary costs. The outbreak of the Civil War played havoc on commodity prices and allowed him to apply his mind to the problem of purchasing goods cheaply in one market and selling them to desperate buyers in another.

While Brush was still in school, Rockefeller set his sights on a new commodity bubbling up from the Appalachian Plateau in western Pennsylvania. Rock oil, or petroleum, was known by many names, including "Seneca Oil" for its use among the Haudenosaunee, who applied it as a mosquito repellent and salve.[47] Rockefeller's own father, William, likely hawked petroleum, along with other questionable remedies, as a type of traveling salesman who would be parodied for generations and give rise to the term "quack" as a particular kind of charlatan that thrived in the unregulated opening decades of consumer capitalism in America. The younger Rockefeller, however, spied the true potential of the mysterious, viscous fluid as an illuminant. At the time, there weren't many good options for extending the light of day into the Ohio night. Various plant or animal oils used in candles or lamps offered limited utility. Beef tallow candles were dim and produced excessive smoke. Lamps filled with whale oil provided superior illumination, but they were tied to market prices, which skyrocketed as vessels from New England hunted whale populations to extinction in the Atlantic and chased them into the Pacific and all the way to the Bering Sea by the 1840s. When Herman Melville published *Moby-Dick* in 1851, whale oil prices placed it beyond the reach of most consumers.[48] Beginning in 1863, Rockefeller entered the oil trade, converting the black liquid rock oil into kerosene, an illuminant that burned brightly and at a fraction of the cost.

The realization and adoption of this new commodity shattered the existing relationship between civilization and nature. Humans had mastered the use of fire for over one hundred thousand years, but they had failed to concentrate and amplify it much beyond the glow of a candle or campfire. The effect of the widespread adoption of a powerful illuminant was perceptible even to passersby. When Elizabeth Cady Stanton and Susan B. Anthony passed through Cleveland on a train while organizing for women's rights, they were astonished at the intensity of light that filled their train car at night. They questioned the conductor about the effect and were informed that kerosene had allowed people to illuminate their homes at night and complete tasks as though bathed in sunlight. By 1880, Rockefeller's Standard Oil Company in Cleveland was refining an astonishing 90 percent of all petroleum in the United States and making preparations to conquer a global market.

For all its benefits, kerosene lacked the intensity to illuminate much more than interior rooms. At the same time Rockefeller was spreading the gospel of illumination and devouring his competition, Charles Brush was unlocking the secrets of electricity that would allow entire cities to bathe in its glow. While working at the Cleveland Telegraph & Supply Company, he perfected a dynamo using four electromagnets. Filed as US Patent #189,997 in 1876, he declared he had "invented certain new and useful Improvements in Magneto-Electric Machines."[49] Sales were sluggish at first. The dynamo provided more than enough energy to power telegraph machines and alarms, the few electric appliances available at the time. But Brush had developed a source of power for tools that had yet to be invented. Continuing to tinker in his laboratory, he sought to improve on awkward arc light prototypes being developed in Europe. A year later, he won a patent for metal-plated illuminating points that unlocked the ability to transform electricity into a glowing light of great intensity. From his workshop on the top of a building at the corner of St. Clair and Ontario, a block north of Cleveland's Public Square, he had prepared his arc light and used the opportunity provided by a passing parade for his first public demonstration. When the light bathed the street below, the assembled crowd cried in terror, the parade came to a halt, and Brush was soon confronted by angry policemen who demanded him to "turn out that damn light!"[50]

Three years later, he arranged with the city government of Cleveland for a full demonstration of the arc light's ability to illuminate entire city blocks. Brush arranged twelve lights around the Public Square (then called Monumental Park) and wired them to the dynamo at the nearby Cleveland Telegraph & Supply Company's headquarters. At 7:55 p.m. on April 29, 1879, they flickered on, stunning an assembled crowd numbering in the thousands. A shout was raised among the onlookers, a band greeted the blazing glow with a tune, and artillery on the lakeshore fired a salute in honor of the achievement. Decades later, an historian writing of the event remarked somewhat haughtily, "And thus, in the quaint chronicle of the period, electricity was first found to the service of man in Cleveland."[51]

Over the next few years, Brush found his dynamo market as businesses and municipal governments sought to replace gas lamps with his arc lights. In 1881, Cleveland signed a contract for five masts, some three hundred feet tall, and constructed of iron and steel boilerplate, that would produce the equivalent illumination of twenty-five thousand candles. According to a story in the *Cleveland Leader*, each mast would "be sufficient to light the territory in the immediate neighborhood of the mast for a radius of half a mile in every direction, or a circle of one mile in diameter." Although the technology was widely discussed, the phenomenon of what many called "artificial moonlight" appeared almost magical for a population accustomed to measuring power in units, like horsepower, rooted in flesh and bone.[52] By this time, Brush had incorporated his own company, Brush Electric, and would carry his invention throughout the country, manufacturing 80 percent of all arc lights on the market. They illuminated Niagara Falls during a July Fourth celebration in 1879. Like a mischievous child, Brush set up an array of lights on the roof of a Jersey City railroad depot and fired a beam across the Hudson River to announce his arrival to pedestrians in New York City. He beat out fellow Ohio inventor Thomas Edison in illuminating the Big Apple, as arc lights transformed Broadway into the "Great White Way" and made the amusement park at Coney Island glow.[53]

Edison would have the last laugh, however. Kerosene lamps were dirty, and they often exploded. Standard Oil would eventually find a new market by converting petroleum into gasoline for "horseless carriages," fueling the automobile age. Brush sold his company in 1889, ten years after his public demonstration in Cleveland. It would eventually become a subsidiary of Edison's General Electric corporation, which preferred incandescent bulbs and direct current over the alternating current arc lights required. Nevertheless, these transitionary technologies profoundly changed the economy and mainstream culture of America. In her history of artificial light, writer Jane Brox argues, "arc lights had conditioned people to a new level of brightness."[54] Kerosene lamps and arc lights gave people a taste of something that proved insatiable. The day-night cycle that had governed the evolution and behavior of life-forms for billions of years had been broken by two entrepreneurs whose efforts caused a second sun to rise every night across the earth.

The Geography of Nowhere

At the dawn of the twentieth century, the project of remaking northeast Ohio into a utopian vision governed by market relations had succeeded. The initial land surveys provide us with a precontact baseline ecology. In 1800, 94 percent of the state was covered in forest. A century later, that figure had dropped to 15 percent. Eighty-seven percent of Cuyahoga County's population resided within Cleveland's city limits by 1900. A third of the land was covered in cultivated crops, with most of the rest dedicated to industry, commercial buildings, streets, and residential neighborhoods.[55] Cleveland, which had earned the nickname "Forest City" for the great forest that had made its rise possible, witnessed its last stand of old-growth trees die in the 1890s, strangled, according to a professor of botany from Purdue University, by "the smoke from the large manufacturing establishments, and especially from the oil refineries."[56]

While industrial titans such as Rockefeller and Brush were able to live in affluent enclaves, such as the strip of Euclid Avenue known as Millionaires' Row, the hunger for fossil fuels that their businesses unleashed would reorganize the landscape, creating a new geography of sickness known as air pollution. Although Brush used a wind turbine he'd invented to power his own home on Euclid Avenue, his dynamos and the power plants required to electrify America were fueled by burning American soft coal from Appalachia. Rockefeller's refineries were such a nuisance to surrounding communities that citizens in Cleveland's Seventh Ward successfully petitioned the city's Board of Health to block the construction of a new refinery that would "endanger the health of the people."[57] The destruction of the environment had not been a mistake or accidental: it was an intentional choice. During the canal-building boom in the 1830s, the *Cleveland Herald* celebrated a petition to Congress that declared the hope that "the busy hum of the mill and manufactory will drown the noise of waterfall and ripple on the many brooks that are now dancing merrily over rock and pebbly bed."[58] For early settlers such as the Kingsburys, the land's natural condition had nearly killed them, and it did not inspire a sense of romance or reverence.

Progress had come at a cost that advocates of settlement had no way of imagining might be possible. The habitat that held communities of life together had been replaced with a new system that sought to buy and sell commodities that grew ever more estranged from their location in nature. Brush's magical arc lights and Rockefeller's kerosene lamps had once been plant and animal life, but millions of years' worth of pressure and geological processes had transmuted them into a raw fuel that would usher and sustain the automobile age and electrify the darkest valleys of America.

What was gained? Nearly every activity you engage in today, in some way or another, would be impossible without the burning of fossil fuels. Remove them from modern life and our economy, forms of recreation, and culture would collapse. The old world has been replaced with a landscape that one writer has dubbed "the geography of nowhere," a place without distinguishing characteristics that has "ceased to be a credible human habitat."[59] I'll leave to each reader whether they share the same acute sense of loss. Regardless of what your brain thinks, your body experiences environmental changes in ways we are just beginning to understand. In 2003, philosopher Glenn Albrecht coined the word "solastalgia" to describe the emotional distress caused by landscape changes. Two years later, he and a team of mental health experts detailed how coal mining and a climate change-induced drought caused qualitative changes in the mental health of nearby residents in Australia. One Indigenous man described how landscape destruction changed his own behavior. "It is very depressing," he told the team of researchers. "We take different routes to travel down south just so we don't have to see all the holes, all the dirt…because it makes you wild."[60]

Most Americans have lived in built environments their entire lives, which begs the question: Can we miss a landscape we never experienced? History suggests we can. The infamous fire on the Cuyahoga River on June 22, 1969, served as a shock to the culture's conscience. Many Americans had accommodated landscape change, but a burning river triggered deep distress. Call it solastalgia if you like, but Americans had a dawning sense in the 1960s that the narratives of progress that filled their history books had failed to explain the situation they found themselves in. In a sense, the culture snapped out of the haze of the settler narrative and realized just how far the war against nature could carry civilization toward environmental ruin. Narratives are critical to our sense of identity as individuals and as a culture. If reality was no longer matching up with the promises of the old narratives of progress, what new narratives best fit the world most Americans found themselves in?

Revisionist History

Russell Means was arriving at an answer in the summer of 1971. Having organized the Cleveland American Indian Center in the basement of St. John's Episcopal Church, he often collaborated with resettled Indigenous people at the Club 77 bar on the corner of Detroit Avenue and West Seventy-Seventh Street.[61] That summer, the Early Settlers Association of the Western Reserve had planned a celebration to lift up Cleveland from the reputational blow it received from being the poster child of urban environmental disaster. The cause for celebration, according to the association, was the super sesquicentennial, the 175th anniversary of the arrival of Moses Cleaveland on the banks of the Cuyahoga. The association had planned a full day of festivities, including a re-creation of Cleaveland landing on the river by Clay Herrick, president of the association. Bob Hope, who spent his childhood in Cleveland, would give a speech exulting the city and lead a parade as the grand marshal. The event was meant to remind the city of the narrative of progress that justified its existence. Means and the activists at the center had paid little mind to the party until the phone rang in their office at 4:00 p.m. the day before the event. Dennis Bowen, the youth director at the center, answered the phone. After listening for a minute, he smothered the mouthpiece with his hand, turned to Means, and said, "You're not going to believe this, but they want to know if we'll come down to where 'Moses Cleaveland' is going to land and *dance* for them tomorrow." According to his autobiography, Means immediately replied, "Tell them we'll be there."[62]

The next day, in an effort to play the part of Cleaveland, Herrick donned a colonial-era suit, complete with tricorn hat, and jumped aboard the *Goodtime II*. As the vessel made its way to Settlers Landing, where West Superior Avenue ends at the Cuyahoga River, he must have sensed his day was about to go sideways. Along with the expected assembled media, twenty activists from the center had arrived wearing red berets and bearing signs shaming the baseball team for its use of the racist Chief Wahoo mascot, evoking the memory of those killed in the Wounded Knee Massacre, and calling out the FBI, which a band of activists in Media, Pennsylvania, had only months earlier shown to be infiltrating groups, including the American Indian Movement, through a program dubbed COINTELPRO.[63] The association had requested two representatives of the Indigenous community to welcome Herrick with a dance so the party at Public Square could get underway.

As the *Goodtime II* attempted to find a landing, Means screamed at Herrick from the shore, "We might be 175 years late, but we're imposing an immigration law. Go back!" The anger of the activists caused the skipper of the *Goodtime II* to hesitate, not feeling the situation safe to bring the vessel to a shore filled with a hostile crowd. Herrick pleaded with Means to let him land. The police stood by shocked, unwilling to intervene as national media reporters and television cameras captured the chaos. Desperate, Herrick asked Means what it would take to let the ceremony continue. Means demanded that three speakers from the center be allowed to address the crowd congregating downtown ahead of the parade. Herrick agreed and stepped off the boat. Gathering himself, Herrick unfurled a parchment scroll and read an address to the Indigenous representatives. The full speech has been lost, but when Herrick read the words, "We come in peace and want to deal fairly and justly with you," Means wrote that Bowen "lost it." Bowen grabbed Herrick with both hands and yelled in his face, "You liar! You never keep your treaties!"[64]

As Means prepared to speak at the parade, he summed up the previous 175 years of history to a reporter for Liberation News Service, an underground press agency aligned with the New Left. Means blamed the white man for destroying nature because "he has not learned to live with it—only to conquer it."[65] For the Early Settlers Association of the Western Reserve, the event was a catastrophic failure. Rather than validating the old narrative of heroic progress over nature, they had given Indigenous people a platform to voice a very different narrative. That narrative interrogates the assumptions underneath colonial ideas of progress and asks who benefited from the destruction of the relationship forged between Indigenous communities and the environment for thousands of years. From the perspective of 1971, few in Cleveland could hold their heads very high. Mired in pollution, poverty, and racial violence, the city would default on its loans in 1978, the first major city to do so since the Great Depression. While Means spoke at the super sesquicentennial, members of the American Indian Movement passed out pamphlets to the crowd titled "Super Sesqui to Celebrate Mistakes." By then, the moniker "Mistake by the Lake" had already taken hold in the public imagination to describe a city that had failed in its mission, in Ben Franklin's words, to use its "natural advantages" to become "a populous and powerful dominion."[66] Although the city had succeeded in creating power and growing a large population, it had come at a cost that many felt was growing too steep to bear.

CHAPTER 5
The Land

The price we pay for progress accumulates on the streets of Cleveland every spring and fall in the hours before dawn. During the heart of the migration season in the spring of 2019, I would wake up at 4:00 a.m., drive downtown, and walk the lonely streets of Cleveland looking for dead birds. Although the light was dim, a distant splash of yellow on the sidewalk one morning caused my heart to jump. From afar, it could have been a candy wrapper or a leaf, but as I approached, the unmistakable shape of a bird came into view. It was frozen in a cartoonish pose. Lying on its back with its legs sticking up perpendicular to its body, the bird lay motionless as I prepared a specimen bag to collect yet another traveler that had died before it could reach its nesting grounds in Canada for the summer. It was one of an estimated billion birds that die each year in North America as a result of window collisions.

The particular bird I found that spring morning was a Nashville warbler, whose only connection to its namesake is the fact that naturalist Alexander Wilson first identified the bird at that location in 1811. It had spent the winter in Mexico and flown approximately 2,300 miles north before slamming into a window on the side of the Huntington Convention Center in downtown Cleveland. I reached for the fragile gold and gray creature, only to have it hop up and look around in a daze. Using a bander's grip, I carefully picked up the bird and placed its back to my palm with its head poking out between my index and middle finger. I could sense its soft warmth in my hand before I placed it in a paper bag. It joined several other bags in a large tote. This was the toll from that morning's migration, a stream of birds on their voyage north that had to pass through the gauntlet of our built environment.

I made my way east to the southwest corner of Superior and East Twelfth Street. Several unhoused people huddled around steaming-hot manhole covers on the sidewalk next to the Oswald Centre. I stepped around them and made my way to a brown clump at the base of the building's large exterior windows. From a distance, it looked like a pile of feces, but as I approached, I realized it was a bat (*Eptesicus fuscus*, to be precise) huddled up against the window. I pulled on a blacksmith's glove to protect my hand. Bats are carriers for many zoonotic diseases that can make your life the subject of a Health Alert Network bulletin from the Centers for Disease Control and Prevention. Unlike most birds, bats react unpredictably when handled and confined to a small bag. On a recent "necro-birding" date with my wife, as she likes to call them, we rescued another big brown bat from the sidewalk around Rocket Mortgage FieldHouse, and, while we were driving to the wildlife center, it crawled its way out of the bag and flew into her hair. I carefully folded the top of the bag over twice and applied several paper clips to prevent another misadventure.

This particular morning, I was acting as a volunteer for the organization Lights Out Cleveland. I, along with another half dozen or so volunteers, had assembled downtown at 5:00 a.m., and we were assigned routes that would take us past locations with the highest volume of bird strikes. Each volunteer wears a reflective vest and is equipped with specially designed nets for safely capturing injured birds and bats. The volunteers come from all walks of life, but many are at retirement age and looking to invest time in their passions. On my first day monitoring, I walked the streets with Rich. There's a few decades between our ages, but we made fast friends. I asked how he got interested in this project. He blamed his daughter for why he was up hours before dawn scanning the sidewalks for dead and injured birds. She had bought him a backyard bird feeder years ago, and that became his gateway into the birding world. This was a common story among my fellow volunteers.

Rich introduced me to all the hot spots in the city where birds are most prone to collide with windows. The official position of the organization is to avoid "naming and shaming" the specific buildings, but all the volunteers know the worst offenders. On Twelfth Street, I found an American woodcock huddled in a doorway. The sky was overcast with a low cloud ceiling hovering just over the top of Key Tower. These conditions push migrating birds to the ground and amplify the effects of light pollution, which causes the clouds to glow and further disorient birds. Once they descend into the city, they run through a gauntlet that millions of years of evolution never prepared them for: glass is invisible to the avian eye. Some buildings are designed with cavernous interior lobbies that birds try to access without sensing the glass. I walked by the Huntington Bank building on Public Square and spied several small lumps on the cement. As I approached, fumbling for my flashlight, I heard the sickening "thud" of a bird colliding with the curtain of glass in front of me. This is not an uncommon experience for volunteers on a busy day. At the worst times, the bodies literally rain from the sky.

Our built environment interacts with the natural world in unexpected ways. Our lights attract insects, which flit about in their beams. Bats are attracted to the insects, sometimes feasting for hours. Their echolocation allows them to avoid collisions, but they get disoriented in cities and rest for the night in areas that expose them to danger. One day I cut through the parking lot of the 5/3rd building from Vincent Avenue to East Sixth Street and nearly stepped on two bats sleeping in a parking spot—not an ideal roost.

Some birds have adapted to city life. Rock pigeons, of course, thrive in proximity to humans. Gulls from Lake Erie are notoriously opportunistic. Lights Out Cleveland volunteers have seen gulls swallow stunned or dead birds shortly after they strike windows. They became the subject of high-level talks at Progressive

Field during the 2009 Major League Baseball season. Attracted by the buffet of fries, hot dogs, and other concessions, the gulls became a nuisance by stealing food and showering fans in droppings. When a line drive hit a flying bird, altering the outcome of a game in early June of that year, the team decided to set off fireworks between innings to shoo flocks away. The strategy had mixed success.[1]

For the past few decades, Terminal Tower has served as an aerie for generations of peregrine falcons. The raptors plunge off the tower and dive toward their prey, at times reaching speeds in excess of two hundred miles per hour. I've found the remains of several falcon kills, including the decapitated head of an American woodcock. I located the severed wing of a pigeon in the shadow of Terminal Tower one morning, another likely falcon victim. When I picked it up to place it in a specimen bag, a passerby gasped and yelled at me in disgust, "Don't touch that! What are you doing!?" I calmly explained my purpose, but most folks only understand dead wildlife as little more than roadkill. Hold your breath and look the other way.

After months of scanning the pavement for birds and bats, you walk the city differently. Foragers describe getting "mushroom eyes," the ability to apprehend fungus from the background forest litter. I suppose I gained the equivalent for dead wildlife in urban environments. One of the reasons the Lights Out monitoring crew starts scanning the city so early is because pedestrians lack this vision and trample nearly everything underfoot. A warbler stunned by a window collision might recover and carry on after an hour, so long as it isn't crushed by one of the thousands of people rushing to get to work in the morning. Like the birds, we have our own blind spots. We are oriented toward the market like never before. We chase it to work. It follows us on our phones. Do we still have eyes for anything else?

Flight Maps

Humans have observed and commented on bird migrations since ancient times, but the science explaining the phenomenon is still in its infancy. In general, changes in day-length and temperature provide the cues for birds to begin their journey. Once they take flight, they use several tools to guide them to their destination: sight, smell, and even magnetic fields. Light is a critical component too, as birds use the sun as a sort of compass to orient themselves. Prior to the advent of high-intensity, artificial lighting developed in the late nineteenth century, few sources of light could compete with the sun or moon. Throughout history, humans have recorded swarms of birds attracted to lighthouses, sometimes colliding violently with the structures, but our species had not been able to harvest and focus energy on a large scale until Charles Brush came on the scene.

When the Statue of Liberty was unveiled in 1886, the torch was fitted with nine arc lights to serve as a beacon for navigation.[2] Emma Lazarus cited the technological marvel in her famous poem, "The New Colossus," referring to the statue's flame as "imprisoned lightning." Almost immediately, it served as a magnet for migrating birds. So many died that the groundskeepers sold the bodies to local milliners to festoon fashionable hats. Colonel A. C. Tassin, the military officer in command of Bedloe Island (now Liberty Island), began to send the bodies of the birds to the Smithsonian in Washington, DC, for investigation. In 1887, the curator of the National Museum received 260 specimens from Tassin comprising forty different species "killed by flying against the electric light of the statue of Liberty."[3] When 1,400 birds died in a single night in 1888, Tassin ordered *all* the birds to be delivered to scientific institutions in order to explore the cause.[4] Warning signs about the effect of electric lighting on wildlife were apparent from the advent of the technology.

The science describing bird migrations blossomed in the twentieth century with the help of amateur birders from unlikely backgrounds. J. P. "Perk" Perkins of Conneaut, Ohio, began serving on steamships carrying iron ore over the Great Lakes for the US Steel corporation in the 1930s. Perk took notice of birds alighting on his vessel far out in America's inland sea early in his career and hatched a wild idea. He purchased small trees from landscapers, potted them in large containers, and set them out on the deck of his ship to provide habitat for his avian travelers. When his experiment paid off by attracting entire flocks of birds, he began to expand the number of trees. He attempted to recreate different ecological niches on the deck of his ship, purchasing berry-laden trees and even a large, dead log so woodpeckers could find a familiar home amid the waters. His crewmates referred to the eccentric assembly as "Perk's National Forest," and they invited purple finches and rusty blackbirds into their quarters to clear out flies.

By the time Perk was promoted to captain in 1962, he had assembled an incredible catalog of data on migration patterns over the Great Lakes. He identified seventeen different flyways and recorded more than two hundred distinct species of birds navigating the lakes. He captured birds on video, and his path-breaking work was published in *Audubon Magazine*. When traveling through a flyway, the air could become thick with migrating birds. He wrote, "at times there were so many on the bridge deck that the lookout had to be careful not to step on them." When his duties required him on the bridge, "the watchman would pick up a bird and hold it up to the open front window where I would identify it by flashlight."[5] Like the Lights Out volunteers, Perk found bird-watching to be a consuming passion that leads people down strange paths.

Today, we would recognize Perk as a citizen scientist, a new term for amateur volunteers who collaborate with professional scientists to collect data. His efforts revealed that the Great Lakes did not act as barriers to migrating birds and also established the importance of habitat near the lakeshore. Every spring, as migrating birds gather on Lake Erie's southern edges, shoreline habitat is the last opportunity to rest and eat before embarking on a fifty-mile, uninterrupted journey. When making the return voyage every fall, birds will look to any available habitat to rest after the long trek. The lakeshore is the last rest stop before venturing across one of America's largest inland seas, and the habitat it provides is crucial for avian wildlife. But that habitat has undergone rapid changes in the last century.

Let There Be Light

By 1920, only forty years after Brush debuted the first electric streetlights in Cleveland, just over a third of all urban and suburban homes enjoyed some form of electric service. The passage of the Rural Electrification Act during Roosevelt's New Deal rapidly expanded electric service throughout the country, and by the end of World War II, more than 90 percent of Americans were connected to the grid.[6] Ever since, electricity has insinuated itself into our homes and communities and ushered in an era of appliances that liberate us from the backbreaking labor once necessary to cook, clean, entertain, and work. Night still came each day, but it competed with the glow of our new tools that blinded us to its charms. One consequence has been that few modern Americans have experienced a truly *dark* night sky.

Astronomers were the first ones to sense the effects of light pollution. Founded in 1880 in Cleveland, the Warner and Swasey Company manufactured gun sights and range finders for the US military, as well as the high-powered telescopes necessary for precise astronomical observations and measurements. Urban universities big enough to support astronomy programs required observatories fitted with the kind of large optical telescopes Warner and Swasey produced. Cleveland's Case Institute of Technology, while ambitious, did not have the support of more established schools in the East. When the Warner and Swasey Company became trustees of the college, they decided to rectify the problem by gifting the campus a modern observatory fitted with a 9.5-inch refracting telescope produced at their factory on Carnegie and East Fifty-Fifth, not far from where Samuel Huntington had fought off a pack of wolves a century earlier.

Opened in 1920, the observatory held a commanding view from the heights on North Taylor Road, just two blocks south of Euclid.[7] The observatory served the campus for decades and made significant contributions to our understanding of the universe, including confirmation of the theory that the Milky Way was a spiral galaxy. By the 1950s, however, the widespread adoption of electric lighting made optical astronomy at the location nearly impossible.

Barbara Wherley grew up in Cleveland Heights and remembers her father taking her on night outings to the observatory in the 1960s. The view did not impress her. "You really had to struggle to see what they were showing you," she remembers. "I have to admit, it wasn't captivating." She strained to see even the brightest of objects in the night sky during her trips. "I remember really having to look at Venus," she says.[8] In 1957, in an attempt to outrun the spread of light pollution, Case built a new observatory thirty miles to the east in Geauga County. By 1979, however, even that location was untenable, blinded by the growth of suburban sprawl. The facility was eventually moved to Kitt Peak National Observatory, fifty miles southwest of Tucson, Arizona.

By the 1980s, so few locations remained free of light pollution that astronomers organized the International Dark-Sky Association to educate the public about the loss of the nighttime environment. Technology had offered one solution, and many astronomers had switched to telescopes that used radio waves to detect signals outside the visual range. When the Hubble Space Telescope reached low earth orbit in 1990, astronomers had fully escaped the problem of artificial light pollution by abandoning earth as a viable base for optical observatories. Light pollution, however, made amateur astronomy nearly impossible in urban centers. Without access to expensive observatories or satellites, the days of backyard stargazing seemed at an end.

To get a sense of the problem, you need to map it. In 2001, the amateur astronomer John Bortle created a scale for those of us bound to look at the sky with our feet on the ground. Starting at class one and ascending to class nine, the Bortle scale describes the level of light pollution and the effect it has on our ability to observe the night sky. At a nine, which is common in most inner cities, only the moon, planets, and a few of the brightest stars are visible to the naked eye. The sky itself glows from the diffuse light from concentrated artificial light sources. At eight, the sky still glows so bright you can easily read a book by its ambient light. From five to seven, which is most common in suburban environments, clouds appear to glow by reflecting light pollution, and you can easily navigate your surroundings without the aid of a flashlight. Only in rural environments, which rank at a three or four, does the Milky Way begin to appear as a distinct splash across the sky overhead, although the horizon is still marred by domes of light from nearby cities. A class-one night sky provides profound darkness, the likes of which few of us have ever experienced. The Milky Way is so bright in class-one skies that it casts observable shadows. Venus and Jupiter appear as stunning points of light that require your eyes to readjust to the darkness after staring at them, like cosmic headlights.[9]

The same year Bortle published his scale, an international team of astronomers published the first world atlas of light pollution using data collected from satellites. They found that 99 percent of Americans live under light-polluted skies, and only 56 percent "live where it becomes sufficiently dark at night for the human eye to make a complete transition from cone to rod vision."[10] For many of us, the evolutionary hardware bestowed on us by millions of years of surviving the dark of night is no longer relevant in our blinding built environment. Most of the skies above Cuyahoga County today are classified as class eight or nine. Only a few locations deep within Cuyahoga Valley National Park and along the Chagrin River rank as low as a five. The nearest class-one skies are five hundred miles away in Michigan's Upper Peninsula, unless you hop on a boat and make your way out to the middle of Lake Huron near the border with Canada.

When we think of the forces of "habitat change," our thoughts are drawn to tools such as bulldozers, dams, chainsaws, and slabs of concrete that replace one landscape with another. The dark of night has been a critical and overlooked habitat. All bats, most rodents, and 80 percent of marsupials are nocturnal. These species have coevolved with darkness, using it to their advantage in order to hide from predators or stalk prey. These animals contain so few cones in their retinas that even low-level artificial light is sufficient to temporarily blind them. Because of the moon's twenty-eight-day cycle, most nocturnal animals match their behavior to light levels, restricting their activity during a full moon and becoming more gregarious near the new moon phase. Although humans are diurnal—meaning we've evolved to take advantage of daylight—our bodies are governed by circadian rhythms that synchronize with the local day-night cycle. This process, called entrainment, is why we experience jet lag when we travel to a different time zone.

A full moon is about the upper limit of illumination that our eyes can receive before our bodies halt production of certain hormones, including melatonin.[11] Low melatonin levels are associated with insomnia, and many Americans struggling to find a good night's rest turn to synthetic supplements to make up for what their bodies would normally produce under the veil of darkness. In an environment lacking artificial night light, our pineal glands begin producing melatonin around 9:00 p.m. until it reaches peak production around 3:00 a.m. before trailing off by dawn. Artificial night light can severely dysregulate our body's release of melatonin. In one study, researchers discovered that a group of rats exposed to light pollution at night produced

87 percent less melatonin, barely better than the 94 percent decline experienced by another group subjected to twenty-four hours of light.[12] Aside from regulating circadian rhythms, melatonin also suppresses tumor growth. A 2012 study found that female night-shift nurses who experienced prolonged exposure to high-intensity light at night (LAN) experienced a 73 percent higher incidence of breast cancer than populations exposed to low-levels of LAN. The study's authors suggested these risks could be mitigated by "the development of new lighting technologies and shift-work policies" that would allow workers to experience periods of darkness necessary for healthy melatonin production.[13] Some of us are literally dying for the light.

Although some workplaces are beginning to take LAN seriously, animals have no choice but to operate in the new, brilliant nighttime environments we've created. The situation has become so alarming that science journalist Joshua Sokol has compared light pollution to the effects of pesticides like DDT and called for a "Silent Spring moment" for the night sky. In an article published in *Scientific American*, he describes how artificial LAN has made moths and caterpillars more susceptible to predators, deterred nocturnal pollinator activity, stimulated mosquitos to become more active, disrupted courtship signals between fireflies, and even stunted the growth of vital reef-building coral. Although habitat loss and the proliferation of pesticides throughout the landscape have diminished insect life throughout our ecosystems, artificial LAN has played havoc with the stability of the day-night cycle critical to survival strategies. "Light pollution is almost certainly hastening the so-called insect apocalypse," he argues.[14]

The Swedish conservation biologist Jens Rydell spent most of his thirty-year career studying bats. He described the behavior of bats feeding off insects attracted to artificial lights as "so common and widespread among bats that it must be considered part of the normal life habit of many species."[15] Peek out at the sky this summer near the twilight hour at dusk and you will find a flurry of activity as bats fill Ohio's skies, often circling streetlamps in search of an easy meal. Although light pollution is placing big brown bats like the ones I've picked up off the sidewalks of downtown Cleveland in harm's way, they are also adapting and perhaps evolving to a landscape filled with lights. The bats are feasting for now, but adaptation has its limits.

The Cult of Glass

When we think of the technologies that threaten wildlife, we probably imagine novel chemicals or fossil fuel-powered machines that can devour entire mountains or forests. But even something as mundane as window glass can have a dramatic impact when duplicated throughout a landscape. For much of history, windows served primarily as ventilation for dwellings. In fact, the etymology of the word "window" comes from the Old Norse words for "wind eye." Not until the twelfth century did European architects begin to implement glazed window glass in their designs for cathedrals. Well into the modern period, it remained a luxury good available only to the rich, who were assessed a special tax for each glazed window they had in their homes. The tax wasn't repealed in England until 1851, when industrial production made glass more commonplace. When London hosted the Great Exhibition of the Works of Industry of All Nations that same year, the centerpiece of their industrial chest-beating was a stunning 990,000-square-foot structure composed entirely of cast iron and fitted with sixty thousand panes of glass. Dubbed "the Crystal Palace," the building covered nearly eighteen acres of land and calibrated architectural design to a new aesthetic of shimmering glass facades.

Much has changed in subsequent years, but today, many architects sacrifice function for form, defaulting to designs that feature curtains of glass despite the extra costs. A 2004 report commissioned by the US Department of Energy found that the traditional purpose of windows, to provide light and fresh air, had been made obsolete by modern lighting and ventilation technologies. On most modern buildings, windows cannot be opened, they cost more than simply filling the space with a bare wall, and they bleed energy. The windows themselves have a life span of twenty to thirty years, requiring further costs throughout the life of a building. The report found that energy loss via windows accounted for "over 5 percent of the total national energy use." Why, then, with all these downsides, would an architect or building owner choose a window-heavy design? The answer is because all parties view windows as an "aesthetic element."[16] The cult of glass is quite strong.

Nearly all of Cleveland's architectural landmarks constructed over the past century feature the heavy use of glass. When the Louis Stokes Wing of the Cleveland Public Library was completed in 1997, its main architectural highlight was a central glass cylinder. When the Cleveland Museum of Art remodeled and connected its various wings in 2012, it created an atrium of glass large enough to be used as an aircraft hangar. The lobby of the Rock & Roll Hall of Fame is enclosed by a glass pyramid. The Tinkham Veale University Center on the campus of CWRU even earned a Leadership in Energy and Environmental Design (LEED) Gold Status from the US Green Building Council for its design, which featured a vegetative roof covering a rectangular curtain of glass.

The combination of artificial LAN and an infatuation for glass design has had a profound effect on migratory birds. Citing a 2014 study, the US Fish and Wildlife Service estimates that between 365 and 988 million birds die each year in the US as a result of colliding with glass buildings.[17] Bird deaths briefly rose to the level of national politics during the final presidential debate between Donald Trump and Joe Biden in October 2020. When the topic of green energy came up, Trump smeared wind turbines. "It's extremely expensive," he said. "Kills all the birds."[18] Although wind turbines account for approximately a quarter million bird fatalities each year, that pales in comparison to the threat of glass. Since 1970, North America has lost 29 percent of its bird population, a staggering three billion birds that are no longer in our skies.[19] If Donald Trump can acknowledge the need to prevent unnecessary bird deaths, why has there been so little traction for a seemingly bipartisan issue?

I met with Brendon Samuels to learn why birds struggle to apprehend the threat of glass and what we can do to make our built environments less fatal for them. Samuels is a PhD candidate in biology at Western University in London, Ontario. He also volunteers with the Fatal Light Awareness Program (FLAP), which, since its foundation in 1993, has been patrolling the streets of Canada's major urban centers. Samuels studies how birds see window glass and react to it, and he hopes his work will inform future building designs so architects can implement visual cues that alert birds to glass surfaces. His goals are also more immediate, however; he wants the Province of Ontario to update its building codes to implement bird-safe designs as a regulatory standard.

I asked him about the LEED certification and its impact on wildlife, and he scoffed. Buildings designed according to LEED standards, he told me, "might as well be floating in outer space" because of how little regard they have for plant and animal communities. Although the US Green Building Council does have a pilot credit for bird-safe designs, the LEED program does not require the use of any bird-safe designs or materials. For now, LEED measures only energy inputs and outputs, an important but insignificant metric if the building kills wildlife by failing to acknowledge their presence.

Considering the price tag for LEED certification can run in the tens of thousands of dollars, existing bird-safe technology is well within the reach of architects. One way to make buildings safer is to use our understanding of bird vision to create signals that only they can see. Human color vision is trichromatic, producing images based on the assembly of different shades of blue, green, and red light. Birds, however, have tetrachromatic vision. Their eyes contain four types of cones, which include the three we possess and one that can perceive ultraviolet wavelengths. Companies are already producing glass that reflects UV patterns so birds can see the window as a barrier while humans keep their unobstructed views.

Although treated glass remains an expensive option for bird-safe design, there are a plethora of affordable alternatives to make existing windows less fatal to wildlife. When the law library at Cleveland State University grew concerned about the number of birds killed by its large, plate-glass entrance, it reached out to several advocacy organizations to find a solution. When I began as a volunteer for Lights Out Cleveland, I regularly checked the sidewalks surrounding the entrance for dead or injured birds soon after they treated their windows with a dot matrix film. For both the spring and autumn migrations, I never found a single bird near the library. Placed two inches apart, the dots succeeded in preventing bird collisions at a location that had once been a hot spot. By the end of the year, we rarely checked the building in order to direct our resources where they were most needed. A few stickers can save a lot of lives.

Even low-cost measures make a difference. Hanging strips of twine over exterior windows two inches apart is enough of a deterrent to prevent collisions. Adding a dot or line pattern to the exterior of windows with a grease pencil is another cheap solution. Moving feeders and outdoor plants away from untreated windows can also reduce the chance birds will mistake a reflection for actual habitat. Some ornithologists have even recommended to the stingiest of building owners to simply stop washing their windows, as the film of dirt and water marks can be sufficient to deter collisions.

Lights Out Cleveland has taken a nonconfrontational approach by meeting and working with building owners to build partnerships. Organized in 2014, the program has enlisted over two dozen buildings to shut off their external lights from midnight until dawn through the spring and autumn migration seasons to reduce the sky glow in Cleveland. Harvey Webster was there from the beginning. Webster, who is now serving as ambassador emeritus for the Cleveland Museum of Natural History (CMNH), attended a conference in Chicago and first learned about the efforts of Lights Out Chicago to create partnerships between building owners, scientists, and local volunteers to reduce bird fatalities. He told me the organization began with a single volunteer for the Lake Erie Nature and Science Center (LENSC), who would walk the perimeter of the Huntington Building, right across the street from where Charles Brush held his first crowd-stunning demonstration of the arc light. During the mid-2000s, this volunteer collected over six hundred dead birds around the footprint of that single building by herself. Webster believed the programs in Canada and Chicago could find a home in Cleveland as well.

He remembers giving a public talk on the topic in 2009 at the Western Reserve Land Conservancy. In the audience was writer Connie Schultz and her husband, Senator Sherrod Brown.

When Webster told them he was organizing his own program and intended to call it Lights Out Cleveland, the senator urged him to reconsider the name. "Whatever you do, Harvey, don't call it that," he said. Brown had won his senate seat by appealing to working-class voters suffering from a declining manufacturing base in the heart of the rust belt. "It sounds like we're turning out the lights on our economy," he offered. The nation was in the grips of the "Great Recession," when Cleveland's Slavic Village neighborhood experienced the highest foreclosure rate in the country, resulting in a staggering residential vacancy rate of 33 percent.[20] In that economic environment, did light pollution really rank as a high priority?

Webster's solution to Brown's suggestion was to name the program Smart Light Safe Flight. The problem was, he couldn't recruit enough buildings to make a meaningful impact. Some buildings would sign up initially, only for Webster to find their lights back on at 5:00 a.m. "They wanted to have a lit skyline for the early morning news," he told me with a look of exasperation. At the time, he grew frustrated and found himself sidetracked by work on the opening of the new Perkins Wildlife Center at CMNH. A vibrant group of scientists and activists stepped in to help. Matt Shumar at Ohio Bird Conservation Initiative, Tim Jasinski at LENSC, Andy Jones at CMNH, and Jen Brumfield (JB) with Cleveland Metroparks came together to provide an institutional backbone to the project.

Redubbed Lights Out Cleveland, the organization trains around fifty volunteers each year to maintain the downtown monitoring program. The process of collecting data is simple enough. After a volunteer bags a dead or injured bird, it is conveyed to LENSC, where Jasinski coordinates a small team of volunteers to give it the best chance at recovery. The monitoring program collects an average of three thousand birds each year off the streets of

Cleveland. For 2019, the year I volunteered, Jasinski achieved a 95 percent recovery rate for the birds that arrived at LENSC alive. I spent a couple months helping him with the inglorious work of animal rehabilitation. We washed a duck that had been covered in oil with Dawn dish soap, cleaned cages, fed birds, and checked medication schedules for injured animals. The birds that survive and recover are banded and released into Huntington Reservation on the lakeshore in Bay Village to complete their migration. Dead birds are placed in cold storage and conveyed to CMNH, where they make up over 10 percent of the museum's ornithological collection. The entire outfit operates on a shoestring budget and is held together by passionate volunteers. By the time I attended the training session, staff warned the incoming volunteers about the potential for developing PTSD from watching the animals they love suffer and die every day of migration season. One volunteer admitted she left the Facebook group because the endless feed of dead birds was just too much to bear.

The scale of the problem is also an invaluable opportunity for research. Lights Out Cleveland collects so much data that researchers are willing to travel long distances to do fieldwork here. Emily Webb, a biology PhD candidate at Arizona State University, joined the monitoring crew during the 2019 autumn migration. She set up a mobile lab in the back of an SUV parked on East Sixth Street to dissect and collect tissue samples for her dissertation research on carotenoid allocation in birds. There are few places where you get to see citizen scientists collect a dead bird still warm to the touch, walk it a block, and hand it over to a researcher who dissects it, collects tissue samples, and updates her database, all within the time it takes to make an espresso drink at Starbucks.

Although the threats are well documented, not everyone has such a grim view of artificial night lighting. In a 2017 article, environmental historian Sara Pritchard argued that activists and scientists focused on light pollution have not paid "adequate attention to vital social justice issues including the benefits of artificial lighting and the ways in which darkness can index low standards of living, even dire poverty." The "trouble" with the movement to reclaim darkness, Pritchard argues, is that it "may end up reproducing (neo)colonial forms of conservation that place landscapes of tourism, leisure, and aesthetics for wealthy outsiders at odds with ensuring local livelihood and improving basic standards of living." Instead, she believes we should consider the problem of "lighting poverty" when we consider conserving darkness.[21]

On the political right, legislators have fought tooth and nail to oppose any efforts at habitat conservation. As the policy director at Audubon Great Lakes, Marnie Urso has been giving a voice to wildlife for her entire adult life. She is a veteran environmental activist. She can lace up muddy hiking boots and show you some of the best bird habitat on the lakeshore, but she can just as easily don a sharp blazer and press Republican senators to support environmental legislation. She has a talent for sizing power brokers up, speaking their language, and finding common ground across the no-man's-land of the culture wars. Even if you despise environmentalism, she will seize upon your passion for hunting, gardening, or even a summer job at a local park from your youth and turn you into a conservationist before you know it. Despite the threats posed to wildlife habitat, she is also surprisingly optimistic. When I was casting about for a new research project that wasn't as grim as my last book, she said she had just the idea. "Birds!" she told me over drinks at Happy Dog. "And the bird lovers who fought for them," she added. This book started that day.

As I was collecting dead birds off the streets of Cleveland in the autumn of 2019, Urso was testifying on Capitol Hill in front of the House Natural Resources Subcommittee on Water, Oceans, and Wildlife. She was there to support two bills that would protect migration corridors "at risk due to habitat loss or fragmentation." In the hearing, she provided ample scientific evidence demonstrating the risk to habitat posed by urban development and climate change. During questioning, Republican senators went to extreme lengths to avoid engaging in the science of habitat loss and instead played to conservative fears of "big government." Tom McClintock, a climate change-denying Republican representing California's Fourth Congressional District, which includes Yosemite National Park, disparaged federal control of habitat as "decrepit" and advocated for "actively managed private and local land." He sidestepped Urso's testimony and instead identified the "principle cause of bird mortality: cats."[22] Without strong bipartisan support, both bills died in committee.

According to the US Fish and Wildlife Service, house cats kill an estimated 2.4 billion birds every year, more than doubling the fatalities caused by glass. Globally, the domesticated cat has been linked to the extinction of at least forty bird species.[23] With approximately eighty-six million cats in America, the scale of the problem is significant.[24] But to recruit these feline predators to the cause of neoliberal policies that seek to privatize as much land as possible and avoid regulating land use is disingenuous at best. When a Democrat-sponsored bill in Maine sought to apply the state's animal trespass laws to cats to curtail the problem, animal rights groups and conservative media went wild. The Maine Animal Coalition opposed the bill because cats "treasure their outdoor time."[25] A story about the proposal published on the Fox News website included reader comments criticizing "over-regulating" Democratic lawmakers and racist comments about the threat to cats posed by Asian restaurants.[26]

CHAPTER 5: THE LAND

Lights are a far less politically charged topic than house pets, but the public still struggles to grasp the weight of their impact on the ecosystem. Chris Ronayne, the Cuyahoga County executive, seems to have little appetite for dimming the city's lights to save migrating birds. In a 2017 article published in *Cleveland Magazine*, he urged the city to "reject the darkness of winter" and celebrate Cleveland's role as the "first city of light." Ronayne views light as a plaything we should delight in using. "Each year Cleveland could have a light concert on Public Square," he argued, to "beam lights off office spires and the spire of the Old Stone Church choreographed with a fusion of rock and classical music."[27] We've come a long way from the time when the police threatened to arrest Charles Brush for beaming light over a parade on Ontario Street.

Environmental activists have had varying ideas about how to bring communities together. Beginning in 2007, the World Wildlife Fund (WWF) initiated Earth Hour, an annual event where buildings are invited to shut off their lights for sixty minutes during the last Saturday in March. The WWF acknowledges the limits of the program as an "iconic action" to inspire and empower people across the globe, not as a solution to climate change or energy waste. Each year, Key Tower joins the Pyramids at Giza, the Acropolis, and the Eiffel Tower in dimming its lights for Earth Hour. Although critics are quick to mock the sacrifice of a single hour, the action does force us to contemplate a tantalizing thought. Unlike greenhouse gasses, light pollution isn't stored in our atmosphere. If we were to stop emitting CO_2 today, it would take up to one thousand years for the accumulated emissions from the Industrial Revolution to work their way out of our atmosphere according to NASA's Jet Propulsion Laboratory.[28] If, however, we were to eliminate sky glow by directing light where it is needed, the dark of night would return and the brilliance of the

Milky Way would shine on our cities once again. As the black-out of 2003 demonstrated, the only thing separating us from the night sky that astonished our ancestors can be something as small as a single computer keystroke.

Wastelands

What happens in the sky is determined by how we use the land and water. Needless to say, Cleveland has had a fraught relationship with the lake. While light pollution has made the little wildlife habitat that is still intact less safe, Lake Erie and its near-shore wetlands remain a vibrant ecosystem fifty years after they were commonly known as "North America's Dead Sea."[29] It wasn't for lack of trying. Since the days when men like Ben Franklin dreamed of American colonies along its shores, Lake Erie has been viewed through utilitarian eyes. Although settlers understood it first as a passage for commerce and then as a fishing ground, the lake eventually became a barrier to development.

Take a look at a map of Cleveland and you'll begin to sense the frustration of urban developers. From outer space, you can see that the city is laid out like half a wagon wheel, with neighborhoods connected through streets, railroads, rivers, canals, and now interstates. The logic of the grid could obliterate most land-forms and even fell mighty forests in search of real estate profits, but it had no answer for bodies of water the size of Lake Erie. While the city and commercial interests invested in shipping harbors on the Old River at Whiskey Island and along the Flats, the lakeshore on the Cuyahoga's east bank fell into neglect.

Railroads had been given right-of-way on the marginal land near the lakeshore and began to explore the potential to make their own real estate by creating wharfs and filling in the water with soil. The Illinois Central Railroad Company had already provided a proof of concept on the Chicago lakeshore, making hundreds of acres of new land by filling in the open water between its causeway and the shore. If you've ever been to one of Chicago's lakeside parks, chances are you're standing on land that was thrown into the lake following the Great Chicago Fire of 1871.[30]

By the early twentieth century, railroads began to eye similar possibilities in Lake Erie. The lake's natural shoreline was just a few feet north of the present railroad tracks that run parallel with Marginal Road. From Edgewater Park in the west to Gordon Park in the east, the railroad was the edge of the world for Cleveland until a century ago. By then, the maps of Cleveland told a new story in the city's history. Cleveland began to grow into the lake in dramatic fashion as railroads filled the shore with soil and waste to create land for facilities. If you have ever visited Edgewater Park or Wendy Park, caught a Browns game, stopped by the Great Lakes Science Center or the Rock & Roll Hall of Fame, or fished from the East Fifty-Fifth Street Marina, you have stood on land that was once an open lake 150 years ago.

The railroads developed land so quickly into the lake that the state of Ohio grew alarmed and sued them to cease, citing English common law, which reserves all "submerged territory" as belonging to the people, prohibiting the enclosure of the lake for any private use that would threaten the free flow of navigation or access to fisheries. *State v. Cleveland & Pittsburgh Railroad* reached the Ohio Supreme Court in 1916. In writing the unanimous decision, Justice James Granville Johnson affirmed the right of landowners to "wharf out to navigable waters" because, without them, "the operations of commerce would be seriously weakened." American jurisprudence has a deep, historic bias toward viewing development as a benefit for the commonwealth of all.

Johnson did hedge his decision, however, by acknowledging that "the state holds the title to the subaqueous land of navigable waters as the trustee for the protection of the public rights therein." If a landowner has a right to develop the shoreline, and the state holds title to the land they develop, what is the legal status of this newly "made" land? Johnson looked to the legislature to make suitable laws governing this very issue. "The state has power to regulate navigation and fishing," he wrote, but he admitted that "our general assembly has enacted no legislation providing such regulations." If the purpose of a judiciary is to interpret laws, Justice Johnson seemed to be saying, pass some laws that define how the lake can be developed.[31]

Within a decade, the Ohio legislature passed a bill granting the powers of the state to all submerged lands along the lakeshore. The city of Cleveland could now demand lease agreements on the new land and shape the development of the city's shoreline. With the railroads firmly in control of the shore from Whiskey Island to West Third Street (formerly Seneca Street), the city focused on creating land north of the new courthouse and city hall buildings on Lakeside Avenue. William R. Hopkins, Cleveland's city manager through much of the 1920s, created an ambitious plan to use land-making technology for the betterment of the community, envisioning what would become the Cleveland Memorial Shoreway. Although the project was estimated to cost over $6.5 million, the 450 acres the city would reclaim from the lake, Hopkins believed, would be worth at least $25 million, "and in the course of 10 years would actually be a source of very large profit to the city in the matter of tax income."[32]

The city council grew to fear the power Hopkins had accumulated and eventually removed him from office in January of 1930. His plans lived on, however, as the city began to fill in the lakeshore with municipal waste. As hundreds of acres of land rose from the lake, the city constructed Cleveland Municipal Stadium as a way to proclaim victory over the environmental limits that had held back development. Completed in 1931 at a cost of $2.5 million, the stadium could accommodate over seventy-eight thousand spectators, more than any other outdoor arena at the time. Unfortunately, the Great Depression had wrecked Cleveland's manufacturing base so that when the stadium was completed, one-third of the city's workers had been laid off. The unemployment rate in the worst-hit census tracts topped 90 percent. Unable to afford rent or even purchase food, workers turned to edge environments near the new stadium. A 1933 survey by one Cleveland charity identified at least nine shantytowns, most of them located on the lakefront or riverbanks.[33]

Sometimes referred to as "Hoovertown" or "Tin Can Plaza," the camp just east of the stadium was the city's largest shantytown. Located at the dump where East Thirteenth Street meets the lake, the camp held a population of over two hundred people and even elected their own mayor. In his history of homelessness in Cleveland, historian Daniel Kerr describes how shantytown residents foraged for food and supplies from the city dump and accepted donations from local businesses. Members of the shantytowns, he noted, "employed more traditional commons strategies to supplement their diet: they fished, hunted birds, and tended small gardens."[34] This experiment in survival outside of the market along the lakeshore would soon come to an end. With the stadium complete, the city wanted to extol its industrial leadership by hosting a Great Lakes Exposition and the Republican Party's national convention in 1936. Using New Deal programs to offer temporary employment to some residents, the city sought to clear the shantytowns and build an airport on the land created by the waste dumped on the lakefront. By 1936, workers employed through the Works Progress Administration and Civil Works Administration had cleared the camps and prepared the land for the energetic future the city envisioned.

Although the exposition attracted approximately seven million visitors, few of its landmarks remained by the end of the decade, except for the 3.5 acres of manicured gardens designed by A. Donald Gray. Gray, who had worked with Frederick Law Olmsted's architecture firm, had designed the landscaping for some of the cultural gardens in Rockefeller Park and nearby Forest Hill Park. Like Olmsted, Gray sought to make the country pastoral aesthetic of English estates accessible to urban populations. His garden remained along the lakeshore just north of the stadium, a rare slice of habitat in a landscape dominated by commerce, entertainment, and transportation.

The gardens stood in stark contrast to the surrounding rail yards, docks, and dump. Although Cleveland Municipal Airport (now Cleveland-Hopkins) opened in 1925 as the first city-owned airport in the US, the Lakefront Airport (now Burke) had been built out enough to officially open in 1947. Hoping to attract wealthy tourists, the Lakefront Airport struggled to grow fast enough on inputs from the municipal waste stream. By the 1950s, the US Army Corps of Engineers (USACE) had built a steel bulkhead retaining wall and deposited dredgings, also known as "spoil," from the harbor and navigation channel on the Cuyahoga River. Scooped out of the river with a clamshell bucket, the dredge spoil was a slurry of fine silt that could be pumped onto the site like pancake batter, where it would drain and form new soil. It wasn't the only source of "made" land. When the *Cleveland Press* constructed a new office in 1957, they sent 135,000 tons of excavated dirt directly to the airport to build it out further into the lake.[35]

The lakefront remained the city's primary waste dump into

the 1950s, but by that time, nearby residents and motorists on the shoreway were no longer willing to suffer the nuisance. The lakeshore dump stretched from East Twelfth down to East Forty-Ninth Street and was often ablaze to help reduce the mounds of rubbish to more compact ash. When a spring snowstorm in April 1957 dumped "black snow" on Cleveland's downtown, the city's streets commissioner morbidly predicted, "It will get worse before it gets better." Citing construction of the inner-belt freeway and other projects, Commissioner A. J. Preusser told a reporter for the *Cleveland Press*, "the amount of burning will be stepped up." Maintenance workers used vacuums on city streets, and the smoke and soot became so bad that motorists had to use their headlights to see during daylight hours. One Brooklyn resident, miles from the lakeshore, found his freshly painted house speckled with ash.[36] In a withering editorial, the *Cleveland Press* mocked the city for condemning its citizens to the same fate as Pompeii by being buried under toxic ash: "Will the same thing happen to Cleveland before city officials blast themselves out of their lethargy and quench the lake-front dump first?"[37]

The city fired four watchmen at the dump tasked with burning refuse and promised a cleaner operation. Mayor Anthony Celebrezze attempted to secure funding for a modern incinerator to handle the volume of trash, but the project hit a snag when it came in a million dollars over budget. The smoke reduced visibility on the shoreway to such an extent that it caused a four-car pileup that resulted in a $95,000 suit against the city. Desperate for a solution, members of the city council went on a field trip to Chicago to learn about the apparently novel technology of landfills. One newspaper was so unfamiliar with the concept that it awkwardly described them to readers like this: "the city [would] dig big holes and bury the rubbish."[38]

As Cleveland braced itself for yet another winter and the possibility of more black snow, the courts stepped in and demanded action by New Year's Day, 1958. A three-judge panel from the Cuyahoga County Court of Appeals declared the practice of setting fire to the dump as a "public nuisance" and wrote a scathing critique of the city's environmental record. "There is no reason why the thousands of motorists passing…between E. 12th St. and E. 49th St. should endure the acrid fumes, noisome smoke and offensive fly ash belched forth by these open fires." They urged the city to stop using the lake as a dumping ground, which they called "as outmoded and old-fashioned as the use of a horse and buggy."[39]

The traditional narrative of American history describes an awakening to environmental consequences following the Cuyahoga River fire of 1969, the first Earth Day, and the establishment of the EPA in 1970. Clevelanders were well aware of the dire state of their land, air, and water prior to those watershed events, however. The decline in the urban environment combined with the rapid development of suburbs following World War II to heighten preexisting anxieties as cities began to aggressively gobble up the countryside.[40] Cleveland reached its demographic high-water mark in the 1950 census, boasting a population of 914,808 people, making it the seventh-largest city in America. But was size necessarily a marker of success if it was purchased at the price of the quality of life of those residing in the metropolis?

Part of the reason why the city was able to grow its lakeshore by only relying on dredge spoils was the sheer amount of erosion clogging the navigation channel and harbor that the USACE removed each year. A 1963 report demonstrated that replacing forest or farmland with housing developments or highways increased soil erosion by a factor of twenty thousand to forty thousand.[41] Plants—even row crops—serve a vital ecological service by anchoring soil in place, a lesson the nation had supposedly learned during the Dust Bowl. When you bulldoze the soil bare and expose it to the elements, it washes into waterways until a new community of plants can take root. All of that soil washed into the nearest stream and eventually into the Cuyahoga. By the beginning of the twenty-first century, the USACE was dredging 330,000 cubic yards of spoil from the Cuyahoga River every year, enough silt to fill Municipal Stadium to the brim.[42]

The farmland threatened by urban sprawl was also undergoing rapid changes. After my father's family emigrated to the US in 1950, they settled in the small farming village of Archbold in Ohio's far northwest corner. Having been farmers in Soviet Ukraine prior to World War II, my family took to the area because it resembled home. For the first time in a decade, my great-grandfather was able to keep dozens of beehives, which helped him find something familiar in this new land. My father took summer jobs walking the row crops at local farms and pulling out milkweed by hand. He graduated from high school and enlisted in the air force in 1966. When he returned in 1970, the sleepy northwest corner of Ohio had changed dramatically. Farmers no longer employed local kids to patrol their fields for unwanted plants and instead turned to the broadcast spraying of herbicides and insecticides. When my father discovered that my great-grandfather's bee population had been reduced to only two hives, he was told the reason for the drop was simple: everyone was spraying their crops now. From 1960 to 1980, American farmers more than tripled the amount of pesticides they used on their land.[43] The application of industrial processes allowed chemical companies to reduce prices and place pesticides within reach of many farmers.

You're probably familiar with what happened next. Many pesticides, such as DDT, were not water-soluble, and they concentrated in the bodies of animals. As these chemicals washed off Ohio's farms and into our rivers and Lake Erie, they entered the food chain. Organochlorine pesticides build up in the fatty tissues of birds, reducing the available calcium in their body that they use for egg production. If those levels drop low enough, eggshells become so thin that the body of a nesting bird can crush their own eggs. By 1963, just a year after Rachel Carson published *Silent Spring*, the US Fish and Wildlife service reported that only 417 nesting pairs of bald eagles remained in the lower forty-eight states.[44] By the end of the decade, a team of biologists declared peregrine falcons extirpated east of the Mississippi River.[45] Farm yields skyrocketed, but the cost to native plants and wildlife was significant. Although the chemical industry smeared Rachel Carson as a "hysterical woman" in the media, she was no prophet of doom. "It is not my contention that chemical insecticides must never be used," she wrote. She simply wanted the country to understand the consequences of using them so broadly. "The public must decide," she wrote, "whether it wishes to continue on the present road, and it can do so only when in full possession of the facts."[46] It took time for the nation to learn these lessons.

Concern over the health of the environment eventually reached the level of national politics. By the 1950s, the League of Women Voters became concerned with water pollution in the Great Lakes.[47] As early as the 1930s, Lake Erie experienced such intense algae blooms as a result of sewage runoff that one observer described how it "looked as if it were coated with green paint."[48] When untreated waste enters the lake through combined sewage overflows, such as the one at Walworth Run, microscopic algae feast on the nutrients in the waste. When all the nitrogen and phosphorus has been converted into energy, the algae dies. Microorganisms then decompose it, sucking in dissolved oxygen from the lake during the process. When the bloom is big enough, dissolved oxygen levels can plummet to almost zero, spelling disaster for marine life.

Having human waste in a body of water that a community uses as a source of drinking water and a swimming hole also isn't ideal. By 1968, the *Plain Dealer* published a "Beach Bacteria" chart to alert the public about bacteria counts at beaches throughout the region. Officials in Cleveland closed any beach with a measurable coliform count over one thousand. That summer, measurements from the White City Beach in Collinwood revealed a coliform count of five thousand. Edgewater Beach reported a count of 110,000. To give a sense of just how inflated those figures are, when the EPA first set a safety standard for coliform levels in recreational waters, they put the upper limit at two hundred and later revised it down to thirty-five.[49]

Intent on showing leadership and providing the city's citizens with an environmental amenity during the summer of 1968, Mayor Carl Stokes secured a $325,000 grant from the Federal Water Pollution Control Administration, a forerunner of the EPA. Stokes used the money to create a "swimming pool in the lake" at White City Beach. Separated from the polluted lake water by vinyl curtains, the pool required four thousand gallons of liquid chlorine before its coliform count dropped below one thousand, and additional daily supplements of 350 pounds of powdered chlorine to maintain those levels. To demonstrate the safety of the new amenity, Stokes joined a crowd of swimmers for a dip in the pool on the final day of July.[50]

Although the pool offered residents a semblance of normality, it did nothing to address the deeper issue: Cleveland had developed in such a way that essential environmental amenities had become a threat to public health.

Making the Wasteland Bloom

In retrospect, the city's decision to pursue the project of creating land from trash on the lakeshore did prove profitable, but it failed to provide the economic security promised by City Manager Hopkins. The construction of Municipal Stadium, Lakefront Airport, and the Great Lakes Exposition meant little to the Clevelanders foraging for food amid the burning trash beside Lake Erie. When boom times returned following World War II, the prosperity was purchased at the expense of the natural amenities that had first attracted white settlement to the region. With beaches closed due to high bacteria counts, and with the air filled with choking soot from trash fires, the burning of the Cuyahoga in the summer of 1969 was just another symptom of a city at odds with its landscape. Historians David and Richard Stradling summed up Cleveland in the postwar years when they described it as "a good place to find work but a poor place to live."[51]

Mayor Stokes wanted to change that, but he faced a century of accumulated decisions that had willingly sacrificed environmental stability for economic growth. Growing public dissatisfaction was already moving federal agencies to review long-standing policy. In response to the attention paid to the impact of water pollution, the USACE revised its regulations in 1968 and announced that dredging permits would be subject to "an evaluation of all relevant factors, including the effect of the proposed work on navigation, fish and wildlife, conservation, pollution, aesthetics, ecology, and the general public interest."[52] When Congress amended the Federal Water Pollution Control Act in 1972, section 404 encoded into law the new regulatory framework in use by the USACE for dredge spoil disposal. Now known as the first "Clean Water Act," the legislation had the effect of prohibiting the long-standing practice of dumping toxic dredge spoil in Lake

Erie without first building a confined disposal facility (CDF) that was walled-off from the open waters by steel bulkheads and composed of layers of rock and sand that would filter toxins.

Planning lakefront development now became a matter of necessity for the city. It didn't take an environmental engineer to know that the Cuyahoga River was full of pollutants. When the city commissioned an environmental impact statement for a CDF to extend the lakefront airport in 1986, a chemical analysis of sediment at eighteen sites within Cleveland Harbor found all but one "highly polluted" with lead, arsenic, oil, grease, and chromium. All the sites were "highly polluted" with cyanide.[53] The scale of the problem became apparent quickly. The USACE has a mandate to dredge the harbor to a depth of twenty-eight feet, and the first six miles of the Cuyahoga to a depth of twenty-three feet, to maintain navigation. All of that dredge spoil would need to go into CDFs after the passage of the Clean Water Act. In the coming decades, the city of Cleveland would gain permits for three CDFs: the first would build out the dump at the edge of Gordon Park, and two more would add on to Lakefront Airport. In total, the USACE would build forty-five CDFs throughout the Great Lakes as rivers and harbors became full of the consequences of unregulated industrial growth.

The CDF at the end of Gordon Park received immediate attention. In the early 1960s, the city had scuttled two iron ore freighters to create a break wall for the boat launch at the park and to serve as a supporting structure to extend the dump. With the passage of the Clean Water Act, the city decided this would be the location of the city's first CDF. Designated "Dike 14," the location became an aquatic construction zone during the late 1970s just as the city faced economic collapse. Cleveland was confronted with a vicious cycle as mounting costs to maintain infrastructure was met by a shrinking tax base due to wealthy residents fleeing for the suburbs. The municipal government cut services to the bone. The city sold management rights for Municipal Stadium to Browns owner Art Modell in 1974, a decision that would eventually result in the franchise leaving for Baltimore two decades later. City parks fell into disrepair due to budget shortfalls, leading the city to relinquish control of all of its parkland to the Ohio Department of National Resources in exchange for a single dollar and the hope that state funds could prevent the lands from complete devastation. Despite these desperate attempts, Cleveland officially defaulted on $14 million worth of loans in December 1978. It was the first major city since the Great Depression to financially collapse. Combined with the Cuyahoga River fire of 1969, the default sealed Cleveland's reputation as the "Mistake on the Lake."

Something unexpected happened during this low point in the city's history. Suffering from years of neglect and falling into disrepair, the Donald Gray Gardens became a sanctuary for migrating birds and a hot spot for Cleveland birders. Without active management, ornamental plants gave way to native species, such as grapevines, that provided critical forage for birds. With the state in control of Cleveland's parks, in 1979, they commissioned a bold plan to bring people back to the lakeshore. Dike 14 would play a pivotal role. Prepared by Behnke Landscape Architecture, the state planned to convert the CDF to a park upon completion. It even proposed the creation of a "series of islands" near Dike 14 dedicated to "wildlife habitat and environmental education."[54] Cleveland, with a helping hand from the state, had charted a course to a future that acknowledged the need for urban parkland and wildlife habitat.

Over the next twenty years, the USACE filled Dike 14 with 5.7 million cubic yards of dredge spoil, enough to create an eighty-eight-acre peninsula with a high point of thirty-nine feet.[55] Even before the site was completed in 1999, birds were at-tracted to the mudflats created by the dredge spoil. As portions of the CDF filled in and drained, seeds locked away for years burst into new life at the site. New England aster, jewelweed, Virginia creeper, milkweed, and sunflowers transformed the mudflats into prairie. The highest areas supported communities of sandbar willow, eastern cottonwood, white pine, and black locust trees. Although plant communities grew in fits and starts as new dredge spoils piled up every year, birders didn't wait for the site to of-ficially close and become a park. By the 1980s, bird-watchers were already trespassing on the CDF to spy rare birds during the seasonal migrations. "They simply jumped the fence," Marnie Urso told me with a mischievous smile. Guerrilla birding on a toxic waste dump fit the new underdog attitude that Cleveland embraced in the last years of the twentieth century.

When the city ceased dumping at Dike 14 and switched to a CDF at Burke Lakefront Airport in 1999, birders began to collect data on the new patch of habitat on Cleveland's shore. Both amateur birders and field ornithologists from the Kirtland Bird Club and the Audubon Society documented 278 species of birds at Dike 14, including twenty-three of the twenty-nine species on the Ohio Division of Wildlife's endangered species list. The data convinced Audubon Ohio to designate the site as a National Audubon Important Bird Area in 2000. In a press re-lease, Audubon Ohio described Dike 14 as a "premier migratory staging site" that "provides the necessary habitat requirements essential to allow migrating birds to rest and refuel before con-tinuing on their passage."[56] Within the span of two decades, a patch of toxic waste had been converted into a vibrant habitat. The wasteland had bloomed.

Dike 14 should have become a park soon after it stopped receiving dredge spoils in 1999, but it did not open to the public until 2012. The story of what happened in the intervening years could fill a book of its own. Cleveland citizens formed the Dike 14 Environmental Education Collaborative to push the city of Cleveland to hold true to the 1979 plan for the site. Representatives from Audubon Ohio, Cleveland Metroparks, CMNH, LENSC, the Cuyahoga Soil and Water Conservation District, the Cuyahoga Valley National Park Association, the Nature Center at Shaker Lakes, and the Earth Day Coalition attended dozens of meetings, wrote letters to policymakers, and penned editorials to local newspapers, urging the designation of the site as a wildlife preserve. Several developers floated wild plans at the time, including a sculpture garden, bike trail, and barbecue pits. There were rumors that a golf course was in the works. Urso was in those meetings and rolled her eyes when I asked her about the proposals. "None of it made much sense," she told me. "You can get all those things by walking a few blocks to Gordon Park or the cultural gardens at Rockefeller Park. What we didn't have on the lakeshore was space dedicated to *habitat*."

The environmental collaborative printed field guides and won permission to escort students from the Glenville and St. Clair-Superior neighborhoods on nature walks. Chris Trepal, cofounder of the Earth Day Coalition, helped organize the field trips. The daughter of a union organizer, Trepal grew up on East Seventy-Ninth Street and told me "environmental justice was always at the core of [her] work." If the city was going to preserve land, she wanted it to serve the immediate communities. But there were challenges. "You'd be surprised how many kids were afraid," she said. She told me about one field trip where Harvey Webster invited the kids to touch a northern brown snake. "Some of them ran away screaming," she told me while laughing. "But others wanted to try it." For many kids, it was their first time seeing a deer or certain flowering plants. Trepal relished those early days of bringing students out to witness nature reclaim what was basically a dump. "They were enchanted," she said.

No one was a stronger advocate for the conservation of wildlife habitat at Dike 14 than Barbara Martin. Martin was an active member of the League of Women Voters of Cleveland, an organization that took an early interest in the health of the Great Lakes. Sadly, she passed away just months before I began researching this project. Martin and several other activists were present for the ribbon-cutting ceremony on a cold and windy February day in 2012. The officials from the port and city of Cleveland congratulated themselves in front of the assembled media without ever acknowledging the work of people like Martin, Trepal, Urso, and Webster to bring the nature preserve to fruition. When I met Barbara's husband, Ken, and several other activists at her house in Berea, I was offered all of her notes from the years she spent working to secure Dike 14 as a wildlife habitat. When Ken opened the door to the storage closet, it contained two dozen legal boxes full of documents, including emails, meeting minutes, newspaper clippings, USACE correspondence, and even audio cassette tapes of phone calls she made to local officials and fellow environmental activists. The mountain of files represented fifteen years' worth of labor toward a single issue: providing habitat for wildlife and an opportunity for environmental education for the surrounding neighborhoods. It was a testament to just how much Clevelanders can care for their community. Martin's notes are being cataloged as a collection by the Western Reserve Historical Society for future scholars to discover. Some of us preserve habitat. Others preserve the story of how it was created.

Crime Pays but Botany Doesn't

After spending a year volunteering with Lights Out Cleveland and caring for animals at LENSC, I earned a reputation among my friends as a kind of eccentric birder. Friends alerted me to injured birds that struck windows at their office, which I would then come collect and transport to LENSC. I was happy to help, but the truth is, I'm not very good at identifying species. Sure, I can distinguish a northern flicker from a downy woodpecker, but most species just look vaguely familiar to me. Once you've been around folks who can identify a species by a single chirp or flash of a wing, you gain an appreciation for the depth of sensory knowledge required to distinguish one bird from another.

What I understand much better is the connection between habitat and wildlife because the formula is simple: animals will eventually show up if the plants that sustain them are allowed to grow. The plants we choose to grow in our yards, if we are fortunate enough to control those decisions, can play an important role in sustaining wildlife. "Home-improvement store clerks are on the front lines," Brendon Samuels told me during our interview. The stock available at garden centers determines what most people plant in their yard. With just a little knowledge, these outlets could steer consumers toward native plants that support local wildlife or shielded light fixtures that prevent sky glow. Instead, many garden centers and home-improvement stores offer non-native plants, some of which are invasive. For instance, many of my neighbors have planted ornamental silvergrass (*Miscanthus*), which can reach heights of over twelve feet. Easily identifiable by their feather-like inflorescences, the grass has escaped my neighborhood and colonized the adjacent metropark. Not to be confused with the taller and even more aggressive common reed (*Phragmites australis*), which can be found in just about every low-lying area in northeast Ohio, silvergrass is available at nearly every home-improvement store.

Whether through government action or personal consumer decisions, restoring habitat in the Great Lakes region has global impacts. The milkweed that my father pulled from fields in the 1960s coevolved with monarch butterflies, whose larvae eat and ingest the plant's toxins to protect them from predators. As milkweed habitat declined and pesticide use rose, monarch populations in the eastern US declined by 80 percent between 2007 and 2017, according to the US Geological Survey (USGS). Monarchs migrate and overwinter in Mexico, requiring habitat along their flight corridors. Scientists estimate that it takes approximately 28.5 milkweed plants to give a single butterfly a chance to make it to Mexico. Unfortunately, we are about 1.8 billion plants shy of a habitat necessary to sustain a healthy monarch population.[57] The situation has become so dire that the monarch now has a significant chance of going extinct in the eastern US over the next

fifteen years; in 2014, the US Fish and Wildlife Service recommended the population be listed as "threatened" under the Endangered Species Act.[58] The butterfly effect, used to describe the impact of seemingly small actions on large systems, will take on new meaning if we lose a species that has defined the landscape for millions of years.

Joey Santore, an amateur botanist, has described nonnative plants like silvergrass as "horticultural atrocities" on his YouTube channel, *Crime Pays but Botany Doesn't*. Deriding "parking-lot slums" and the destruction of wild habitat by housing developments, Santore has earned over three hundred thousand subscribers for his videos offering down-to-earth lessons on botany, geology, and ecology. With a punk aesthetic, he applies a DIY ethic to botany, with frequent instructions on how to gather wild seeds and proliferate them through guerrilla gardening. Like Chef Umansky and Alexis Nikole Nelson, Santore is part of a growing movement that seeks to rediscover lost knowledge about the land by deepening our understanding of the connections between plant and animal communities. He says his mission is simple. He wants to "show people how incredible the natural world is and kind of get them out of that narrow-minded myopia of only knowing things that are in human society, because if that is all you know about planet earth, that's fucking bleak, man."[59]

Santore's irreverent view is actually rooted in science. In one longitudinal study, researchers found that children who spend the first ten years of life in environments with little to no green space are 55 percent more likely to develop mental illnesses than children with abundant access.[60] According to the media research firm Nielsen, Americans spend an average of just over ten hours a day looking at some form of electronic screen.[61] Increasingly, school, work, and entertainment are operating in digital environments disconnected from the land. The journalist Richard Louv coined the term "nature-deficit disorder" to describe the cluster of symptoms that develop as a result of alienation from plant and animal communities.[62] Although medical institutions have not embraced the term, studies have demonstrated that spending as little as two hours per week in green spaces or other natural environments imparts a greater sense of well-being and health.[63] The might of our culture often blinds us to the fact that, as animals, humans also require healthy, undeveloped habitats, and our brains don't function as well without them.

Even if you can dismiss the mental health benefits and fate of wildlife, the economic effects of habitat restoration are sufficient to undertake concerted effort. In a 2007 study, the Brookings Institution estimated that restoration of habitat throughout the Great Lakes would provide over $6 billion dollars in revenue from tourism, fishing, and recreation, and raise coastal property values by $12 to $19 billion. The report documented substantial evidence "that people are willing to pay more to locate in areas with high environmental amenities."[64] The zero-sum thinking that environmental stability must come at the cost of economic growth is withering, but it remains strong. The defeat of recent bills that would protect and expand habitat demonstrates that old ideas die hard in today's political environment.

* * *

I'm happy to embrace the DIY spirit from fellow environmental activists instead of waiting for a changing of the guard in Columbus or Washington, DC. Every autumn, I harvest milkweed seeds from familiar spots and scatter them in areas I know will be spared from mowing and herbicide application. Waste places in the Flats, abandoned lots in Cleveland's poorest neighborhoods, and park prairies are great milkweed habitats. If you think the birds have it rough crossing the lake, imagine doing it on the energy stored in the body of a single monarch butterfly that weighs about half a gram. When I see a cluster of milkweed stalks poking up in a new area I seeded the previous year, the existential dread lifts a bit. Considering my father's milkweed-destroying youth, I suppose it's also a form of generational reparations to the land.

Walking the paths through parks in northeast Ohio reveals how just a little bit of habitat can make a big difference. At Hinckley Reservation, you can spy the gnawed stumps of giant trees laid low by a family of beavers who constructed a lodge and dam near one of the bloodiest battlefields in Ohio's war against nature. You can spot the giant aeries of bald eagles along the Towpath Trail, where DDT once washed into the Cuyahoga River. In the past thirty years, there have even been several sightings of black bears along the Chagrin River, once a hub for the transatlantic fur trade. In my own backyard on the southern edge of Cleveland's city limits, wild turkeys often claw at the ground to take dirt baths, and I sometimes catch a glimpse of a pack of coyotes as they lope through my garden. Like a glacier, the inertia of natural systems is slow but relentless, and it will grind our concrete and asphalt to substrate for future forests. Take hope in that.

From our perspective, the prospects of a rebound seem dim. We are so often attracted to technological fixes that ignore underlying causes. Like Mayor Stokes's swimming pool in the lake, we judge our impact by direct experience and often lose sight of the state of the larger system. When you combine the biomass of all the land mammals on earth, humans and our livestock account for 98 percent of the total, while wild animals comprise the remaining 2 percent.[65] Are we prepared to rethink our relationship with the environment and view ourselves as another animal embedded within the community of life? Can we spare a little room (and a little darkness) for life-forms that represent our planet's genetic legacy? Human decisions, not natural processes, decided the fates of the passenger pigeon and bald eagle. Which model we adopt going forward will determine whether the land has a chance to heal or whether it will become haunted by ghosts that only exist locked behind the glass displays of museum exhibits.

Duty of Care

How would you tell the story of northeast Ohio? Is it one of astounding success or incomprehensible failure? I think it has been both, and everything in between. That perspective won't satisfy those looking for stark binaries of progress and failure, but the data does suggest at least one clear pattern. Many of the human failings in this story were the result of the adoption of new technology that fundamentally transformed a culture's relationship with the environment. From paleo points to the arc light, humans have often learned about unintended consequences the hard way. Indigenous societies modified their cultures to view plants and animals as vital members of the same community they inhabited. Mainstream American culture has struggled to do the same, despite benefiting from scientific knowledge that has revealed the secrets of the universe. How can a civilization so advanced fail at something so basic, so necessary for survival?

I contend the problem is one of consent. Although nature should not be assigned a consciousness in the human sense, it does organize itself according to certain laws. Indigenous cultures recognized the patterns at work in the environment and constructed societies (with notable exceptions) that operated within those limits. How have colonial societies fared in comparison? On paper, the United States government is founded upon the "consent of the governed." Over the past 250 years, the right of the individual to act without hindrance has been the primary goal of the American project. Not until passage of the Endangered Species Act of 1973 did the federal government recognize the need to preserve the integrity of the living world for its own sake.

And what about the way we relate to one another? A nation of individuals without an ethic of duty to community has been a toxic brew throughout American history. Our devotion to individual freedom has blinded us to its casualties. Perhaps the greatest example of this is the racist economic system of chattel slavery that persisted for much of the first century after the American Revolution. Stripping one group of people of their property rights was less palatable than liberating another group of people from a system that viewed them *as* property. The rights of a few to do as they please have often come at the cost of the consent of the many. The philosopher Isaiah Berlin described societies that value liberty over community best when he wrote, "Freedom for the wolves has often meant death to the sheep."[1] Many Americans consent to the system because they imagine themselves as wolves without ever looking in the mirror.

The health of the environment has rebounded since the grim days of the past century. Fish are returning to Ohio's rivers and lakes, some endangered birds have returned from the brink of extinction, and our air and water are cleaner than at any point since the Industrial Revolution. Our relationship with the environment seems on the mend, but it is still brokered by a few, powerful forces. Since the days when steel mills and oil refineries filled Cleveland's Flats, industry still has a heavy impact on our life in the land. FirstEnergy, the company responsible for the 2003 blackout, funneled $60 million into an organization controlled by the Republican speaker of the Ohio statehouse in return for a $1.3 billion bailout. The US attorney for the Southern District of Ohio called the boondoggle "likely the largest bribery, money laundering scheme ever perpetrated against the people of the state of Ohio."[2] That's quite a feat considering that Ohio gave birth to the Standard Oil Company, notorious for buying both the competition and legislators.

When a Norfolk Southern train derailed about eighty miles southeast of Cleveland in East Palestine, Ohio, it rekindled apocalyptic scenes of the rust belt on fire. Video documenting the burning of over one hundred thousand gallons of vinyl chloride spread across social media in early February 2023. Just as cleanup crews were conducting a controlled burn of the vinyl chloride on February 6, I met with Eddie Olschansky at Tommy's in Coventry Village to learn more about the state of Cleveland's environment. Olschansky looks like a dock worker from Cleveland's past, sporting a knit beanie, sweatshirt, and ragged jeans. He grew up in Walton Hills, close enough to "throw a baseball from my childhood bedroom to the Cuyahoga Valley National Park," he tells me. If his name doesn't sound familiar, it's because he is the mostly anonymous force behind the Instagram account known as @trashfish_cle. He spends his days in a kayak on the Cuyahoga, mostly in the five miles or so closest to the lake, fishing trash out of the water with a grabber and filling bag after bag with garbage. The TrashFish account documents the troubling and sometimes humorous side of water pollution. "I have an odd collection of sex toys I've fished out of the river," he tells me while digging into a falafel sandwich. "Anything that's in your bathroom that might get flushed down the toilet, I'm gonna find it." Used condoms are so common he refers to them as "river snakes."

Irreverent at times, Olschansky went to school for journalism and knows how to frame a story for different audiences. He has been interviewed by national media, gives talks to local schools, and has a fleet of fifteen kayaks so everyone from grandmothers to children can join him on the river. When discussing the problems of trash, he's very clear about who is to blame. The bio line of the TrashFish account declares, "'Litter' ain't the issue!" and Olschansky rejects the decades-old messaging that blames consumers for litter. "We can't recycle our way out of this problem, we need to stop producing this stuff," he says. Although he identifies single-use plastics as the most common trash he pulls out of the river, he's deeply concerned about the rise of what he calls "zero-use plastics."

Olschansky is referring to nurdles, or tiny plastic pellets that resemble the candy Nerds. Think of nurdles as the ingots of plastic manufacturing. One step removed from petroleum refining, they are shipped to businesses throughout the world, where they are melted down and poured into molds for everything from electronics to toys to the recycling bin you throw your single-use plastics into. Take a look around you. Chances are there is something within six feet of you that was once hundreds or thousands of nurdles. Although they never enter the consumer market, Olschansky has been skimming nurdles off the river and off the beaches of Lake Erie for years now. "The day you find your first one in the wild," he says, "you will never stop seeing them." Olschansky says he now has a sixth sense, that he can almost smell nurdles and knows where they collect in waterways. I found them within minutes at Wendy Park near the mouth of the river. Go to any beach and locate the area where sticks collect on the sand. Scatter them a bit and I guarantee you will find nurdles of every shape and color lurking in the sand below.

As tough as bottles and condoms are to fish out of the river, nothing compares to the problem of collecting a plastic pellet just under five millimeters in size. Nurdles insinuate themselves into every conceivable nook and cranny along the river. Olschansky uses an aquarium net to painstakingly retrieve as many as he can. While we are eating, he pulls a small glass jar out of his pocket and places it on the table. "I've got a bottle in my truck with about twenty thousand of them in it," he said.

Olschansky had always found meaning on the water. "There's a world down there that you don't understand until you are engaged with it," he told me. Although he is the type of guy who can't walk by a stray shopping cart in a parking lot without returning it, he understands that individual action is not the solution to environmental problems. All of us have responsibilities that reduce our individual capacity. For instance, a new mom reached out to him, asking for advice on how to make the world a bit cleaner for her child. She asked, "I got an eighteen-month-old at home, I'm seeing all the plastic garbage that being a mother generated in my child's small life, like, what can *I* do?" Olschansky recognizes that individual action shouldn't come at the expense of what we value most. "I was like, okay, you could get cotton diapers and wash them out every day," he tells me, "or you could not stress too hard about it. Take that effort and treat your child well with it instead." He practices what he preaches by taking little steps to limit his waste. He brought a reusable water bottle with him to the restaurant, but he doesn't live a monk's life. He wants to direct his energy where he feels it is needed most: the river.

Olschansky believes the responsibility for waste ultimately rests with producers. "I get more demoralized when I go to Costco and I see the stack of water bottles that are just floor to ceiling, and I know that that gets delivered there every three days, or whatever," he says. "I don't see the consumer as the problem anymore." Although he doesn't express it in these words, he is describing the moral responsibility that legal scholars describe as a "duty of care," which recognizes that each individual has a responsibility to prevent harm to others through our actions (or inaction).

When you shovel snow from the sidewalk in front of your house or apartment, you are fulfilling your duty of care. That duty may even be codified in municipal ordinances, and neglecting your duty may run you afoul of the law. All of us practice the duty of care when we enter into relationships, have a child, adopt a pet, or purchase a plant. Scholars have identified it as a hardwired behavior in all humans. The Russian polymath Peter Kropotkin argued against the misconception of Darwinian evolution as "survival of the fittest" in his work *Mutual Aid*. Relying on his observations of the animal world, Kropotikin argued that cooperation, not competition, was the most successful evolutionary strategy and the basis of all animal behavior.[3] Even the most die-hard capitalist feeds their children without demanding compensation in return.

Although we practice mutual aid in our relationships, our legal system has struggled to incorporate a duty of care into law. For example, there is no law regulating the safe handling of nurdles by businesses. Olschansky shared with me second-hand stories from a friend in the plastic production business. "It's not uncommon for them to spill a cool million of these and they're just swept into a drain," he told me with frustration.

Days after our interview, the National Traffic Safety Board (NTSB) released its initial assessment of the derailment at East Palestine in a televised press conference, and they identified a surprising cause for the catastrophe. NTSB Chair Jennifer Homendy identified train car number twenty-three as the source of the accident. Although most of the media focused its attention on the cars full of vinyl chloride, car twenty-three carried one item: nurdles. "It was the combination of the hot axel and the plastic pellets which started the initial fire," Homendy reported to the assembled media.[4] When I shared the video with Olschansky, his reaction summed up the feelings of many in the region. "What a fucking mess," he said.

TrashFish is an example of a project to remediate the environment and spread awareness using digital media. Olschansky has resisted attempts by venture capital to monetize it; instead, he relies on both small donors and grant funding. For-profit businesses in the region are also experimenting with new ways to solve environmental problems. Chef Jeremy Umansky, who we met earlier, has sustained his restaurant, Larder Delicatessen, for five years by crafting menu items from local, sometimes foraged foods. He has earned multiple nominations for James Beard Awards in a city that has redefined itself as a foodie destination.

While Umansky is trying to shorten the feedback loop with the land in his sourcing methods, Daniel Brown is getting Clevelanders to close their waste loops by redirecting kitchen scraps from landfills to composting facilities. I interviewed him over coffee at Phoenix on Lee Road. Wearing a battered cap and jacket, he looks like he could have just rolled off a freight train. He was immersed in the farm-to-table movement while working at Spice Kitchen & Bar after college. By day, he would intern and run a community garden, and at night, he would shift to food service. He had a chance conversation with his neighbor, Drew Ullman, a community organizer with the Detroit Shoreway Development Organization, about the potential for composting within the city. As Brown filled trash bags with food scraps each night from the restaurant to build soil in the garden, he felt there was an opportunity to close a waste loop within the city that had been neglected for over a century. As he and his roommates bounced the idea around, they encountered an immediate problem: "How do we get the food scraps that we see an abundant amount of through our daily work back to community gardens and back to farms?"

Brown and his friends raised about $2,000, which got them a "really beefy mountain bike." After a friend welded a trailer onto it, Rust Belt Riders was born. The next problem to tackle was how to attract customers. Would anyone pay them to collect and compost food scraps? Brown first approached Ben Bebenroth, the chef and owner of Spice, who was happy to pay a little so his food waste would create soil at local gardens. "And then we just sort of went from cafe to cafe," Brown told me. News traveled fast through Cleveland's tight-knit service industry that a few workers from a local restaurant were offering to collect food waste for a small fee. Rust Belt Riders soon gained customers throughout the city. "What it's turned into far surpasses what we expected it to be," Brown admitted.

Brown and his fellow cofounder Michael Robinson hadn't been prepared for the kind of growth the business enjoyed. "I studied ethics, he studied social and political philosophy. We didn't have a business class between us," Brown told me. They both had experience in nonprofits, but Brown had a different idea for the future of the small business. "We believed worker-ownership would be really cool, and we needed a for-profit vehicle to do that." Brown and Robinson gained valuable mentoring through the Social Enterprise Accelerator offered by the Columbus-based SEA Change organization. The model they created for Rust Belt Riders was so innovative they won a $20,000 prize after competing in a *Shark Tank*-style pitch competition. "That pretty quickly transformed this thing we would do outside of our other jobs to us deciding to dive headfirst into this," Brown said. Rust Belt Riders were soon in action full-time, collecting coffee grounds from local cafes and food scraps from kitchens. "What we're doing would have been totally unnecessary not that long ago," he admitted. "It is a by-product of modern supply chains where roughly 40 percent of all food that is grown in this country is thrown away and never consumed."

Prior to World War II, food scraps were fed to livestock and pets or collected for compost at truck gardens. With the spread of municipal trash collection and the development of sanitary landfills, all waste went into a single stream. The problem with this, Brown will point out, is that if organic matter decomposes in the absence of oxygen, the bacteria that specialize in that process create methane (CH_4), which is twenty-five times more powerful than carbon dioxide (CO_2) in trapping heat in our atmosphere. "If the city of Cleveland has a climate goal of reducing greenhouse gasses, I've got an answer," Brown says. "Stop sending food to landfills."

Rust Belt Riders are providing one solution to the waste problem Olschansky encounters at the river, but their success is entirely dependent upon enthusiastic buy-in from the community. Large local businesses have been early adopters. "Every year when Great Lakes Brewing Company brews their Christmas Ale, we get sixty-four-gallon bins full of ginger and cinnamon sticks," Brown says with a smile. "It's amazing." Rust Belt Riders have also expanded their service to residents, who have the option to either drop off their food scraps at two dozen locations throughout Cuyahoga County or sign up for weekly curbside pickup. With a worker-owner model, Brown has no qualms in using a for-profit platform for the mass adoption of diverting food waste from landfills. As the business grows, every employee shares in its success.

The mountains of compost the company has produced go directly to urban farms, such as Ohio City Farm, which is just north of the parking lot for the West Side Market. Brown knows the challenges of urban farming in a rust belt city. "The soil sucks," he tells me. Building up nutrients in the earth after a century or more of neglect and abuse opens the door to new possibilities for a landscape many wrote off as dead at the height of the environmental crises of the twentieth century.

Protecting the Land and Ourselves

If Brown and Olschansky are resurrecting land and waterscapes from centuries of harm and neglect, Western Reserve Land Conservancy (WRLC) is working to safeguard land from the perils of reckless development. On a frigid January morning in the Chagrin River Valley, I drove by fields glazed with rime to meet with Pete McDonald at the nonprofit's central office. McDonald has a gentle manner and a warm, deliberate tone when he speaks. He grew up on a farm in Munson Township, not far from Hambden Orchard Wildlife Area and Punderson State Park. "When I was a teenager I watched all these developments come in," he told me. As Cleveland's growth spread eastward into Geauga County, it threatened the community's identity. When McDonald described the distress that landscape change caused his family, it reminded me of the research on solastalgia. "My dad has cherished and hunted on that land," he told me. "It's just devastating to him and my mom to see."

McDonald studied biology at the College of Wooster, did field research in the Rocky Mountains, and learned how to build digital maps with geographic information systems (GIS). He joined the land conservancy in 2005, and his training in GIS is evident. Whenever we would talk about a certain location, he would pull up a color-coded map projected on the wall that displayed all the acreage within the land conservancy's portfolio. As he zoomed out to a satellite view of Ohio, areas protected by the land conservancy stretched across twenty-eight counties. By the end of 2022, the organization had protected over seventy thousand acres of land in the state, an area 130 percent larger than the city of Cleveland.

I asked McDonald how they had accomplished it. He takes his time considering how to answer. "So, I'm going to get technical here," he begins with a grin. What he reveals is that an overlooked amendment to the US tax code that was passed during the final weeks of the Carter administration allowed landowners to earn an income tax deduction for setting aside land from development. The legislative session had already passed the largest expansion of protected federal lands and created the Superfund program, but Section 6 of Public Law 96-541 may be one of the most radical environmental laws in American history. McDonald deflects any attempts to politicize the work of the land conservancy. "I call it an interesting endeavor in property law," he offers.

The idea of land trusts predated the 1980 amendment to the tax code, but the new law provided a powerful incentive to landowners to protect some or all of their property with permanent legal restrictions. By doing so, the landowners stripped themselves and all future owners of the property from developing the designated parcel. Once a conservation easement is created, it cannot be subdivided, and the level of protection can never decrease. McDonald's job is to make sure everyone is living up to their promises. His team captures aerial imaging of properties, walks the land with the owner, and files reports on any changes they observe every calendar year. Some properties only require an in-person visit once every five years, but McDonald says his team likes to meet with landowners annually if they're interested. "My team's job is relationship building," he says.

Those relationships are critical when navigating conflicts that arise in a culture that holds property rights as an almost sacred covenant. "There are people who argue that this law is unconstitutional because you're tying the hands of future landowners, and that's not American," McDonald tells me. He has three responses to that sentiment. The first is to recognize that the American tradition of granting a property owner total freedom to determine how their land is used led to the creation of this law. "Second of all," he continues, "there's other things that tie a future landowner's hands, like third-party oil, gas, and mining leases that you don't have control of, so it's buyer beware." If you can sign away access to subterranean resources to a corporation, why shouldn't you be able to give those same rights to a land trust? Finally, he admits, "there are inevitable lawsuits that are going to come up." That's why his team is building legal defense funds for when future landowners decide to test the restrictions placed upon them. McDonald tells interested landowners that when they join the land trust, "you're essentially giving a voice to the land." Sometimes that voice has to pass through the mouth of a lawyer for it to be heard.

Nationwide, the approximately 1,700 land trusts in the US have preserved over sixty million acres of land, more than twice the size of the state of Ohio. McDonald isn't just looking for raw acreage, though; he is focused on creating habitat corridors in the region to support wildlife. The land conservancy has been quietly accumulating adjoining lands in some areas to add to existing habitat preserves. WRLC locations host breeding populations of endangered species that will require concerted effort to protect.

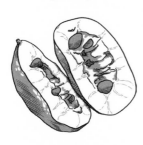

The land conservancy has also been responsible for expanding the tree canopy in the Forest City. Despite the efforts of Cleveland Metroparks, approximately three-quarters of Cleveland's tree canopy potential is on private land. With their Trees4CLE adoption program, the land conservancy helped city of Cleveland residents plant over 1,200 native trees. My backyard has six pawpaw (*Asimina triloba*) trees from the program. Producing the largest edible fruit native to the continent, the pawpaw tree was once spread by hungry megafauna, like mastodons, that stalked Ohio's forests. Now the tree offers critical habitat to the zebra swallowtail butterfly (*Eurytides marcellus*), whose caterpillars feed exclusively on pawpaw leaves.

McDonald has found a sense of peace and security in his work by rebuilding habitat acre by acre. He's moved back to the family farm, installed some solar panels, and planted a pollinator habitat in the backyard. "It's amazing," he tells me. "It's like, how can I be so lucky, you know?" He wants everyone to be able to enjoy the sense of stability that comes with cultivating a connection with the land that leaves it in better shape for future generations.

* * *

Though it's possible to restore the land to fertility and revive wildlife habitat, can we foster a culture that places the health of the community above our own self-interest? We may have no other choice if we wish to secure the standard of living our parents enjoyed. The country has crashed into the limits of progress in recent years, and the effects are cascading through society. From 2015 to 2017, the US experienced a sharp downturn in average life expectancy. According to a study published in the medical journal *BMJ Open*, this wasn't just a blip but "the longest sustained decline since 1915–1918."[5] The main drivers for the decline were so-called "diseases of despair." Defined as drug overdoses, alcohol-related deaths, or suicides, diseases of despair rose by 68 percent between 2009 and 2018. Although the researchers admit that the "concept of despair remains largely unstudied," they provide ample evidence for what is driving people to desperation. Declining economic opportunity, stagnant wages, the erosion of social safety nets, a "generalised cultural rise in loneliness, depression, alienation and anxiety," rising rates of gun ownership, and racial resentment among poor whites are all creating a sense of hopelessness that is driving Americans to desperately seek comfort any way they can find it.

Ohio has done worse than the national average, particularly in metropolitan environments. Deaths of despair rose 89 percent in Ohio, claiming over fifty-three thousand lives and robbing our communities of a collective 1.9 million years that we could have spent with our loved ones and neighbors.[6] Nearly every adult Ohioan knows at least one person who has died from one of the diseases of despair. I have mourned several, but the last was by far the worst. In the autumn of 2021, my nineteen-year-old son, Aleks, was being intentional about keeping in touch with his friends after our family moved from Cleveland's westside to Slavic Village. Many of his friends live in Lakewood, where they could enjoy the few green spaces the city has to offer, such as Kaufman Park. One friend had been struggling with substance abuse and had recently left a rehab facility. Aleks was able to reconnect with him and let him know how happy he was to see him again. A week later, his friend died after snorting cocaine that had been cut with fentanyl. With a lethal dose equivalent to no more than a few grains of sand, fentanyl causes you to lose consciousness and cease breathing. By the time he was discovered, it was too late. At just nineteen, one mistake cost him and his loved ones an entire lifetime of experiences.

The loss was incomprehensible, and in my grief, I discovered Thrive for Change, a Cleveland-based organization that offered free harm-reduction courses. I was desperate to find some tool, any tool, for processing my grief. I signed up for a Harm Reduction 101 class. During the course, I learned how to order and administer Narcan nasal spray, an opioid antagonist, that can buy enough time to get someone experiencing an overdose to a medical facility. The two course instructors had lived experience with opioid use and spoke of it without shame or judgment. Bethany Roebuck, Thrive for Change's executive director, had herself been rescued from an overdose by Narcan and admits she wouldn't be here today without it. Ashley Rosser, the harm reduction specialist at the organization, has been distributing Narcan for years because it wasn't available when a loved one needed it most.

I met Rosser at a cafe near Thrive's old office in Solon on an unseasonably warm spring day. She has dark hair highlighted by a shock of green dye. With a "straight outta narcan" sticker on her laptop, her personal effects are emblazoned with harm-reduction messages. If you are unfamiliar with the term, Rosser has a simple explanation. "People can't recover if they're dead," she says. She shares her trauma and the story of her path to Thrive for Change with the public often, but she colors in some details during our interview that resonate with me.

Her story goes like this: Several years ago, she had moved in with her boyfriend at his parent's house, where they would use a variety of drugs. Eventually, Rosser found her way to treatment. "I tried twelve-step groups, because that's all there is in Portage County," she tells me. "I really wanted to give it a shot so I decided I needed to leave and we broke up." She stayed in recovery. "I went to detox, did my thing, didn't look back, and here I am today," she says, spreading her arms out.

Her boyfriend continued to use and overdosed in 2018. The loss was traumatic, but exactly how he died changed the trajectory of Rosser's life. "His parents found him and he was out," she tells me. "He was surrounded by paraphernalia: syringes, cotton balls, and the drugs themselves." Rosser says his parents were so terrified that the police would blame them that they spent precious minutes cleaning up the scene before calling 911. "By that time, it was too late. People can't be down for too long," she says. "They just didn't know what to do." The experience shifted her view on drug abuse and recovery. Rosser is accustomed to speaking to the media, the public, and at corporate training seminars. She articulates ideas with a polish you would expect from a college professor, but she lets her mask down a bit and vents her anger when describing the impact of the loss. She tells me the experience infuriated her. "There's no fucking way we have to live like this. We're just watching people die."

After some research, she learned about Narcan and the strategy of harm reduction that was generated in response to the drug war's zero-tolerance policy. "I felt sick to my stomach that all we needed this whole time was a $40 box of Narcan," she says, shaking her head. She took it upon herself to get as many boxes of Narcan into her community as possible. She illegally distributed them, along with syringes, from her house for a time until Roebuck contacted her with a job offer in 2020. Although she had to stop distributing needles, Rosser is getting Narcan into the hands of far more people today.

Rosser relives her trauma often when educating people, and I ask her how she can maintain that level of emotional vulnerability. She admits it's easy to get burned out. "What keeps me going," she says, "are the people that I meet who reach out to me to say, 'I ended up using this Narcan,' or, 'My friend is alive today because we distributed Narcan to them.'" It can't make up for the loved ones she's lost, but saving others gives Rosser a powerful incentive to stay active in the fight. In 2023, Thrive for Change trained over 4,700 people and distributed twenty-two thousand Narcan kits. These efforts are literally saving lives. The organization confirmed that their kits were responsible for forty-three cases of overdose reversal over the course of the year.

The war on drugs began the same summer that Russell Means and activists from the Cleveland American Indian Center crashed the super sesquicentennial in 1971. Predicated on the idea that severe punishment would curtail drug use, the war on drugs vilified users and created a system of mass incarceration. Although the US accounts for less than 5 percent of the world's population, the country is responsible for nearly 25 percent of all incarcerated people worldwide.[7] During the decade that followed the declaration of war, wages stagnated and became completely decoupled from worker productivity. The city of Cleveland would default on its debt, and the economic security that had made the dismantling of the environment tolerable had evaporated. The old social contract was in shambles. What do the great fortunes accumulated by Charles Brush or John D. Rockefeller mean for a city with the highest child poverty rate in the country? An astonishing 45.5 percent of children in Cleveland live in poverty, more than double the national average.[8] Although Kropotkin may be correct about mutual aid in nature, our economy is organized as a winner-take-all system.

Many have responded to drug abuse with the same attitude they hold toward poverty. "People still believe it's a moral failing," Rosser tells me. "I hear it all the time, even from people who are in recovery themselves. Some of us have internalized years of drug war rhetoric." The most venomous attitudes arise from deeply conservative law enforcement officers like Butler County Sheriff, Richard K. Jones. Since he was first elected to the post in 2004, he has refused to supply his officers with Narcan or other naloxone products. In an interview with the *Washington Post* in 2017, he declared, "I'm not the one that decides if people live or die. They decide that when they stick that needle in their arm." Despite his willingness to let his own community members die, Jones won reelection in 2020, and his official state bio declares his "dedication and commitment to the safety of everyone in Butler County."[9]

This rhetoric of purity and corruption infuses American culture and is applied to sexuality, addiction, and the environment. Protect what is pure and cut loose what is not before it corrupts the little good left, the thinking seems to go. As an environmental historian, many of my activist friends have given in to a sense of despair that the struggle against habitat loss and climate change is hopeless. Every time we cross yet another point of no return for the planet, some activists get the sense that we are attempting to resuscitate a corpse. Some have even become "accelerationists," believing that because collapse is inevitable, the sooner society collapses, the better.

I have felt the pull toward that grim line of thinking myself.

But it too is a kind of disease of despair. The principle of harm reduction works for the planet just as surely as it works for ourselves. By rehabilitating our land and water, Clevelanders like Brown and Olschansky are forging a new duty of care beyond the human community to the larger world. By giving a voice to the land, McDonald is knitting vital habitats back together so wildlife has a chance to return and thrive in the region. By delivering life-saving resources to Ohio's most vulnerable populations, Rosser is literally saving lives and providing a powerful model for community building. These individuals are engaged in cultural experiments that could reconnect society to environments and communities neglected for generations. I like to think that Lewis Mumford would have recognized his hope for civic and environmental reengagement in the work undertaken by the current generation of Clevelanders.

* * *

Walking the trail on the Cleveland Lakefront Preserve as a cool spring breeze tickles the sandbar willow leaves, I was reminded of what Rosser said about her own path to healing. Our past mistakes do not need to define us. We can learn from them, and they can inform how we build a better world for the next generation. It is easy to give up. When stripped of the back-slapping mythology, American history is not a story that inspires trust in our institutions. Our culture readily provides us with scripts for anger, victim-blaming, and bitterness. We seek the fairy tale because we aren't very good at redemption arcs. Once a landscape or a person has fallen in the American mind, it is gone for good. Just as Narcan has brought people back from the brink of death, our technology can also help us bring back toxic landscapes. Our desire for easy technological fixes has also prevented us from structural change. A dose of Narcan and Mayor Stokes's swimming pool in the lake are both stopgaps. We need to acknowledge the roots of our problems. That journey begins with an understanding of how we got here.

In the meantime, we can reduce as much harm as possible. The warblers darting through the trees on the old Dike 14 don't care that the habitat bloomed from a wasteland. The bald eagles nesting on the Cuyahoga don't mind that beneath the soil below are great mounds of slag from Cleveland's steel mills. Like the Indigenous cultures that occupied this land long before Cleveland became a city, we can find wisdom in nature and apply it to our own communities. For my part, I've learned this much: Everyone and every place deserves a second chance.

NOTES

Prologue

[1] *New York Times*, Retro Report. "Blackout: The Power Outage That Left 50 Million Without Electricity." YouTube video, 2:44.

[2] "Memories of the 2003 Summer Blackout," *19 News*, August 14, 2013, https://www.cleveland19.com/story/23139422/memories-of-the-2003-summer-blackout/.

[3] Jo Ellen Corrigan, "Blackout 2003 Anniversary: Stories from the Dark," Cleveland.com, August 12, 2013, https://www.cleveland.com/metro/2013/08/blackout_2003_anniversary_stor.html.

[4] "Final Report on the August 14, 2003, Blackout in the United States and Canada: Causes and Recommendations," US-Canada Power System Outage Task Force, Washington, DC, April 2004.

[5] Lewis Mumford, *The City in History: Its Origins, Its Transformations, and Its Prospects* (New York: Harcourt, Brace & World: 1961), 4.

Chapter 1: Here Be Dragons

[1] Russell Means with Marvin J. Wolf, *Where White Men Fear to Tread: The Autobiography of Russell Means* (Brooklyn: Antenna Books, 2015), 225.

[2] Ibid., 206.

[3] Ibid., 253.

[4] Alan Buis, "Milankovitch (Orbital) Cycles and Their Role in Earth's Climate," Jet Propulsion Laboratory, NASA, January 7, 2023, https://climate.nasa.gov/news/2948/milankovitch-orbital-cycles-and-their-role-in-earths-climate/.

[5] Peter U. Clark, et al., "The Last Glacial Maximum," *Science* 325 (2009): 710–714.

[6] Ian Joughin, "Greenland Rumbles Louder as Glaciers Accelerate," *Science* 311 (2006): 1719–1720.

[7] Michael C. Hansen, "The Ice Age in Ohio," Educational Leaflet No. 7, ODNR, Division of Geological Survey (2020).

[8] William J. Broad, "How the Ice Age Shaped New York," *New York Times*, June 5, 2018.

9 Jessica E. Tierney, et al., "Glacial Cooling and Climate Sensitivity Revisited," *Nature* 584 (2020): 569–573.

10 Bob King, "Vega, the Star at the Center of Everything," *Sky & Telescope*, September 7, 2022, https://skyandtelescope.org/astronomy-news/vega-the-star-at-the-center-of-everything/.

11 Jon D. Miller, et al., "Public Acceptance of Evolution in the United States, 1985–2020," *Public Understanding of Science* 31, no. 2 (2021).

12 Thomas Jefferson, "A Memoir on the Discovery of Certain Bones of a Quadruped of the Clawed Kind in the Western Parts of Virginia," *Transactions of the American Philosophical Society* 4 (1799).

13 Charles Whittlesey, *Early History of Cleveland, Ohio* (Cleveland: Fairbanks, Benedict & Co., Printers, 1867), 18–19.

14 Brian G. Redmond, et al., "New Evidence for Late Pleistocene Human Exploitation of Jefferson's Ground Sloth (*Megalonyx jeffersonii*) from Northern Ohio, USA," *World Archaeology* 44, no. 1 (2012).

15 Jeff St. Clair, "Exploradio: Dining on Ground Sloth in Ohio," WKSU radio, March 12, 2012. Web, April 7, 2014.

16 Jefferson, 252.

17 Robert E. Bieder, *Science Encounters the Indian, 1820–1880: The Early Years of American Ethnology* (Norman: University of Oklahoma Press, 1986), 67.

18 Vine Deloria, Jr., *Red Earth, White Lies: Native Americans and the Myth of Scientific Fact* (New York: Scribner, 1995).

19 Kevin F. Kern and Gregory S. Wilson, *Ohio: A History of the Buckeye State* (Hoboken: Wiley-Blackwell, 2014), 23.

20 The team has published thirteen articles based on these findings and maintained a website at https://www.noblespondpaleo.info/index.html to keep the public informed as they process the tens of thousands of artifacts from the site.

21 Mark F. Seeman, "Intercluster Lithic Patterning at Nobles Pond: A Case for 'Disembedded' Procurement among Early Paleoindian Societies," *American Antiquity* 59, no. 2 (April 1994): 283.

22 Mark F. Seeman, et al., "Evaluating Protein Residues on Gainey Phase Paleoindian Stone Tools," *Journal of Archaeological Science* 35 (2008): 2742–2750.

23 Bradley T. Lepper, "Forensic Mystery: The Burning Tree Mastodon," *Timeline* 23, no. 4 (2006): 22.

[24] Joshua H. Miller, et al., "Male Mastodon Landscape Use Changed with Maturation (Late Pleistocene, North America)," *PNAS* 119, no. 25 (June 13, 2022).

[25] Peter Brannen, "A Mystery That Took 13,200 Years to Crack," *Atlantic*, June 22, 2022.

[26] Laura Arenschield, "Bacteria from Burning Tree Mastodon Survived 13,000 Years," *Columbus Dispatch*, April 28, 2016, https://www.dispatch.com/story/news/technology/2016/04/28/bacteria-from-burning-tree-mastodon/23657700007/.

[27] Hilary H. Birks, et al., "Evidence for the Diet and Habitat of Two Late Pleistocene Mastodons from the Midwest, USA," *Quaternary Research* 91, no. 2 (2018).

[28] Lepper, 29.

[29] Gary Van Sickle, "This Ohio Layout Proves to Be Dinosaur of a Course," *Sports Illustrated*, July 19, 2022, https://www.si.com/golf/travel/this-ohio-layout-proves-to-be-dinosaur-of-a-course.

[30] Dr. Nigel Brush, "The Martins Creek Mastodon: An Ice Age Story," *Holmes County Traveler* 9, no. 4 (1997).

[31] Dr. Nigel Brush, "The Martins Creek Mastodon: An Ice Age Story (Part II)," *Holmes County Traveler*, 10, no. 1 (1998).

[32] Nigel Brush and Forrest Smith, "The Martins Creek Mastodon: A Paleoindian Butchery Site in Holmes County, Ohio," *Current Research in the Pleistocene* 11 (1994).

[33] Rémy Crassard, et al., "The Use of Desert Kites as Hunting Mega-Traps: Functional Evidence and Potential Impacts on Socioeconomic and Ecological Spheres," *Journal of World Prehistory* 35 (2022).

[34] M. T. Boulanger, et al., "Neutron Activation Analysis of 12,900-Year-Old Stone Artifacts Confirms 450–510+ km Clovis Tool-Stone Acquisition at Paleo Crossing (33ME274), Northeast Ohio, USA." *Journal of Archaeological Science* 53 (2015).

[35] Connie Barlow, *The Ghosts of Evolution: Nonsensical Fruit, Missing Partners, and Other Ecological Anachronisms* (New York: Basic Books, 2000).

[36] Deloria, 67–92.

[37] Dan Flores, *Wild New World: The Epic Story of Animals & People in America* (New York: W. W. Norton & Company, 2022): 64.

[38] Stephen R. Kellert and Edward O. Wilson, eds., *The Biophilia Hypothesis* (Washington: Island Press, 1993).

[39] Morten Rasmussen, et al., "The Genome of a Late Pleistocene Human from a Clovis Burial Site in Western Montana," *Nature* 506 (February 13, 2014).

[40] Vladimir V. Pitulko, et al., "Early Human Presence in the Arctic: Evidence from 45,000-Year-Old Mammoth Remains," *Science* 351, no. 6270 (2016).

[41] Yi-Fu Tuan, *Space and Place: The Perspective of Experience* (Minneapolis: University of Minnesota Press, 1977), 4–6.

[42] Deloria, 67–92.

[43] John Neihardt, *Black Elk Speaks* (Lincoln: University of Nebraska Press, 1961), 4.

Chapter 2: Ground Rules

[1] So long as you don't dig in the ground to extract a plant or roots.

[2] Jim McCormac, "Zombie Fungus a Most Effective Killer," *Columbus Dispatch*, August 30, 2014, https://www.dispatch.com/story/lifestyle/home-garden/how-to/2014/08/30/zombie-fungus-most-effective-killer/23907618007/.

[3] Makiko Orito, et al., "Activities Concentration of Radiocesium in Wild Mushroom Collected in Ukraine 30 Years after the Chernobyl Power Plant Accident," *PeerJ* 6, no. 4222 (January 5, 2018).

[4] Roderick Nash, *Wilderness and the American Mind*, 3rd ed. (New Haven: Yale University Press, 1982), 341.

[5] Sarah Maslin Nir, "White Woman is Fired after Calling Police on Black Man in Central Park," *New York Times*, May 26, 2020, https://www.nytimes.com/2020/05/26/nyregion/amy-cooper-dog-central-park.html.

[6] Manoush Zomorodi, "Meet Alexis Nikole Nelson, The Wildly Popular 'Black Forager,'" National Public Radio, September 9, 2021, https://www.npr.org/sections/codeswitch/2021/09/09/173838801/meet-alexis-nikole-nelson-the-wildly-popular-black-forager.

[7] Margharita Mussi, et al., "A Surge in Obsidian Exploitation More Than 1.2 Million Years Ago at Simbiro III (Melka Kunture, Upper Awash, Ethiopia)," *Nature Ecology & Evolution*, January 19, 2023.

[8] Brian G. Redmond and Brian L. Scanlan, "Archaeological Investigations at the Burrell Orchard Site (33Ln15): 2008 Season," Archaeological Research Report, no. 156 (2009), Cleveland Museum of Natural History.

[9] Brian G. Redmond, "Late Archaic Ritualism in Domestic Contexts: Clay-Floored Shrines at the Burrell Orchard Site, Ohio," *American Antiquity* 82, no. 4 (2017), 698.

[10] Ella Deloria, *Dakota Texts* (New York: American Ethnological Society, 1932).

[11] Joseph Campbell, *Historical Atlas of World Mythology: Volume I; The Way of the Animal Powers, Part 2: Mythologies of the Great Hunt* (New York: Harper & Row, 1988), 234.

[12] Johnny Marks, ed., et al., *Shanyaak'utlaax̱* (Juneau: Sealaska Heritage Institute, 2017).

[13] Robert M. Goslin, "Cultivated and Wild Food from Aboriginal Sites in Ohio," *Ohio Archeologist* 2, no. 2 (1952): 23.

[14] T. Douglas Price, "Late Archaic Subsistence in the Midwestern United States," *Journal of Human Evolution* 14 (1985): 457.

[15] Ronald Wright, *A Short History of Progress* (Cambridge: De Capo Press, 2004), 8.

[16] Jared Diamond, "The Worst Mistake in the History of the Human Race," *Discover*, May 1987.

[17] Robert J. Braidwood, *Prehistoric Men*, 3rd ed., Chicago Natural History Museum Popular Series, Anthropology, Number 37 (1957).

[18] Eun Jin Woo and Paul Sciulli, "Degenerative Joint Disease and Social Status in the Terminal Late Archaic Period (1,000–500 BC) of Ohio," *International Journal of Osteoarchaeology* 23, no. 5 (2013).

[19] Kamil E. Barbour, et al., "Vital Signs: Prevalence of Doctor-Diagnosed Arthritis and Arthritis-Attributable Activity Limitation—United States, 2013–2015," *MMWR Morb Mortal Wkly Rep.*, 66, no. 9 (2017).

[20] John O'Connor, "Carpal Tunnel," *Classic Labor Songs from Smithsonian Folkways* (2006).

[21] Dan Flores, *Wild New World: The Epic Story of Animals & People in America* (New York: W. W. Norton & Company, 2022), 90–91.

[22] Judith A. Habicht-Mauche, "The Shifting Role of Women and Women's Labor on the Protohistoric Southern Plains," in *Gender and Hide Production*, eds. Lisa Frink and Kathryn Weedman (Lanham: Altamira Press, 2006), 37.

[23] William Bartram, *Travels* (Dublin: J. Moore, W. Jones, R. McAllister, and J. Rice, 1793), 38.

[24] Paul A. Delcourt, et. al., "Prehistoric Human Use of Fire, the Eastern Agricultural Complex, and Appalachian Oak-Chestnut Forests: Paleoecology of Cliff Palace Pond, Kentucky," *American Antiquity* 63, no. 2 (1998).

[25] Michelle D. Anderson, "Juniperus virginiana," *Fire Effects Information System*, US Department of Agriculture, Forest Service (2003), https://www.fs.usda.gov/database/feis/plants/tree/junvir/all.html.

[26] Charles C. Mann, *1491: New Revelations of the Americas before Columbus* (New York: Vintage Books, 2011), 302.

[27] Joel Greenberg, *A Feathered River across the Sky: The Passenger Pigeon's Flight to Extinction* (New York: Bloomsbury, 2014).

[28] Nancy E. Tatarek and Paul Sciulli, "Comparison of Population Structure in Ohio's Late Archaic and Late Prehistoric Periods," *American Journal of Physical Anthropology* 112 (2000).

[29] Richard Asa Yarnell, "Aboriginal Relationships between Culture and Plant Life in the Upper Great Lakes Region," *Anthropological Papers*, no. 23, Museum of Anthropology, University of Michigan (1964): 20.

[30] A. Dini, et al., "A Compositional Study of Chenopodium Quinoa Seeds," *Die Nahrung / Food* 36, no. 4 (1992).

[31] Yarnell, 103.

[32] David W. Zeanah, "Foraging Models, Niche Construction, and the Eastern Agricultural Complex," *American Antiquity* 82, no. 1 (2017).

[33] Kevin C. Nolan, et al., "A Late Woodland Red Ochre Burial Cache from Madison County, Ohio," *North American Archaeologist* 36, no. 3 (2015).

[34] Louise Phelps Kellogg, "Copper Mining in the Early Northwest," *Wisconsin Magazine of History* 8, no. 2 (1924).

[35] S. H. Blatt, et al., "Dirty Teeth and Ancient Trade: Evidence of Cotton Fibres in Human Dental Calculus from Late Woodland, Ohio," *International Journal of Osteoarchaeology* 21 (2011).

[36] Jerome Kimberlin and John T. Wasson, "Comparison of Iron Meteoritic Material from Ohio and Illinois Hopewellian Burial Mounds," *American Antiquity* 41, no. 4 (1976).

[37] "Superfund Site Profile: Mound Plant (USDOE) Miamisburg, OH," EPA website, https://cumulis.epa.gov/supercpad/SiteProfiles/index.cfm?fuseaction=second.cleanup&id=0504935.

[38] Kevin F. Kern and Gregory S. Wilson, *Ohio: A History of the Buckeye State* (Hoboken: Wiley-Blackwell, 2014), 32.

[39] James C. Scott, *Against the Grain: A Deep History of the Earliest States* (New Haven: Yale University Press, 2017).

[40] Kern and Wilson, 42.

[41] Bridget Coyne and Michael Dodrill, "Archaeological Excavations at the Fort Hill Earthwork Complex," *Undergraduate Research Posters* (2018).

[42] J. M. Heilman, et al., "Exploring for Ancient Culture: Dayton's Prehistoric Indian Village," *Museum Anthropology* 14, no. 1 (1990).

[43] Kern and Wilson, 43.

[44] Mann, 295–304.

[45] Andrew R. Thompson, et al., "New Dental and Isotope Evidence of Biological Distance and Place of Origin for Mass Burial Groups at Cahokia's Mound 72," *American Journal of Physical Anthropology* 158, no. 2 (2015).

[46] Biloine Whiting Young and Melvin Fowler, *Cahokia: The Great Native American Metropolis* (Chicago: The University of Illinois Press, 2000), 148.

[47] David P. Pompeani, et al., "Severe Little Ice Age Drought in the Midcontinental United States during the Mississippian Abandonment of Cahokia," *Scientific Reports* 11 (2021).

[48] Joseph Campbell, *Historical Atlas of World Mythology, Volume II; The Way of the Seeded Earth, Part 2: The Mythologies of the Primitive Planters: The North Americans* (New York: Harper & Row, 1989), 206.

[49] UNESCO, Hopewell Ceremonial Earthworks, https://whc.unesco.org/en/list/1689/.

Chapter 3: Apocalypse

[1] "Building upon the 2020 Growth in Visitation," Cleveland Metroparks (April 2021), https://www.clevelandmetroparks.com/getmedia/a725610d-aa00-4df1-9cf3-4ebdcd30a3e9/04-Marketing-20210415-Board-Mtg-Update.pdf.ashx

[2] Meg Shaw, "Cleveland Metroparks Ravaged by COVID-19 Impact, Seeks Donations for Trail Improvement," *News5Cleveland*, July 23, 2020, https://www.news5cleveland.com/news/local-news/oh-cuyahoga/cleveland-metroparks-ravaged-by-covid-19-impact-seeks-donations-for-trail-improvement.

[3] Dyani Lewis, "COVID-19 Rarely Spreads through Surfaces. So Why Are We Still Deep Cleaning?" *Nature* 590 (January 29, 2021).

⁴ Zoe M. Volenec, et al., "Public Parks and the Pandemic: How Park Usage Has Been Affected by COVID-19 Policies," *PLoS ONE* 16, no. 5 (2021).

⁵ Jennifer Valentino-DeVries, Denise Lu, and Gabriel J. X. Dance, "Location Data Says It All: Staying at Home during Coronavirus Is a Luxury," *New York Times*, April 3, 2020, https://www.nytimes.com/interactive/2020/04/03/us/coronavirus-stay-home-rich-poor.html.

⁶ Meagan C. Fitzpatrick et al., "Two Years of US COVID-19 Vaccines Have Prevented Millions of Hospitalizations and Deaths," *Commonwealth Fund*, December 13, 2022.

⁷ Joshua L. Laughner, et al., "Societal Shifts Due to COVID-19 Reveal Large-Scale Complexities and Feedbacks between Atmospheric Chemistry and Climate Change," *PNAS* 118, no. 46 (2021).

⁸ "2022 Nationwide COVID-19 Infection- and Vaccination-Induced Antibody Seroprevalence (Blood Donations)." Centers for Disease Control and Prevention. COVID Data Tracker. Atlanta, GA: U.S. Department of Health and Human Services, CDC; November 9, 2023, https://covid.cdc.gov/covid-data-tracker.

⁹ Walter Scheidel, *The Great Leveler: Violence and the History of Inequality from the Stone Age to the 21st Century* (Princeton: Princeton University Press, 2017), 297–313.

¹⁰ David Quammen, *Spillover: Animal Infections and the Next Human Pandemic* (New York: W. W. Norton & Company, 2012), 383–489.

¹¹ Alfred W. Crosby, *Ecological Imperialism: The Biological Expansion of Europe, 900–1900* (New York: Cambridge University Press, 1994), 201.

¹² F. Fenner, et al., *Smallpox and its Eradication* (Geneva: World Health Organization, 1988), 2–50.

¹³ Philippe Biagini, et al., "Variola Virus in a 300-Year-Old Siberian Mummy," *New England Journal of Medicine* 367, no. 21 (2012).

¹⁴ D. A. Henderson, *Smallpox: The Death of a Disease* (Amherst: Prometheus Books, 2009).

¹⁵ Mann, 74–105.

¹⁶ Lawrence A. Clayton, ed., et al., *The De Soto Chronicles: The Expedition of Hernando de Soto to North America in 1539–1543*, vol. I (Tuscaloosa: University of Alabama Press, 1993), 82–83.

¹⁷ Alfred W. Crosby, "Virgin Soil Epidemics as a Factor in the Aboriginal Depopulation in America," *William and Mary Quarterly*, Third Series 33, no. 2 (1976): 296.

[18] Reuben Gold Thwaites, *The Jesuit Relations and Allied Documents*, Vol. XIX (Cleveland: Burrows Brothers Company, 1898), 89.

[19] Ibid., 92–93.

[20] Thomas R. Dale, ed., *Native Peoples, and the Natural Landscape* (Washington, DC: Island Press, 2002).

[21] Alfred W. Pollard, ed., *Chaucer's Canterbury Tales* (London: MacMillan and Co., 1907), 14.

[22] Stephen L. Carter, "Abraham Lincoln's Top Hat: The Inside Story," *Smithsonian Magazine*, November 2013, https://www.smithsonianmag.com/history/abraham-lincolns-top-hat-the-inside-story-3764960/.

[23] Timothy Brook, *Vermeer's Hat: The Seventeenth Century and the Dawn of the Global World* (New York: Bloomsbury Press, 2008): 41–45.

[24] Reuben Gold Thwaites, *The Jesuit Relations and Allied Documents*, Vol. IV (Cleveland: Burrows Brothers Company, 1897), 255.

[25] Reuben Gold Thwaites, *The Jesuit Relations and Allied Documents*, Vol. VIII (Cleveland: Burrows Brothers Company, 1897), 2.

[26] Reuben Gold Thwaites, *The Jesuit Relations and Allied Documents*, Vol. VI (Cleveland: Burrows Brothers Company, 1897), 297–299.

[27] Richard White, *The Middle Ground: Indians, Empires, and Republics in the Great Lakes Region, 1650–1815* (Cambridge: Cambridge University Press, 2011), 97–141.

[28] Bruce G. Trigger, *The Children of Aataentsic: A History of the Huron People to 1660* (Kingston: McGill-Queen's University Press, 1987), 627.

[29] Reuben Gold Thwaites, *The Jesuit Relations and Allied Documents*, Vol. XLII (Cleveland: Burrows Brothers Company, 1899), 111–113.

[30] White, 143.

[31] Alexander Koch, et al., "Earth System Impacts of the European Arrival and Great Dying in the Americas after 1492," *Quaternary Science Reviews* 207 (2019).

[32] "Sieur de Saguin" and "Chagrin River," *Encyclopedia of Cleveland History*, https://case.edu/ech/.

[33] Gregory Evans Dowd, *A Spirited Resistance: The North American Indian Struggle for Unity, 1745–1815* (Baltimore: Johns Hopkins University Press, 1993), 34.

[34] R. David Edmunds, *The Shawnee Prophet* (Lincoln: University of Nebraska Press, 1983), 33.

[35] Jeffrey Amherst to William Johnson, July 9, 1763.

[36] John W. Harpster, ed., *Pen Pictures of Early Western Pennsylvania* (Pittsburgh: University of Pittsburgh Press, 1938), 103–104.

[37] Julian P. Boyd, *The Papers of Thomas Jefferson*, vol. 6 (Princeton: Princeton University Press, 1952), 613–616.

[38] R. Douglas Hurt, *The Ohio Frontier: Crucible of the Old Northwest, 1720–1830* (Bloomington: Indiana University Press, 1996), 114–119.

[39] Charles Whittlesey, *Early History of Cleveland, Ohio* (Cleveland: Fairbanks, Benedict & Co., Printers, 1867), 449.

[40] Dudley P. Allen, "Pioneer Medicine on the Western Reserve—V," *Magazine of Western History*, vol. III (1885): 286.

[41] Mark Alan Wright, "Joseph Smith and Native American Artifacts" in *Approaching Antiquity: Joseph Smith and the Ancient World*, ed. Lincoln H. Blumell, et al. (Salt Lake City: RSC/Deseret Book Company, 2015); and Robert V. Remini, *Joseph Smith: A Penguin Life* (New York: Viking Penguin, 2002), 33.

[42] Remini, 110.

[43] Whittlesey, 33.

[44] Ash Ngu and Andrea Suozzo, "Does Your Local Museum or University Still Have Native American Remains?" *ProPublica*, January 11, 2023, https://projects.propublica.org/repatriation-nagpra-database/

[45] Nancy Kelsey, "Native Human Remains Should Be Returned to Tribes, Not Held in Museums," *Cleveland.com*, February 17, 2023, https://www.cleveland.com/opinion/2023/02/native-human-remains-should-be-returned-to-tribes-not-held-in-museums-nancy-kelsey.html.

[46] Kavitha Cardoza and Clare Marie Schneider, "The Importance Of Mourning Losses (Even When They Seem Small)," NPR, June 14, 2021, https://www.npr.org/2021/06/02/1002446604/the-importance-of-mourning-losses-even-when-they-seem-small.

Chapter 4: The War on Nature

[1] D. Armson, et al., "The Effect of Street Trees and Amenity Grass on Urban Surface Water Runoff in Manchester, UK," *Urban Forestry & Urban Greening* 12, no. 3 (2013).

[2] *Cleveland Leader*, February 5, 1883, 1, 6.

[3] Henry David Thoreau, *The Maine Woods* (Princeton: Princeton University Press, 1972), 219.

4 Roxanne Dunbar-Ortiz, *Not "A Nation of Immigrants": Settler Colonialism, White Supremacy, and a History of Erasure and Exclusion* (Boston: Beacon Press, 2021).

5 Kathryn M. Flinn, et al., "From Forest to City: Plant Community Change in Northeast Ohio from 1800 to 2014," *Journal of Vegetation Science* 29, no. 2 (2018).

6 Benjamin Franklin, "A Plan for Settling Two Western Colonies," *The Papers of Benjamin Franklin*, vol. 5, ed. Leonard Labaree et al. (New Haven: Yale University Press, 1962), 457.

7 Robert A. Wheeler, ed., *Visions of the Western Reserve* (Columbus: The Ohio State University Press, 2000), 23–35.

8 Charles Whittlesey, *Early History of Cleveland, Ohio* (Cleveland: Fairbanks, Benedict & Co., Printers, 1867), 241.

9 William Ganson Rose, *Cleveland: The Making of a City* (Cleveland: The World Publishing Company, 1950), 34.

10 Whittlesey, 267.

11 Ibid., 400.

12 Ibid., 386.

13 Ibid., 400.

14 Ibid., 398.

15 W. H. Perrin, J. H. Battle, and W. A. Goodspeed, *History of Medina County and Ohio* (Chicago: Baskin & Battey, 1881), 415.

16 Dan Flores, *Wild New World: The Epic Story of Animals & People in America* (New York: W. W. Norton & Company, 2022), 82–118.

17 Ibid., 298.

18 William Ganson Rose, *Cleveland: The Making of a City* (Cleveland: The World Publishing Company, 1950), 98.

19 *Cleveland Herald*, June 15, 1833, 3.

20 Mark J. Price, "Local History: Great Hinckley Hunt of 1818 Was a Slaughter Like No Other," *Akron Beacon Journal*, December 23, 2013.

21 Perrin, 608–610.

22 Ibid.

23 Ibid.

24 Ibid., 611.

25 Rose, 85.

26 Perrin, 540.

27 *Cleveland Herald*, November 11, 1830, 3.

[28] "McIlrath Tavern," *Encyclopedia of Cleveland History*; Rose, 51.

[29] Vernon C. Applegate and Harry D. Van Meter, "A Brief History of Commercial Fishing in Lake Erie," United State Department of the Interior, US Fish and Wildlife Service, Fishery Leaflet 630 (April 1970): 9.

[30] *Cleveland Leader*, November 9, 1858, 1.

[31] *Cleveland Herald*, February 12, 1839, 2.

[32] *Cleveland Herald*, November 21, 1839, 3.

[33] *Cleveland Herald*, January 17, 1840, 2.

[34] *Cleveland Herald*, January 6, 1847, 2.

[35] Perrin, 542.

[36] Ibid., 560, 662.

[37] Joel Greenberg, *A Feathered River across the Sky: The Passenger Pigeon's Flight to Extinction* (New York: Bloomsbury, 2014), 70–72.

[38] *Cleveland Leader*, October 27, 1862, 3; *Cleveland Leader*, November 8, 1862, 3.

[39] Rose, 403.

[40] A. W. Schorger, *The Passenger Pigeon: It's Natural History and Extinction* (Madison: University of Wisconsin Press, 1955), 40, 44.

[41] Ibid., 45–46, 51.

[42] Ibid., 194.

[43] Flores, 268.

[44] *Cleveland Leader*, December 28, 1869, 4.

[45] *History of Sandusky County, Ohio* (Cleveland: H. Z. Williams & Bro., 1882), 805.

[46] Dan Flores and Sara Dant, "When American Wildlife Was for Sale," *PBS*, https://www.pbs.org/kenburns/the-american-buffalo/when-american-wildlife-was-for-sale

[47] Daniel Yergin, *The Prize: The Epic Quest for Oil, Money, and Power* (New York: Touchstone, 1992), 20.

[48] Jonathan Wlasiuk, *Refining Nature: Standard Oil and the Limits of Efficiency* (Pittsburgh: University of Pittsburgh Press, 2017), 17–18.

[49] C. F. Brush. 1877. Improvement in Magneto-Electric Machines. US Patent 189,997, filed November 11, 1876, and issued April 24, 1877.

[50] Ernest Freeberg, *The Age of Edison: Electric Light and the Invention of Modern America* (New York: The Penguin Press, 2013), 21.

[51] *A History of Cleveland and Its Environs: The Heart of New Connecticut*, vol. 3 (Chicago: The Lewis Publishing Company, 1918), 259.

52 *Cleveland Leader*, July 23, 1881, 9.

53 Freeberg, 24.

54 Jane Brox, *Brilliant: The Evolution of Artificial Light* (New York: Mariner Books, 2011), 108.

55 Flinn, "From Forest to City"; Eric McConnell, "Ohio's Forest Economy," *Ohioline*, The Ohio State University (October 5, 2012); D. K. Musgrave and D. M. Holloran, *Soil Survey of Cuyahoga County, Ohio* (1980) US Department of Agriculture, Soil Conservation Service, Government Printing Office, Washington, DC, 2.

56 Wlasiuk, 79–80.

57 Ibid., 64.

58 *Cleveland Herald*, January 18, 1834, 2.

59 James Howard Kunstler, *The Geography of Nowhere: The Rise and Decline of America's Man-Made Landscape* (New York: Touchstone, 1993), 15.

60 Glenn Albrecht, et al., "Solastalgia: The Distress Caused by Environmental Change," *Australian Psychiatry* 15 (2007).

61 Sam Alard, "Native Cleveland: Robert Roche and the Origins of American Indian Activism in Cleveland," *Cleveland Scene*, October 1, 2014.

62 Russell Means with Marvin J. Wolf, *Where White Men Fear to Tread: The Autobiography of Russell Means* (Brooklyn: Antenna Books, 2015), 192.

63 Ibid., 250.

64 Ibid., 192–193.

65 "Hostile Indians Greet Cleveland Ad Man Re-Enacting Landing of City's Founder," *Liberation News Service*, #363 (July 31, 1971): 1.

66 Franklin, 457.

Chapter 5: The Land

1 "Indians Look for Answer to Bird Trouble," *Associated Press*, June 12, 2009.

2 Ernest Freeberg, *The Age of Edison: Electric Light and the Invention of Modern America* (New York: Penguin Press, 2013), 117.

3 Robert Ridgway, "Report on the Department of Birds, US National Museum, 1888," US National Museum (1888): 11.

4 Calista McRae, "The Bird at the Window," *Boston Review*, January 3, 2020.

[5] Sparky Stensaas, "Lake Superior Journal: Perk's Floating Forest," *Lake Superior Magazine*, January 18, 2011.

[6] Paul Bogard, *The End of Night: Searching for Natural Darkness in an Age of Artificial Light* (New York: Little, Brown and Company, 2013), 22.

[7] J. Mark Souther, "Warner and Swasey Observatory," *Cleveland Historical*, accessed May 9, 2023, https://clevelandhistorical.org/items/show/551.

[8] Barbara Wherley. Interview by Mark Souther. *Cleveland Regional Oral History Collection*. Interview 911086. October 6, 2012, https://engaged-scholarship.csuohio.edu/crohc000/668.

[9] John E. Bortle, "Gauging Light Pollution: The Bortle Dark-Sky Scale," *Sky & Telescope* (February 2001).

[10] P. Cinzano, et al., "The First World Atlas of the Artificial Night Sky Brightness," *Monthly Notices of the Royal Astronomical Society* 328, no. 3 (December 2001).

[11] Catherine Rich and Travis Longcore, eds., *Ecological Consequences of Artificial Night Lighting* (Washington, DC, Island Press, 2006), 19–37.

[12] R. T. Dauchy, et al., "Light Contamination during the Dark Phase in 'Photoperiodically Controlled' Animal Rooms: Effect on Tumor Growth and Metabolism in Rats," *Laboratory Animal Science* 47 (1997).

[13] Barbara Dickerman and Jianghong Liu, "Does Current Scientific Evidence Support a Link between Light at Night and Breast Cancer among Female Night-Shift Nurses?" *Workplace Health & Safety* 60, no. 2 (June 1, 2012).

[14] Joshua Sokol, "Saving the Night Sky," *Scientific American* 327, no. 4 (October 2022).

[15] Rich and Longcore, 43.

[16] John Carmody, et al., *Window Systems for High-Performance Buildings* (New York: W. W. Norton & Company, 2004).

[17] Loss, et al., "Bird–Building Collisions in the United States: Estimates of Annual Mortality and Species Vulnerability," *The Condor* 116, no. 1 (February 2014).

[18] Sophie Lewis, "Trump Claims Wind Energy "Kills All the Birds." Cats and Windows Are Actually Much More to Blame," *CBS News*, October 23, 2020.

[19] Kenneth V. Rosenberg, et al., "Decline of the North American Avifauna," *Science* 366, no. 6461 (September 19, 2019).

[20] "Stabilizing Slavic Village in Cleveland, Ohio," *PD&R Edge*, US Department of Housing and Urban Development (November 2015).

[21] Sara B. Pritchard, "The Trouble with Darkness: NASA's Suomi Satellite Images of Earth at Night," *Environmental History* 22, no. 2 (April 2017).

[22] US Congress, House, Natural Resources Subcommittee on Water, Oceans, and Wildlife, *Legislative Hearing on H.R. 2795: Wildlife Corridors Conservation Act of 2019; and H.R. 3742: Recovering America's Wildlife Act of 2019 (RAWA)*, 116th Congress, October 17, 2019.

[23] Tim S. Doherty, et al., "Invasive Predators and Global Biodiversity Loss," *PNAS* 113, no. 40 (October 4, 2016).

[24] Rachel E. Gross, "The Moral Cost of Cats," *Smithsonian Magazine*, September 20, 2016.

[25] Michael Burrows, "An Ethical and Scientific Position against LD 644 An Act to Include Cats in the Laws Governing Animal Trespass," *Maine Animal Coalition*, March 4, 2023.

[26] "Proposed Maine Law Regulating Outdoor Cats Met with Backlash," Fox News, February 27, 2023, https://www.foxnews.com/politics/proposed-maine-law-regulating-outdoor-cats-met-backlash.

[27] Chris Ronayne, "Cleveland Was the First City of Light," *Cleveland Magazine*, February 10, 2017.

[28] Alan Buis, "The Atmosphere: Getting a Handle on Carbon Dioxide," *NASA*, October 9, 2019, https://climate.nasa.gov/news/2915/the-atmosphere-getting-a-handle-on-carbon-dioxide/.

[29] Dan Egan, *The Death and Life of the Great Lakes* (New York: W. W. Norton & Company, 2017), 219.

[30] Jonathan Wlasiuk, "A Company Town on Common Waters: Standard Oil in the Calumet," *Environmental History* 19, no. 4 (October 2014): 697.

[31] *State v. Cleveland & Pittsburgh Railroad*, 94 Ohio St. 61 (1916).

[32] W. R. Hopkins, "Realizing on Our Lake Front," *The Clevelander* (November 1927): 22, 26.

[33] Daniel R. Kerr, *Derelict Paradise: Homelessness and Urban Development in Cleveland, Ohio* (Amherst: University of Massachusetts Press, 2011), 51–54.

[34] Ibid., 54.

[35] "Press Bldg. Dirt Goes to Airport," *Cleveland Press*, April 22, 1957, 7.

[36] "Plans to Speed New Incinerator Hit Snag," *Cleveland Press*, May 1, 1957, 37; "City Fires Four at Dump after Ashes Fly," *Cleveland Press*, July 16, 1957, 11.

[37] "Rain of Filth," *Cleveland Press*, May 1, 1957, 36.

[38] "Dump Fire Tied to Crash, City Sued for $95,000," *Cleveland Press*, July 13, 1957, 1; "Council to Get Plan to Bury City Rubbish," *Cleveland Press*, July 2, 1957, 34.

[39] "City Loses Appeal on Lakefront Dump," *Cleveland Press*, October 17, 1957, 1.

[40] Adam Rome, *The Bulldozer in the Countryside: Suburban Sprawl and the Rise of American Environmentalism* (New York: Cambridge University Press, 2001), 123.

[41] Ibid., 203.

[42] Bradley Campbell, "That Sinking Feeling," *Cleveland Scene*, May 14–20, 2008.

[43] Jorge Fernandez-Cornejo, et al., "Pesticide Use in US Agriculture: 21 Selected Crops, 1960–2008," *Economic Information Bulletin*, US Department of Agriculture, no. 124 (May 2014).

[44] "Can the Bald Eagle Still Soar after It Is Delisted?" *Science* 316 (June 22, 2007).

[45] R. W. Risebrough, et al., "Polychlorinated Biphenyls in the Global Ecosystem," *Nature* 220 (December 14, 1968).

[46] Rachel Carson, *Silent Spring* (Boston: Houghton Mifflin Company, 2002), 12–13.

[47] David Stradling and Richard Stradling, *Where the River Burned: Carl Stokes and the Struggle to Save Cleveland* (Ithaca: Cornell University Press, 2015), 122.

[48] Ted Steinberg, *Down to Earth: Nature's Role in American History* (New York: Oxford University Press, 2009), 165.

[49] "Recreational Water Quality Criteria," *Environmental Protection Agency* (2012): 5.

[50] Stradling, 114.

[51] Ibid., 6.

[52] Jeffery K. Stine, "Regulating Wetlands in the 1970s: US Army Corps of Engineers and the Environmental Organizations," *Journal of Forest History* 27, no. 2 (April 1983): 62.

[53] "Cleveland Harbor, Cuyahoga County, Ohio Confined Disposal Final Facility Project (Site INB—15 Year): Final Environmental Impact Statement and Appendices," US Army Engineer District, Buffalo (1994): EIS-9.

[54] "Cleveland Lakefront State Park: A Positive Statement of the Potential for Cleveland's Lakefront," Ohio Department of Natural Resources, Prepared by Behnke Dickson Tkach (1979): 137.

[55] "Land Management Plan: Cleveland Lakefront Nature Preserve," Davey Resource Group (September 2015): 4.

[56] Audubon Ohio. "The Conservation Value of Dike 14 as an Audubon Important Bird Area," January 29, 2003.

[57] "Billions More Milkweeds Needed to Restore Monarchs," USGS, April 27, 2017, https://www.usgs.gov/news/national-news-release/billions-more-milkweeds-needed-restore-monarchs.

[58] Brice X. Semmens, et al., "Quasi-Extinction Risk and Population Targets for the Eastern, Migratory Population of Monarch Butterflies (Danaus plexippus)," *Scientific Reports* 6 (March 21, 2016).

[59] Joey Santore, "Doing What You Love without Making It Your Job, with Joey Santore," The Joy of Challenge, YouTube Video, 51:37, https://youtu.be/vcArOD2Xjzg.

[60] Kristine Engemann, et al., "Residential Green Space in Childhood Is Associated with Lower Risk of Psychiatric Disorders from Adolescence into Adulthood," *PNAS* 116, no. 11 (February 25, 2019).

[61] Kirsten Weir, "Nurtured by Nature," *Monitor on Psychology* 51, no. 3 (April 1, 2020).

[62] Richard Louv, *Last Child in the Woods: Saving Our Children from Nature-Deficit Disorder* (Chapel Hill: Algonquin Books of Chapel Hill, 2005).

[63] Mathew P. White, et al., "Spending at Least 120 Minutes a Week in Nature Is Associated with Good Health and Wellbeing," *Scientific Reports* 9 (June 13, 2019).

[64] John C. Austin, et al., "Great Lakes: Healthy Waters, Strong Economy," Brookings Institution (September 2007): 6–8.

[65] Yinon M. Bar-On, et al., "The Biomass Distribution on Earth," *PNAS* 115, no. 25 (May 21, 2018).

Epilogue: Duty of Care

[1] Isaiah Berlin, *Four Essays on Liberty* (New York: Oxford University Press, 1970), xlv.

[2] Teo Armas, "GOP Ohio House Speaker Arrested in Connection to $60 Million Bribery Scheme," *Washington Post*, July 22, 2020.

[3] Peter Kropotkin, *Mutual Aid: A Factor of Evolution* (New York: McClure Phillips & Co., 1902).

[4] "NTSB Media Availability: Norfolk Southern Freight Train Derailment, East Palestine, Ohio," NTSBgov, YouTube video, 54:44, February 23, 2023, https://youtu.be/5NN6gjWT7dI.

[5] Emily Brignone, et al., "Trends in the Diagnosis of Diseases of Despair in the United States, 2009–2018: A Retrospective Cohort Study," *BMJ Open* 10 (2020).

[6] Randy Leite, et al., "Ohio Deaths of Despair, 2010–2019," Ohio University (2020), https://878570bd-c4fe-4dfe-8107-669a96dd214b.filesusr.com/ugd/89e8f1_c87f53c4fd3744b3a7445a0cba20b42d.pdf.

[7] Michelle Ye Hee Lee, "Does the United States Really Have 5 Percent of the World's Population and One Quarter of the World's Prisoners?" *Washington Post*, April 30, 2015.

[8] Emily Campbell, "More Reliable 2021 Census Estimates Have Erased Progress on Cleveland Children's Poverty," The Center for Community Solutions, September 19, 2022, https://www.communitysolutions.com/more-reliable-2021-census-estimates-have-erased-progress-on-cleveland-childrens-poverty/.

[9] Cleve R. Wootson Jr., "Why This Ohio Sheriff Refuses to Let His Deputies Carry Narcan to Reverse Overdoses," *Washington Post*, July 8, 2017, https://www.washingtonpost.com/news/to-your-health/wp/2017/07/08/an-ohio-countys-deputies-could-reverse-heroin-overdoses-the-sheriff-wont-let-them/.

ACKNOWLEDGMENTS

This book would not have been possible without the mentorship I received from several distinguished historians. John Grabowski offered me my first editorial job at the Encyclopedia of Cleveland History and has been a passionate advocate for the importance of this city in American history for decades. Dan Flores taught me the importance of place in storytelling and remains a champion for the practice of bioregionalism in his own writing. Ted Steinberg never let me forget that nature has always been a battleground for systems of power. As reference supervisor at the Cleveland History Center of the Western Reserve Historical Society, Ann Sindelar always knows exactly what documents I should be reading to tell my story.

Multiple scientists, activists, and community leaders shared their world with me and breathed new life into this project. As a wildlife rehabilitation specialist at the Lake Erie Nature and Science Center, Tim Jasinski put a broom in my hand and showed me the uncelebrated work necessary to nurse injured animals back to health. Michelle Leighty and all the passionate volunteers at Lights Out Cleveland welcomed me into the group, taught me the routes, and helped me identify bird species. Harvey Webster generously offered his time and provided invaluable context for the evolution of environmental education in Cleveland. Daniel Brown, Pete McDonald, Eddie Olschansky, Ashley Rosser, Brendon Samuels, and Jeremy Umansky all enthusiastically shared their stories through interviews that provided this book with a beating heart.

The members of the Dike 14 Environmental Education Collaborative deserve credit for their fight to prioritize habitat restoration over other interests. William Gruber shared countless emails and documents detailing grassroots activism for habitat at

Dike 14. Chris Trepal shared her story of the struggle for environmental education at Dike 14 and the alliances forged between diverse interests to advance the dream of restoring critical habitat. Ken Martin entrusted me with dozens of boxes of materials (schedules, meeting notes, fliers, petitions) that Barbara Martin cataloged in her quest to transform a former dump into a bird sanctuary. Ken Vinciquerra took me on an hours-long tour of the Lakefront Nature Preserve on a bitterly cold September morning to show me firsthand the efforts of volunteers who contribute to birding surveys.

Marnie Urso has fought for wildlife as both a grassroots activist and now as a senior policy director with Audubon Great Lakes. More than anyone else, she convinced me to abandon my academic detachment and get my boots dirty in order to better understand the compromises and coalition building necessary for lasting social change.

Libby Geboy's illustrations have accompanied my stories since we first worked together for a community-supported fishery based out of Sitka, Alaska. Through her enthusiasm and creativity, she always manages to communicate exactly what my words are grasping for, even when I can't quite figure it out.

The Belt Publishing family has brought this project to fruition. Anne Trubek provided invaluable guidance and embarrassed me with praise through the editing process. Michael Jauchen cleaned up my slapdash prose and sent me back to work on passages beyond the aid of even his help. David Wilson designed a fantastic minimalist cover. Cleveland and the larger rust belt are fortunate to have a publisher specializing in hyperlocal stories. It is fitting that this history of the land was crafted by people from it.

Anna Kiss Mauser-Martinez remains my first reader, editor, and promoter. I cannot thank her enough.

About the Authors

Jon Wlasiuk was born in the Black Swamp region of northwest Ohio and earned a PhD in environmental history from Case Western Reserve University. He has taught at colleges throughout the Great Lakes and lives in Cleveland's Slavic Village neighborhood.

Elizabeth (Libby) Geboy was born and raised in Wisconsin and now resides in Colorado. She holds a master's degree in sustainable food systems and now works for the Colorado Wine Industry Development Board. Through illustration, she translates favorite subjects in the natural world, specifically food, flora, and fauna, in her artistic style.